TWENTY BATTLES

THAT SHAPED MEDIEVAL EUROPE

DEDICATION

To the handful of people who believed in me.
With all my heart.

TWENTY BATTLES

THAT SHAPED MEDIEVAL EUROPE

Georgios Theotokis

ROBERT HALE

First published in 2019 by
Robert Hale, an imprint of
The Crowood Press Ltd,
Ramsbury, Marlborough
Wiltshire SN8 2HR

www.crowood.com

British Library Cataloguing-in-Publication Data
A catalogue record for this book is available from the
British Library.

ISBN 978 0 7198 2873 7

Typeset by Chapter One Book Production, Knebworth

Printed and bound in India by Parksons Graphics

CONTENTS

GLOSSARY

Almohads Islamic Berber tribesmen from North Africa who invaded the Iberian Peninsula in 1145 and maintained a caliphate there until the 1230s.

Almoravids Islamic Berber tribesmen from North Africa who invaded the Iberian Peninsula in 1085, in response to the Christian conquest of Toledo, and maintained a state there until the 1140s.

Angevin Meaning 'from Anjou', applied to the first English kings of the Plantagenet dynasty ie Henry II (1154–89), Richard I (1189–99), John (1199–1216).

battle A division of an army. Typically in the later Middle Ages there were three. On the march they formed van, main body and rear-guard.

burgh Old Germanic word for a walled, fortified site, generally of earth and timber.

Caballeros villanos 'Commoner knights', frontier warriors in Reconquista, Spain.

carroccio An ox-drawn wagon carrying the banner of an Italian city-state.

castellan A man entrusted with the command of a castle.

Catharism A Christian dualist heresy, whose followers believed that the world was created by the Devil. Popular in south-western France around 1200.

chevauchée French term for a mounted raid intended to destroy an enemy's resources, damage.

condottieri Mercenaries employed by fourteenth- and fifteenth-century Italian city-states.

dediticii Barbarians who surrendered themselves to the Empire and were received into the state for settlement.

Fatimids Caliphs and rulers of Egypt from 969 until overthrown by Saladin in 1171. They were of the minority Shi'a form of Islam.

field army Mobile forces, as opposed to those in garrisons in castles and towns.

foederati Barbarians in a treaty (foedus) relationship with the Empire.

Greek fire An inflammable mixture made from a now lost recipe originally known by the Byzantines and later used in the Islamic world and the West.

halberdiers Soldiers carrying pole-arms with blade- or axe-shaped heads, swung in close combat.

Hospitallers The hospital of St John, a charitable foundation, assumed military functions in the mid-twelfth century. Most brothers were Western knights, mainly French, who led a monastic life. They acquired land in the West, and played an important role in defending the crusader states.

housecarl Member of a Scandinavian lord's military household; they are found in England after Cnut's conquest (1016) until 1066.

iq'ta A grant of land or revenues by an Islamic ruler to an individual.

Janissaries The *yeni askeri* ('new troops' in Turkish), raised by the Ottomans in the mid-fourteenth century to provide their largely cavalry forces with reliable infantry.

jihad Islamic holy war, the duty of Muslims to wage war on non-Muslims until they submit.

laager An encampment made by drawing an army's baggage wagons into a circle/square.

laeti Barbarians captured by the Romans and settled on the land.

limes (Lat.) Literally, border or wall.

men-at-arms Heavily armoured soldiers trained to fight as cavalry, by the fourteenth century in addition to knights; these included lesser nobles, such as esquires and gentlemen.

palisade A wall/stockade made from stout timber.

pavisse A tall shield, usually rectangular, used from the twelfth to the fifteenth centuries to give a man complete protection, especially at sieges.

routiers French term for bands of mercenary soldiers in twelfth- to fourteenth-century Europe

schiltron Circular formations of infantry armed with long spears, employed in Scotland at the end of the thirteenth century.

Templars The knights of the Order of the Templar, founded in 1128 for the protection of pilgrims on the route to the River Jordan.

Teutonic Knights A monastic military order founded in the Holy Land c. 1190, invited to Poland where by 1250 it had established an independent Order state in Prussia.

INTRODUCTION

WAR AND MILITARY HISTORY

THIS BOOK IS a history of Europe in the Middle Ages viewed through the lens of the most potent and dramatic aspect of war: battle. It is not designed to give a detailed account of the political or social history of Europe between the fourth and the fifteenth centuries, a period that we have come to identify as the 'Middle Ages', but rather, to work as a general introduction into the basic principles of war, strategy, military equipment and battle tactics of European armies in the aforementioned period. Its central aim is to stimulate the reader's interest in the importance of pitched battles in war, and to explain the geo-political gravity of twenty of them in the shaping of the European Continent as we came to know it in the 'early modern times' that followed.

Warfare has been one of humankind's predominant activities since the dawn of civilization, affecting every aspect of life for millennia. But what, exactly, is war? If you put this question to an enthusiast or a junior scholar of history, you are more likely to receive quotations – or probably paraphrases – ranging from Clausewitz ('War is thus an act of force to compel our enemy to do our will'[1]), perhaps the most influential military theoretician of the gunpowder era, to the oldest surviving military treatise in the world written by Sun-Tzu (fifth century BC). War, however, is a violent form of interaction that has dominated human life for millennia. Therefore, to understand man's 'insanity' of going to war against his own species, other sciences such as psychology, sociology, evolutionary biology and anthropology can add to the theories raised in the past.

In order to explain man's 'pathological behaviour', evolutionary biologists have put the blame on several factors, ranging from a 'selfish gene' most eager to replicate, to excessive amounts of testosterone directly linked to aggressiveness. Psychological explanations put forward by William James as early as 1910 have suggested that warfare was prevalent because of its positive psychological effects, both on the individual and on society as a whole.[2] Forging bonds of communal identity and discipline has been cited as a 'positive' consequence of war on society; on an individual level, however, war is essentially conducive to crime and violence, drastically increasing the levels of adrenalin, and making one feel more alive, alert and awake, often compared to human behaviour under the influence of drugs or alcohol.[3]

Another issue that has been brought up by historians in recent decades is the definition of military history. This is a branch of history that focuses on the core element of war, the battle itself – on military tactics, strategies, armament, and the conduct of military operations – what we may call 'battle narratives'. But in the last two generations, military history has grown up to be much more than a look into the 'art' or 'science' of war. According to the eminent military historian Stephen Morillo:

> A broad definition of military history … includes an historical study in which military personnel of all sorts, warfare (the way in which conflicts are actually fought on land, sea, and in the air), military institutions, and their various intersections with politics, economics, society, nature, and culture form the focus or topic of the work.[4]

Therefore a military historian should focus on three main contexts: first, the political-institutional context that covers the relation between the political and the military institutions within a state, and to what degree an army could be used as an instrument of politics. Then there is the socio-economic context, an area that includes the impact of war on societies (economic productivity, logistics, recruitment, technology and so on), and that of societies on war; and finally, the cultural context that shows the interaction of warrior values with the cultural values of societies in general (glorification or condemnation of warrior values through epic poems, folksongs and tales).[5]

Nevertheless, this book deviates from the 'fashionable' narratives of the so-called 'New Military History' that have dominated historical output since the 1980s, although that does not mean that I am disputing or dismissing the importance of matters such as administration, the institutional framework for warfare, supply systems and logistics, society during war, and the importance of sieges, raids, skirmishes and ambushes to warfare during the Middle Ages. Rather, the emphasis in this study is both on analysis and narratives, and each chapter considers and evaluates campaigns and battles that demonstrate classic and sometimes unchanging aspects of the 'Art of War', as well as illustrating changes in tactics and practices that came as a response to new challenges, weapons and environments.

Therefore it is my intention to reintegrate the operational, tactical, technical and equipment aspects of the conduct of warfare, and to give to the general audience a wider understanding of how significant and decisive pitched battles could be on a *macro-historical* analysis, which seeks out large, long-term trends in world history.

THE CONCEPT OF DECISIVE BATTLE

> Perhaps the interpretation of the Koran would now be taught in the schools of Oxford, and her pulpits might demonstrate to a circumcised people the sanctity and truth of the revelation of Mahomet.[6]
>
> Edward Gibbon (1737–1794) on the outcome of the Battle of Tours (732), in his work *The History of the Decline and Fall of the Roman Empire*

Despite the fact that battles have fallen into disfavour in the last twenty or thirty years, to the point that it has become 'unfashionable' to ascribe global or even regional geo-polit-ical developments to their outcome, yet they have traditionally attracted great attention from scholars because they have demonstrated to have the potential to exert an enormous impact on the course of history. But what is it that makes a battle *decisive*? The answer is straightforward: impact! A decisive battle should have long-term socio-political implica-tions between adversaries, and should profoundly affect the balance of power on more than just the local level. But a specific characteristic of (decisive) battles that makes them invaluable for historians to study, is their *rarity*. And the reason behind this can easily be deduced from the sources:

> It is preferable to subdue an enemy by famine, raids and terror, than in battle where *fortune* ['fortuna'] tends to have more influence than bravery.[7]
>
> > Vegetius, *Epitome of Military Science*, c. 400

> To try simply to overpower the enemy in the open, hand to hand and face to face, even though you might appear to win, is an enterprise which is very *risky* ['τῆς τυχούσης'] and can result in serious harm. Apart from extreme emergency, it is ridiculous to try to gain victory which is too costly and brings only empty glory.[8]
>
> > Emperor Maurice's *Strategikon*, c. 600

> It is good if your enemies are harmed either by deception or raids, or by famine; and continue to harass them more and more, but do not challenge them in open war, because *luck* ['τῆς τύχης'] plays as major a role as valour in battle.[9]
>
> > Emperor Leo VI's *Taktika*, c. 900]

Therefore, the rarity of battles in the pre-industrial era comes as a direct result of a hugely influential factor: chance! Although the outcome of a battle does not necessar-ily prove the social, economic or technological superiority of a 'military culture' over another,[10] other things such as an accidental arrow, unexpected rainfall, fog or a royal horse running astray in the battlefield, could upset the turn of events. This is what Clausewitz called 'friction':

> [T]he only concept that more or less corresponds to the factors that distinguish real war from war on paper ... This tremendous *friction*, which cannot, as in mechanics, be reduced to a few points, is everywhere in contact with chance, and brings about effects that cannot be measured, just because they are largely due to chance.[11]

Bearing in mind that the Middle Ages were a period in history when a king or an emir were at the forefront of fighting, and their units often bore the brunt of an enemy attack, the death of a leader or extensive losses in the battlefield could dramatically upset the balance of power between two forces for many years or even decades – or even for ever. And even if the sources of a polity's material and cultural wealth were not directly harmed by the battle, it could take years to reorganize armies, rebuild morale and inter-national alliances, and train and equip new combatants.

To give a characteristic example: every medieval history enthusiast has heard the famous story of King Harold dying in the field of battle at Hastings as a result of an arrow through his eye (historically accurate or not, I provide an answer in Chapter 10 on the Battle of Hastings). The king's untimely death proved to be the *catalyst* that tipped the scale in favour of the Normans and changed the face of English history for ever. At the Battle of Dyrrhachium some fifteen years later (1081), another Norman invader – Robert 'Guiscard' Hauteville – also defeated the Byzantine Emperor's armies in modern Albania. But even though his Norman knights had the emperor Alexius Comnenus surrounded after he fled the battlefield, the emperor managed to escape and established a rallying point at Thessaloniki. His death would have brought the state to the brink of a renewed civil war, just like the aftermath of the Battle of Manzikert had done ten years before (1071), and the future of the Byzantine Empire would have been very different.

Therefore I firmly believe that, regardless of whether battles are trustworthy or untrustworthy assessments of historical entities and movements, they are rare events, and they form the ultimate 'Darwinian test' for two sides facing each other in a frenzied and violent interaction that would provide history with a winner. They are the *catalyst* that introduces an element of chaos in history, where small inputs can create very large perturbations. And for that reason, I find John Keegan's assertion to be fitting as a concluding remark on the importance of battles in world history:

> For it is not through what armies *are* but by what they *do* that the lives of nations and of individuals are changed.[12]

1 THE BATTLE OF THE FRIGIDUS

The Fatal Blow to the Western Roman Armies

Date 5–6 September 394
Location Near the River Frigidus, modern River Vipava, western Slovenia

THE HISTORICAL BACKGROUND

I WOULD LIKE TO open my discussion into the Battle of the Frigidus with a question: why Frigidus and not Adrianople? Surely a 'barbarian' victory over the Roman army in Thrace should have been considered important (or decisive) enough for this study? The situation after the Battle of Adrianople (378) was, undoubtedly, disastrous for the empire: a Roman emperor had been killed in battle for the first time in over a century; there was a power vacuum in the East; and the Persian frontier was left largely bereft of troops, while the Goths were left roaming around Thrace, free to pillage and destroy. But the latter were inexperienced in besieging fortified cities, something which prevented them from taking advantage of the situation in order to establish themselves firmly in the eastern Balkans; they just had to contend with raiding the Thracian countryside.

The Roman historian Ammianus Marcellinus (died c.391–400) compared Adrianople with Cannae (216BC), Hannibal's great defeat of the Romans.[1] However, the point about Cannae was that, horrific disaster that it was, Rome revived and won the war. That was the case for the period that followed Adrianople: Emperor Theodosius moved the Goths into the empire and enrolled them in the army as *foederati* (allies), following the treaty signed with them on 3 October 382. The 'Gothic Crisis' ended with a Roman victory over the remaining semi-independent Goths of the Balkans in 383.

Theodosius was appointed *augustus* in the East by Gratian, the *augustus* of the West, in January 379, after the political vacuum that followed the disastrous outcome of the Battle of Adrianople in August 378. In the Balkans, Theodosius was given the command of Dacia, Macedonia in eastern Illyricum. In 381, an army sent by Gratian and led by the 'barbarian' (Romanized Franks) generals Bauto and Arbogast drove the Goths out of Macedonia and Thessaly and back to Thrace. Gratian, however, was soon toppled and killed by the Spanish commander of Britain, Magnus Maximus, in August 383; the former had shown extensive favouritism to 'barbarian' soldiers, at the expense of his Roman troops. Gratian's younger brother Valentinian, despite having been declared an heir to the throne of the West in 375, was only thirteen years old, and too young to exercise any independent power.

Following Maximus' usurpation of the throne in the West, and by negotiation with Emperor Theodosius, Maximus was made emperor in Britannia and Gaul, with his base in the German city of Trier, while the young Valentinian retained Italy, Pannonia, Hispania and Africa, with his capital in Milan. However, Maximus' ambitions led him to invade Italy in 387, displacing Valentinian who sought refuge in the eastern city of Thessaloniki; but Maximus was eventually defeated by Theodosius at the Battle of the Save in 388. The main reason behind Theodosius' change of mind in supporting young Valentinian and his mother Justina was the fact that Justina offered Theodosius the prospect of marriage to her beautiful daughter Galla, hence achieving dynastic relations between East and West.[2]

Valentinian II was dispatched to Trier in 388, where he remained under the control of Arbogast, the Frankish *magister militum* appointed by Theodosius. Contemporary primary sources portray the role played by Valentinian in Trier as that of a figurehead under the absolute control of Arbogast, who was the real power broker in the West. Both parties attempted to assert their power from each other; however, the (Romanized) Frankish general could not be crowned *augustus*, so he found a more 'co-operative' Roman aristocrat named Eugenius, a well-educated professor of rhetoric, who made a common cause with him.

But when Valentinian also attempted to break his bonds, he was soon found hanged, and Arbogast quickly proclaimed Eugenius as emperor. Arbogast's action showed how political power in the West had fallen into the hands of Germans. But this was also a challenge to the *augustus* in the East who went too far, and Theodosius had to march west once more to re-establish order.

THE PRELUDE TO THE BATTLE

Preparations for the armed clash between Theodosius and Arbogast went on for a year and a half after Theodosius proclaimed his second son, Honorius, as *augustus* in the West, in January 393. The religious character of the conflict was pronounced when the eunuch Eutropius, one of Theodosius' closest advisers, was dispatched from Constantinople with instructions to seek the wisdom of John of Lycopolis, an aged Christian monk living in the Egyptian town of Thebais. According to the account of the meeting given by Sozomen (c. 400–c. 450), the old monk prophesied that Theodosius would achieve a costly but decisive victory over the pagan Eugenius and Arbogast.[3]

Theodosius' expeditionary army departed from Constantinople sometime in May 394. The Eastern emperor himself led the army, having chosen renowned leaders to be among his commanders, namely Stilicho – the Vandal who later became the guardian of the under-age Honorius in the West – and Timasius, the Visigoth chieftains Gainas and Alaric, and a Caucasian Iberian (modern Georgian) named Bacurius Hiberius.

Theodosius' advance through Pannonia until the Julian Alps was unopposed, and the troops took over a number of key mountain passages that led to the ancient Roman city of Aquileia, at the head of the Adriatic Sea. Based on his experience in fighting the usurper Magnus Maximus in Gaul, Arbogast had thought best to abandon Pannonia and concentrate his forces in northern Italy instead.

At the beginning of September, Theodosius' army descended from the Alps unopposed, heading towards the valley of the Frigidus river to the east of Aquileia. It was in this narrow, mountainous region that they came upon the Western Roman army's encampment on the banks of the Frigidus. Arbogast was careful to dispatch detachments of his army to hold every high point in the river valley, to hinder the Eastern army's ability to manoeuvre freely.

We should bear in mind that the Battle of the Frigidus river took place between Castra and Ad Pirum, two of a series of interconnected Roman fortifications in southern Pannonia that defended the hilly and mountainous eastern approaches to the Italian peninsula; this system of fortifications was called Claustra Alpium Iuliarum (Latin for 'Barrier of the Julian Alps').

The 'Barrier of the Julian Alps' was the mountainous and hilly region from the Julian Alps to the Kvarner Gulf, in modern Slovenia, a defensive system within the Roman Empire that protected Italy from possible invasions from the East.

THE OPPOSING FORCES

Deducing any numbers for the two armies that clashed on the banks of the Frigidus is a futile exercise. Nevertheless, perhaps as many as 20,000 Gothic *foederati* would have been raised by the Gothic leaders Gainas and Alaric, and these would have suffered the highest casualties among the troops from the Eastern armies during the two-day clash. There may even have been some Georgian troops in the ranks of Theodosius' army, for a Georgian officer named Bacurius the Iberian is mentioned in chronicles of the time.

With Arbogast in charge of the Western army, he is very likely to have recruited large numbers of his fellow Gallo-Romans. But the bulk of the troops on both sides would have been Roman, although this is the period when legionaries were beginning to be outnumbered by auxiliaries. As in the Eastern army, cavalry was becoming a larger percentage of the overall number of the Western forces – but not quite in the numbers as in the East.[4] Historians estimate that the Eastern and Western armies that faced each other at Frigidus would have been, more or less, of the same importance and size, in the range of 40,000–50,000 each.[5]

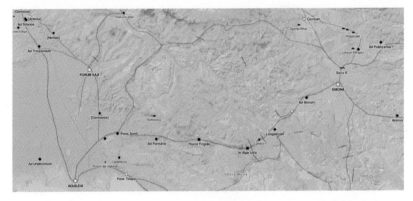

The 'Barrier of the Julian Alps' was made up of a series of interconnected fortifications, with its centre at Fluvio Frigido (modern Ajdovščina, in the Vipava Valley). These fortifications were commanded from Aquileia.

Weapons

The Roman soldiers who faced the 'barbarian invasions' of the fourth and fifth centuries carried weapons that varied little from those of the first-century legionnaires.[6] However, the strategic emphasis that the Romans put on their cavalry forces in the fourth century brought about the gradual replacement of the short *gladius*, the traditional sword of the Roman legionary of the Antonine period (AD96 to AD192), by the *spatha*, a longer sword (up to 75cm long) traditionally used by the Roman cavalry to strike at enemy warriors on the ground. The spear or lance was the primary offensive weapon of the warriors of Antiquity, both cavalry and infantry, and while there is remarkably little evidence regarding the length of Roman spears, their size would have remained relatively consistent, between 2.4 and 2.7m.

There were three types of javelin: the shafted weapon identified as the *speculum*, consisting of a shaft 5.5 Roman feet long (1.63m) and a metal head 9 Roman inches long (200mm); the so-called *verutum*, consisting of a shaft some 3.5 Roman feet long (1.03m), which had a head of 9 Roman inches (200mm); and a third type, more like a throwing dart, called the *plumbata* or *mattiobarbuli*, less than one metre long and with a head averaging between 100 and 200mm.

The spear was also the primary weapon of the fourth- and fifth-century 'barbarians';

it was called a *frameae*, and according to the first-century Roman author Tacitus, 'had short and narrow blades, but so sharp and easy to handle that they can be used either at close quarters or in long-range fighting'. The only thing we can be sure about the 'barbarian' spears is the lack of uniformity in size or shape, with each smith probably creating their own design. Swords were equally important for the 'barbarians' as they were for the Romans, and findings from burial sites point to a variety of types, from longer ones (up to 100cm), to shorter ones (around 40–50cm).

Finally the axe was used by the early 'barbarians', both as a smashing weapon and a projectile. It remained largely in use until the early seventh century, and was adopted by the Romans already from the fourth century; a weapon such as the Frankish *francisca* weighed some 1.2kg, and it could drop an enemy at distances of between 4 to 15 metres.

Armour

While the average 'barbarian' warrior wore little, if no body armour, it was not unusual for chieftains to be in the possession of their own helmets and sophisticatedly decorated armour. They did, however, carry convex wooden shields made of strips of wood covered with leather, measuring between 80 to 90cm in diameter. Roman armour was, of course, much more elaborately designed and manufactured, although the sources of the period complain of many legionaries losing their armour and helmets and relying only on their shields for protection. How widespread this practice was, however, is impossible to determine.

Fourth-century Roman body armour was of two distinct types: the *lorica squamata*, a type of scale armour made of small scales made of iron, bronze, bone, wood, horn or leather sewn to a fabric backing; the other the *lorica hamata*, made of metal rings that were sewn in interlocking rows to a fabric backing. Roman round (or oval) shields had replaced the popular curved rectangular ones of the Antonine period around the turn of the third century, and were largely made of wood.

Finally, the simplest type of Roman helmet was the ridge one, composed of two pieces of metal joined together by a central metallic strip running from the brow to the back of the neck, usually rounded but often having a slightly raised top. It was fitted with neck guards and cheek fittings directly attached to the leather lining of the helmet. But even this ridge helmet would often have been discarded in favour of the 'Pannonian helmet', a leather cap, as Vegetius (c. AD400, author of the famous military treatise *Epitoma Rei Militaris*) informs us, worn by the legionaries under their iron helmet.[7]

THE BATTLE

Regrettably, our sources do not mention anything about the formations of the opposing armies that lined up for battle in the evening of the 5 September. Hostilities commenced when Theodosius ordered his Visigoth *foederati* under Gainas and Alaric, who were deployed in the first line preceding the main division of the Romans, to launch a frontal attack against the enemy infantry across the battlefield. These Gothic troops were therefore sent into the battle more or less as 'cannon fodder', suffering some 10,000 casualties. The rest of the Eastern army then followed in a headlong attack that resulted in heavy casualties on both sides but little gain, with the Iberian commander Bacurius being killed in action.

We are left in the dark about which units followed up the Visigoth attack, but bearing in mind the late Roman army's typical battlefield deployment, according to Vegetius, this would have included the deployment of the main units of Roman infantry in three lines in the centre of the formation, with skirmish troops placed in front of them to 'soften up' an enemy attack. The cavalry units would have been placed on the flanks, first to offer protection against any encircling manoeuvres, and to launch an attack against the enemy at the right moment.[8] Therefore we can only assume that both the cavalry and the infantry units of the first lines would have clashed with Arbogast's units on the first evening of the battle.

While Theodosius spent a sleepless night (5/6 September) praying to God, Western emperor Eugenius ordered a victory celebration in the army camp, sure that the next day the East Romans would be swept from the field. Arbogast was more cautious, however, and dispatched a detachment of élite troops – probably locals who knew the area – to march secretly through a footpath that led to the mountain passes behind the Eastern army's camp, in order to block their retreat and attack them from the rear the following day.[9] However, the commander of this detachment made contact with the Eastern Roman force, and defected to Theodosius after agreeing to a considerable monetary inducement.

This act of defection was viewed by the Eastern emperor as God's answer to his prayers, prompting him to open the second day of hostilities with an all-out attack. The final 'miracle' came in the form of a weather phenomenon called a *bora* – a strong north to north-eastern wind that blows from the mountains to the sea, and an integral feature of Slovenia's Vipava Valley. According to tradition, the storm blew directly into the eyes of the Western army, and was said to be so strong that it caused the javelins and arrows fired to be blown back towards them. At the least it disrupted the movements of Arbogast's army, and when the East Romans charged, the Western Roman units rapidly disintegrated.

CONCLUSIONS

The Battle of the Frigidus has been represented as the triumph of Christianity over the last vestiges of paganism in the Western part of the Roman Empire. Contemporary sources attributed equal importance and glory to the outcome of the Battle of the Frigidus as had been given to the Battle of the Milvian Bridge eighty-two years earlier. Influential Christian writers of the period – such as Sozomen (c. 400–c. 450), Theodoret of Cyrrhus (c. 393–c. 458/466), and especially Rufinus, in his continuation of Eusebius' *Ecclesiastical History* published in 402/3, paint a lavish portrait of Theodosius' campaign

The 'Stilicho diptych', carved around AD395 and kept in the cathedral at Monza. It represents a military man with a spear and shield on one panel, and on the other, a high-ranking woman holding a flower above the head of a small boy, not more than ten years old. It has been generally accepted that these people are the Western Roman general of infantry and cavalry forces (*magister utriusque militiae*) Stilicho (d. 408), his wife Serena, the niece and adoptive daughter of Eastern emperor Theodosius I, and their son Eucherius.

against Eugenius and Arbogast, more or less as some sort of a proto-'Holy War' to suppress the *pagani*.

Recently, however, Alan Cameron cast doubt on the truthfulness and the historical value of the contemporary Christian accounts with regard to the eye-witness reports of the battle, and how these were remembered.[10] Rather, he asserted that these historical accounts have been distorted, based on political and theological considerations, to justify Theodosius' campaign against Eugenius and Arbogast, who were falsely branded as pagans after their defeat. Eugenius was further painted as a 'usurper' (*tyrannus*), a term which after the reign of Constantine the Great in the fourth century had taken the additional meaning of persecutor of Christians, and – on top of that – as a person who was 'by no means sincere in his profession of Christianity': this was undoubtedly false, and gives us an idea of the blatant propaganda that emerges from the Christian accounts of the Battle of Frigidus!

This is further confirmed by the historical manipulation of the *bora*, the storm that blew in the second day of the battle. According to the same study,[11] the earliest source to mention the decisive *bora* was Ambrose of Milan (c. 340–397), but he reports about the storm on the day before any fighting had begun. This could have been picked up by another contemporary source, the poet Claudian (c. 370–c. 404), who, in his propagandistic poetry, moved the wind to the decisive moment of the battle as a sign of godly approval of the emperor's strategy.

Therefore we should put the emphasis of Theodosius' victory at Frigidus on the asserting of control over the Western parts of the empire and the slaughtering of the Western army, rather than on the overthrow of paganism. Considered in sequence with the earlier Battle of the Save (388), where the usurper Maximus was heavily defeated, the units that had been withdrawn from the north-western provinces of the Roman Empire to be used in the gamble for power between the Eastern and the Western *augusti*, lost heavily in the battles with Theodosius' Eastern troops. Large parts of Gaul and the Rhine frontier were left on their own, as there was hardly any time for governmental structures to be reorganized after Maximus' usurpation before troops were again withdrawn for Eugenius and Arbogast's rebellion.

Thereafter the northern regions were seemingly left in a political limbo, while the Roman empire was contracting closer to the Mediterranean Sea.

2 THE BATTLE OF THE CATALAUNIAN FIELDS

Thwarting the 'Scourge of God'

Date 20 July 451
Location Châlons-en-Champagne, perhaps between the source of the River Vannes at Fontvannes and Troyes

THE HISTORICAL BACKGROUND

THE ROMAN HISTORIAN Ammianus Marcellinus (330–c. 400) provides us with a glimpse into the origins, the customs and the appearance of the Huns in a lengthy digression into his work, known as the *Res Gestae* (written in the 380s). He portrays a sedentary Roman's perception of these nomadic warriors from the steppes, a description which, however, should be taken with a pinch of salt due to the numerous cultural stereotypes that emerge from the work, all part of the well-known ethnographic schema of the period, which contrasted the 'barbarian' nomads with the civilized Romans (as regards civilization, laws and so on). And it was not just Ammianus, but also Jerome (AD347–420), Sidonius Apollinaris (d. AD489) and Jordanes (c. 526–c. 575) who felt horrified and repulsed by the appearance and savagery of the Huns.[1]

These peoples, who were quite distinct from the Germans, seem to have broken into the Roman world in the first half of the fourth century, forcing several tribes of the Alans and the Goths that inhabited the regions between the rivers Volga and Don to migrate further west than the River Dniester, and to cross into the Roman Empire and seek refuge as *foederati*. But it would be a mistake to see the Huns as a serious threat to the Empire in this early stage of their infiltration into Europe, because according to Ammianus, the Huns had no king or overall leader, but operated in bands. In fact, not only were individual Hunnic bands recruited into the Roman armies of Valentinian II and Theodosius I (following the battle of Adrianople in 378), but as early as 380 a group of Huns was given *foederati* status and allowed to settle in Pannonia (modern Hungary). They soon developed from 'warbands on the make' and began their attacks into the Eastern empire, directing their most destructive raid against Asia Minor in 395–98.

At the turn of the fifth century, it seems that the increasingly numerous and potent groups of Huns roaming north of the Rhine and Danube rivers were responsible for a Gothic invasion of Italy in 405, and the crossing of the Upper Rhine by hundreds of thousands of Vandals, Sueves, Alans and Burgundians after December 406. In the meanwhile, one of the first names that appear in contemporary sources as a Hunnic leader was Uldin. He headed a group of Huns and Alans defending Italy against the Goths in 405, and he also defeated Gothic rebels under Gainas that troubled the Eastern Romans in the lower Danube around 400–401. In 408, Uldin crossed the Danube and captured a fortress in Dacia Ripensis (the modern Serbian-Bulgarian border region) named Castra Martis (modern Kula), before he proceeded to plunder Thrace. The East's response was to build the new walls of Constantinople in 413.

After this point, relations between the Romans and the Huns would be influenced to a great degree by the Western *magister militum* Flavius Aetius. He spent his youth in the court of the Western Emperor Honorius (AD384–423), and was of such a high status to be sent to the Gothic king Alaric as a hostage, between 405–408, and subsequently to the court of the king of the Huns, again as a noble hostage, where he made friends and connections that were to prove valuable, and where he learned how to fight (and think) in an unconventional (for the average Roman) way.

Aetius thrived in a period (413–55) when generals of Roman extraction held power in the West. He relied upon Hun mercenaries to control other barbarian groups, such as the Visigoths in 425, 430 and 436, the Franks in 428 and 432, and also the Burgundians in 436–7. Primarily he set himself to establish a power base in Gaul, and in 433 he was so strong that he received both the military office of *magister militum* and the civilian title of *patrician*.

The death of the Hun leader Rugila in 434 left his two sons, Bleda and Attila, in command of the confederation of tribes, and responsible for conducting negotiations with Eastern Emperor Theodosius II's envoys for agreeing on a peace treaty (the Treaty of Margus, AD435). The Huns remained out of Roman sight for the next few years while they invaded the Sassanid Empire, with the Persians defeating them in Armenia and putting a stop to their invasion plans. But in the 440s, extreme pressures on the Western empire by the Huns and the Vandals would usher in a twelve-year period of political instability. In 442, the West ceded the prosperous provinces of Africa Proconsularis and Byzacena on the north African coast to the Vandals, a development that diminished the state's tax revenues and had an immediate impact on the military capability of the Western empire.

In the same period, after the Eastern Romans broke the terms of the Treaty of Margus, Attila and Bleda crossed the Danube and in 441 razed the cities of Margus, Singidunum (modern Belgrade) and Viminacium (the capital of the Roman province of Moesia Superior). In the campaigns that followed, Hun armies sacked Naissus (modern Niš), Sardica (modern Sofia), Philippopolis (modern Plovdiv) and Arkadiopolis (modern Lüleburgaz), completely defeating Theodosius II's army in autumn 443.

Because of Aetius, the West had escaped relatively unscathed from the 'Hunnic storm', with Attila (sole leader after 447) directing his attacks against the richer East. By the 440s, however, Rome's hold in the North, and especially Gaul, had diminished significantly. By 434, Britain and northern Gaul had long been removed from any formal links with the Empire, ruled by local warlords whose authority was based upon claimed Roman titles. In 418, the Romans had concluded a treaty with the Visigoth king Walia, which handed over to the Goths the province of Aquitania Secunda, the valley of the Garonne in south-western Gaul. Similarly in Spain the Sueves had tightened their grip on Gallaecia.

Therefore, Aetius' strategy focused on the Rhine frontier and the southern Gaulish coast, with the focal points for the struggle against the Visigoths being the strategic administrative centres of Arles and Narbonne. He destroyed the Burgundian kingdom of the Middle Rhine in 436, giving them land in what we now call Burgundy. Nevertheless, Aetius suffered serious setbacks which restricted Rome's authority in Gaul; instead, he was forced to strike a peace treaty with the Visigoth king Theoderic I, in 439, to free himself to face the Vandals in Africa. The Goths remained quiet for the next decade, and even contributed troops to Aetius' operations against the Sueves in the early 440s.

This fragile balance of power between the two halves of the Roman Empire and the Huns was interrupted in 450. For more than a decade, the Huns had been extorting annual money payments from the emperors in the East by threatening raids into the Balkans. But in 450 there was a new *augustus* in Constantinople, Marcian, an aged Thracian military officer; Marcian took advantage of the peace with the Sassanians in the East, who had their own troubles with the so-called White Huns, to cease the payment of the tribute to the Huns. Rather surprisingly, Attila hesitated to attack Constantinople, but instead moved westwards.

In the same year (450), a Frankish succession crisis following the death of the Salian king Chlodio gave Attila the pretext to get involved in the politics of the West, when a senior claimant to the crown appealed to him for help, while the junior claimant turned to Rome. Surely it would have seemed more profitable an enterprise to install a puppet prince in Gaul than once again descending upon the Balkans. Furthermore, Jordanes writes that the Vandals in Africa were encouraging the Huns to move against the Visigoths.[2] The die had been cast!

THE PRELUDE TO THE BATTLE

Attila crossed the Rhine and invaded Gaul in the spring of 451, at the head of a huge invading army, which also included a branch of the Ostrogoths, under Valamir, Thiudomer and Vidimer, and the Gepids under Ardaric.[3] Most likely his army would have spread into smaller bands to live off the land. Coming from two different directions, from Trier and Strasburg, they merged before the walls of Metz, which they captured and sacked on 7 April.

Regrettably we know very little about what followed from April to June 451. Attila's army cut a swathe through northern France from Metz to the Loire valley, and they, once again, would have operated over a very wide area to ease problems of supply and forage. Attila then headed west across the Meuse and Marne rivers and towards a strategic city on the Upper Loire Valley, Aurelianum (modern Orléans). The siege of the city with battering rams is confirmed by the later account of Gregory of Tours.[4] After four days of heavy rain Attila began his final assault on 14 June, but this was abandoned due to the approach of the Roman coalition.

THE OPPOSING FORCES

Upon learning of the invasion, Flavius Aetius advanced his army rapidly from Italy to Gaul. According to Sidonius Apollinaris, he was leading a 'thin, meagre force of *auxiliaries* without legionaries'.[5] Why Aetius did not have more regular (Roman) troops at his disposal is not clear; perhaps the emperor Valentinian did not want to leave Italy undefended, or maybe he suspected Aetius would use these troops to turn against him. Another reason could have been that the majority of Aetius' army was already stationed in Gaul.[6]

The Roman 'auxiliis' mentioned by Sidonius would probably have been the *auxilia palatina*. These units were formed after the reorganization of the Roman Army during the reign of Diocletian (end of the third century AD), creating regiments out of the old legions, which had an established strength of around 500 men. Aetius' *auxilia palatinae* would have been special units of commando-style, highly trained but lightly armed troops, conducting more mobile operations.[7]

However, according to another theory, these were simply 'barbarian' allied troops that formed some sort of a private guard for those who could afford their services, and Aetius was no exception to the 'trend' of the time. Whatever the case, Aetius' troops would have been too few to stop Attila by themselves, although their exact composition and numbers remain unclear. (I will not go into the details of the Roman soldier's equipment of the period – c. 400 – here, as I have offered a detailed description in the study of the battle of Frigidus (394).)

The Visigoth king Theodoric I (reigned AD418–451) would have been aware that his kingdom was an attractive target for the 'Hunnic storm' descending upon Gaul, hence it was not difficult to persuade him into an alliance against Attila. The Visigoths formed a substantial proportion of Aetius' army in 451, and Jordanes gives the impression that they may even have managed to defeat Attila singlehandedly. Heather suggests that the Visigoths may have been able to field some 25,000 men.[8]

But the Goths who fought side by side with the Romans in northern Gaul in 451 were not the same soldiers in terms of equipment as those who had defeated them at Adrianople in 378. Since their establishment in southern Gaul at the beginning of the fifth century, they had settled down as a warrior aristocracy over the native Gallo-Romans, and they certainly had had access to Roman weapons factories (*fabricae*), which gave them a significant advantage over other Germanic nations. Yet they were still armed with a variety of spears and swords, while their defensive equipment would have improved with the addition of scale or mail armour, similar to the Roman *lorica squamata* or *lorica hamata*, to complement the round or oval wooden shields and

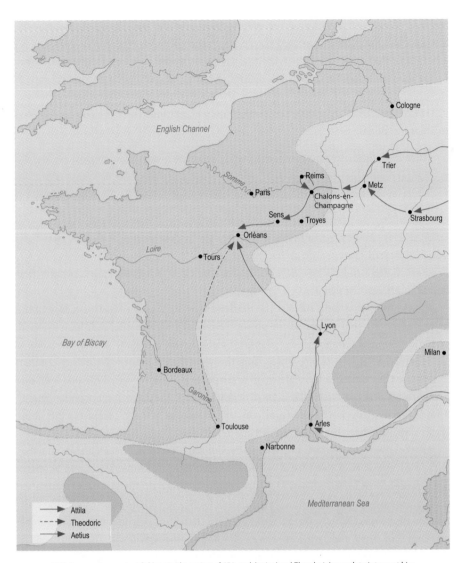

Attila's campaign against Orléans in the spring of 451, and Aetius' and Theodoric's march to intercept him.

metallic helmets. The Visigoths would have fielded few contingents of heavily armed and armoured cavalry, probably manned by native Gallo-Romans, although the sources leave us in the dark about their precise equipment.

Jordanes lists Aetius' allies as:

… the Francii (Franks), Sarmatae (Alans), Armoriciani (Bagaudae from Brittany), Liticiani (*laeti*: defeated enemy troops who were settled in Roman territory owing hereditary military service), Burgundiones (Burgundians), Saxones (Saxons), Riparii (Ripuarian Franks) and Olibrones (they remain a mystery).

Sadly it is impossible to know the composition and size of the allied contingents, although we understand that these would have been *foederati* rather than independent allies, troops who had been given land or pay in return for service in the Roman army under their commanders, although technically, they would have been subordinate to the Roman officers.

For the hordes of troops that descended upon Gaul under Attila's coalition, we read in Sidonius' poem:

> After the warlike Rugian comes the fierce Gepid, with the Gelonian close by; the Burgundian urges on the Scirian; forward rush the Hun, the Bellonotian, the Neurian, the Bastarnian, the Thuringian, the Bructeran, and the Frank, he whose land is washed by the sedgy waters of Nicer.

Sidonius certainly exaggerates his poetic licence in describing tribes that either did not exist or had disappeared at the time of Attila's campaign, such as the Bastarnae, Bructeri, Geloni and Niceri. Nevertheless, we know of other Germanic peoples that fought in Attila's army in 451.

Franks fought on both sides at the Battle of the Catalaunian Fields, because of the princely factions that contested for power after King Chlodio's death. These warriors would have mainly fought in dense infantry phalanxes, and they were renowned for their battle-axes (*franciscae*), which they threw at their enemies just before combat. Otherwise they were not heavily armed or armoured, wearing only light padded body armour and perhaps a metallic helmet or leather cap, and carrying a wooden shield. There were also a number of Burgundians and Alamanni living to the east of the Rhine who would have been forced to join Attila's army.

Of the other contingents mentioned by Sidonius, there were the Germanic tribes who lived under Hun overlordship, the Gepids, Rugians, Thuringians and Scirians. They would have favoured hand-to-hand combat, either on horseback or mostly on foot, as we know from the description of their tactics provided in the Byzantine military treatise called *Strategikon* (c. AD600).[9] The Ostrogoths also formed a formidable contingent in Attila's army, and because of their long association with the Huns and the Alans from the steppes of eastern Europe, they would have fielded large contingents of horsemen, although these would not have been horse-archers but, rather, were armed with missile weapons and long lances, like the Greuthungi at Adrianople seven decades before.

Finally, the Hun warriors would have presented the most disparate part of Attila's army, one that caused fear and awe to the contemporary and later Western authors to the point of conjuring up mythical attributes when describing them. As with all steppe nomads, commentators were struck by their attachment to their horses. Ammianus Marcellinus noted that they were 'almost glued to their horses, which are hardy, it is true, but ugly, and sometimes they sit of the woman-fashion (presumably side-saddle) and so perform their ordinary tasks.' Therefore it is only natural to assume that the Huns' particular attachment to their horses, coupled with the pastoral way of life in the

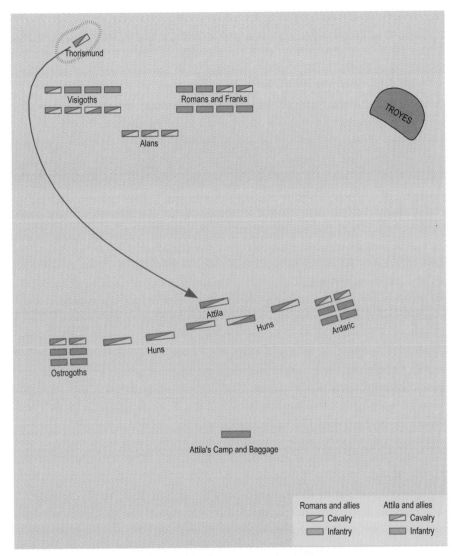

The Battle of the Catalaunian Fields, 20 July 451.

Eurasian steppes, would have shaped the way they fought against their nomadic and sedentary neighbours.[10]

The majority of the Hunnic warriors, at least until the fifth century, were lightly armed horsemen whose main weapon was the composite bow made from layers of horn, wood, sinew and glue, and they would have carried two quivers with around forty to sixty arrows in each one. The composite bow possessed a maximum range of 300m (although the effective range would have been much shorter, at around 100m), and a well-trained horse-archer could discharge up to five arrows in just three seconds. In addition, mounted archers such as the Huns, and their Scythian and Sarmatian predecessors, could effectively shoot from the saddle without the stabilizing effect of stirrups, something which can only affirm the pre-eminence of Hunnic horsemanship.

The Hun nobility would have been better equipped, with mail armour, a metallic helmet, a sword, a lasso and, possibly, a lance for close combat; poorer Huns would have had to make do with padded armour. Yet by the mid-fifth century most of them would have worn Roman equipment, and supplemented their native weapons with those they got from the Romans.

The main characteristic of the Hun way of war was the ability of their armies to move quickly. This was mainly because a typical Hun warrior not only had a single horse for transport, as in Europe, but a string of horses that could be ridden in turn while on campaign. This kind of steppe warfare could qualify as a medieval 'blitzkrieg', reminiscent of the modern military strategy that employed surprise, speed and concentrated firepower to paralyse an adversary's capacity to organize defences.

As was the case with most steppe armies, the Huns applied tactics that aimed to exploit their abilities with the bow and their mobility, usually by staying out of reach of their opponents' weapons. They applied 'hit-and-run' tactics in waves, and showered the enemy with arrows by employing the famous 'Parthian shot'. Their trademark was the feigned retreat tactic, when they pretended to fall back in an attempt to draw their enemies in a disorganized pursuit, only to wheel around and encircle them. However, historians believe that, by the time of Attila, the majority of the Huns would have fought on foot because the Hungarian plains could not have supported more than 150,000 horses, enough for only 15,000 warriors.[11]

Keeping the last point in mind, that the mounted Hun warriors at the time of Attila should not have exceeded 15,000, we come to the hotly debated topic of the numbers that were involved in the Battle of the Catalaunian Fields. We can surely all agree that the army Attila led into France was probably quite large for the time, although Jordanes' half a million is sheer fantasy. Some historians believe that Attila's forces in 451 were in the neighbourhood of 40,000 to 50,000 effectives, while the Roman coalition led by Aetius was of the same size, or perhaps even 50 per cent larger. Others, however, urge caution, and cast serious doubts as to whether early medieval commanders could have coped with the logistical difficulties in putting such large armies in the field for long periods of time. Perhaps a realistic estimate would be something in the region of 20,000–30,000 on each side.[12]

THE BATTLE

When Attila heard the news of the approach of the Roman coalition army, according to Jordanes he 'was taken aback by this event and lost confidence in his own troops'. Jordanes was probably writing with the benefit of hindsight, but we do know that Aetius' arrival forced the Hun leader to reconsider his plans and fall back to Troyes, some 200km (125 miles) to the east. Attila realized that he had no choice but to fight, but he wanted to do this on ground of his own choosing, and while his troops were passing through the flat open grounds of Champagne on their way to Orléans, he would have recognized that this would have made an ideal ground for his armies to take full advantage of the speed and mobility of their cavalry and horse-archers.

Attila may have followed the old Roman road that led east, along the River Vanne and on to Troyes. Aetius pursued Attila from Orléans, and according to Jordanes, the night before the battle, some of the Franks in Aetius' army encountered a band of Gepids in Attila's rear guard, engaging with them in a skirmish. But this account cannot be verified.

The actual location of the Battle of the Catalaunian Fields remains unclear. The current scholarly consensus is that there is no conclusive site, although there have been several attempts to locate it using the meagre information provided by the primary sources and archaeology. We can only say with relative certainty that the two armies clashed in the vicinity of Châlons-en-Champagne, perhaps between the source of the River Vannes at Fontvannes and Troyes, where in modern times the open space allowed for the building of an airport to serve the city of Troyes.

The battle opened on the morning of 20 July, with the scramble by Aetius to occupy the ridge between Fontvannes and Troyes, in modern Montgueux. This would have provided the Roman the opportunity to observe his enemy's deployment before offering battle. But Attila would not have stayed idle, and his scouts would certainly have alerted him to the strategic importance of taking that ridge. According to Jordanes, the Huns sought to take the ridge, but were overtaken by the Goths. This early morning action was only the prelude to the real battle, which was about to unfold a few hours later.

Aetius deployed his Roman contingent on the left wing which, apart from his *auxilia* and the remnants of the Gallic army that he would have collected on the way, would have been complemented by Franks, Armoricans, Saxons and Burgundians. Most would have been infantry, fighting in close order and supported by archers, while Aetius would definitely have kept cavalry in reserve. On the right wing were the Visigoths under the combined command of Theodoric and his eldest son, Thorismund. The latter would have been in charge of a cavalry force held in reserve in the right flank of the main Gothic division under Theodoric, which would have fought on foot forming a dense shield-wall. The Alans would have been placed in the middle, probably because they were of questionable loyalty; they would have fielded both horse-archers and their trademark 'Sarmatian' cataphracts, who combined the mobility of larger horses with the shock effect of charging with the lance, all clad in heavy armour.

Attila would have kept his Huns in the centre of his formation, many of whom would have fought as horse-archers, although they would also have been supported by foot soldiers. Holding the left flank were the Ostrogoths, deployed on horseback and favouring shock tactics, while they would also have been supported by infantry and archers. The Gepids and the rest of the Germanic allies of Attila formed the right wing, comprising a mixed force of heavy cavalry (Gepids) and infantry (Franks, Alamanni, Thuringians and Rugians).

Regrettably, the only detailed account about the battle comes from Jordanes, whose description is limited to the action on the Visigoth wing. Therefore inferential reasoning and conjecture have to fill in the huge gaps left by the historical accounts about this monumental clash between these two coalition armies. MacDowall has suggested that Aetius probably deployed his forces mid-way between the ridge of Montgueux and the plains, adopting a defensive position to await Attila's attack, with his right flank protected by the ridge of Montgueux, which was occupied by Thorismund's Visigoths.[13] If that was the case, then this deployment demonstrates the brilliance of Aetius' strategic thinking, and his experience in defending a position against a highly mobile army such as the Hunnic one.

Jordanes reports the following for the opening stages of the battle: 'Hand to hand they clashed in battle, and the fight grew fierce, confused, monstrous, unrelenting.' Certainly there would have been mayhem and slaughter at the points where the Huns would have attacked the Roman coalition, but Jordanes' description lacks the necessary details (battle manoeuvres and so on) to establish exactly what happened on that summer's day. It is possible that Attila's division would have attacked the enemy centre, where the Alans were deployed, because the position Aetius had chosen would have denied Attila the chance to envelop his enemy. But this is mere speculation!

Jordanes further notes a crucial detail about the course of the battle: 'Then the Visigoths, separating from the Alani, fell upon the horde of the Huns and nearly slew Attila.' This evidence may strengthen the assumption that Attila attacked the Alans in the centre, probably breaking through their ranks and forcing (some of) them to fall back to the relative safety of the ridge, thus exposing the flanks of both the Roman and Visigoth wings. Then Jordanes notes that Theodoric, whilst leading his own men against the enemy Ostrogoths, was killed in action.

It must have been late evening by then, and the outcome still hung in the balance, when the Visigoths fell upon Attila's household unit, forcing the Hun to retreat to the safety of his camp. Jordanes also reports of Thorismund charging down the ridge into the enemy flank 'before the night fell', and we may presume that it was the king's son who led the Visigoth charge and then the pursuit of the Huns. There he was wounded in the late-night fighting before he was rescued by his peers.

It is impossible to reconstruct anything more about the course of the battle, or about what was going on in Aetius' wing. What is certain, however, is that Thorismund's surprise mounted charge into the flank of the enemy engaged to their front would have had a devastating impact, pushing the Huns to fall back to their camp (*laager*: an encampment formed by a circle of wagons). Darkness finally put an end to the slaughtering.

The following day, Thorismund recovered the body of his father 'where the dead lay thickest, as happens with brave men; they honoured him with songs and bore him away in the sight of the enemy': an end befitting a king. Attila was still besieged by the coalition forces inside his *laager*, and we would expect that his situation would have been desperate. Nevertheless, Aetius was a master of diplomacy and knew the Huns were valuable as a counterbalance to the rising Visigoth power in Gaul. So he convinced

Thorismund to return home and secure the throne for himself, instead of seeking to revenge his father's death.

CONCLUSIONS

For the immediate aftermath of the Battle of the Catalaunian Fields, Prosper of Aquitaine (390–463, writing before 455) wrote of an 'incalculable slaughter', while Hydatius (c. 400–c. 469) estimated that the dead from both sides would have reached the impossible number of 300,000. Nevertheless, some modern historians insist that calling Catalaunian Fields a decisive victory is to ignore its aftermath, or to exaggerate the importance of the battle over the successful siege of Orléans, which was actually responsible for pushing Attila out of Aquitaine.[14]

Catalaunian Fields certainly did not prevent the threat of Attila from re-appearing in Europe, as the Hun attacked Italy the following summer (452) at the head of another enormous army, storming Aquileia and destroying Milan and other cities in the north of Italy. He even marched upon Rome before having his famous meeting – shrouded in legend – with a papal embassy led by Pope Leo I, who eventually persuaded him to abandon his plans; other accounts write about Attila and his aristocrats' concerns (following Alaric's death soon after the sack of Rome in 410) that there was a curse on anyone who conquered the city of Rome.

Eventually, Attila drank himself to death in 453, and within a few years his empire had completely fallen apart. However, historians need to be less short-sighted and see the bigger picture of the geo-political consequences that ensued after Attila's defeat in 451.

To me, there is no doubt that the Catalaunian Fields had a profound effect on the history and civilization of western Europe in the fifth century and beyond. First and foremost, it demolished the myth of the Hunnic invincibility in the battlefield in what Halsall calls:

> … the most serious concerted military threat to be launched against the western Empire, and certainly the only such expedition apparently carried out with the avowed aim of its subjugation, probably since the second Punic war.[15]

It cannot be doubted that the European Continent would have looked very different if Attila had succeeded in establishing a kingdom in Gaul, as we know for a fact that the Huns had far less respect and appreciation for Graeco-Roman civilization than most of the other Germanic nations.

For Roman Gaul in particular, the aftermath was explicit in the sense that the battle significantly weakened the military capacity of the Alans and the Romans, which allowed for Visigoth, Frankish and Burgundian hegemony in Gaul to flourish. Following the Catalaunian Fields, the Romans were – practically – unable to field a significant military force to thwart Attila in 452, or to prevent the sack of Rome by the Vandals three years later. Then in 452, the new Visigoth king Thorismund (murdered in 453) campaigned north and decisively defeated the Alans, driving them across the Loire from northern Aquitaine, before turning his attention to Spain.

There is little doubt that if Attila had prevailed at Troyes, his next target would have been the Visigoth kingdom of Toulouse; to the contrary, the allied victory – despite Theodoric's death in the battle – favoured the further expansion of the Visigoth kingdom within less than a decade, from Aquitaine and Spain to the south, to the River Loire in the north, where fifty-six years later they would face the Franks in a battle (Vouillé, AD507) that would establish the polity we now know as France.

The outcome at the Catalaunian Fields also favoured the Frankish expansion into *Gallia Belgica* (modern Belgium, Luxembourg and the Netherlands), under the ambitious Childeric I (457–81/82) and his son Clovis I (481/82–509), and the growing power of the Burgundians in south-eastern Gaul, from Vesontio (Besançon) to Lugdunum (Lyon) and Vienna (Vienne) in less than twenty years (AD455 to 476).

3 THE BATTLE OF VOUILLÉ

The Birth of France

Date Spring, 507
Location Vouillé, 15km (9 miles) north-west of Poitiers, Aquitaine

THE HISTORICAL BACKGROUND

THE MOST IMPORTANT historical development of the fifth century in western Europe was the emergence of the Germanic kingdoms, which had already absorbed the former western provinces of the Western Roman Empire. The main groups that can be identified were the Western Goths (Visigoths), who dominated south-west Gaul and Spain, the Burgundians in the upper Rhone valley, the Salian Franks who were emerging in northern and central Gaul, and the eastern Goths (Ostrogoths), based in Pannonia through the third quarter of the century, who were to take control of Italy at the end of the fifth century.

After the death of the Roman general Aetius, the victor of Châlons (Catalaunian Plains) in 454, imperial power in Gaul rapidly disintegrated. The emergence of the Kingdom of Soissons in northern Gaul (later, Naustria) as a Roman remnant state under Aegidius, a former *magister militum* of Roman Gaul appointed by Emperor Majorian (reigned 457–461) before his murder in 461, increased the chaos of contemporary Gaul, as he maintained his power against Franks to his east and Visigoths to his south; his son Syagrius succeeded his father to the rule of Soissons in 465.

After the middle of the fifth century, the king of the Salian Franks, Childeric (ruled 457–481), became a major power in northern Gaul, and his victories against the Visigoths, Saxons and Alemanni established the basis of the Salian-Frankish State in northern Gaul. He further supported Aegidius in the latter's victory against the Visigoths at Orléans in 463. But it was Childeric's son Clovis (ruled 481–511) who would go on to unite most of Gaul north of the Loire.

By 481, the major geo-political clash in western Europe would be between the three peoples that were competing for predominance in the territory of Aquitaine: the Visigoths in south-western Gaul, the Burgundians in the south-east, and the Franks north of the Loire. Clovis, who had succeeded his father as leader of the Salian Franks of Tournai in 481, gradually brought under his control the territories between the Loire and the Somme; by around 486 he had defeated Syagrius and effectively dissolved the Kingdom of Soissons. This victory provided Clovis with a strongly fortified base – Soissons, a substantial arms factory, and the Roman units that had served Syagrius and were being integrated into his following.

After he gained full control of Neustria (the territories under the former Kingdom of Soissons, between the Loire and the Somme), Clovis turned his attention against a small group of Thuringians in eastern Gaul, just north of the Burgundians, winning a battle in 491. It was quickly becoming apparent that Clovis' expansionist strategy was directed against the Burgundians and the Alamans of the Upper and Middle Rhine. Eventually, he won the Battle of Tolbiac in 496, some 50 kilometres (30 miles) south of Cologne, against an Alamanni invasion of Austrasia and the Lower Rhine.

Although the exact nature of the battle remains obscured in legend, according to Gregory of Tours, Clovis adopted his wife Clotilda's Orthodox (that is, Nicene) Christian faith, having undergone some sort of a religious experience during the battle. Or perhaps it was mere diplomatic manoeuvring that pushed the Frankish king to denounce his pagan past, which always entailed the danger of losing him the support of his pagan followers; historians have emphasized a letter sent by Remigius, the bishop of Rheims who eventually baptised Clovis, in which he pointed out to the Frankish King that 'he would find it advantageous to have the support of the Gallo-Roman church.'

The later 490s saw a series of poorly attested Frankish attacks upon Visigoth Aquitania, which were boosted by an alliance with the Arborychi ('Armoricans') from modern-day Brittany who, probably, provided Clovis improved access to the Visigothic kingdom south of the Loire. But the Visigoths eventually repelled the Frankish attacks, with Gregory of Tours reporting a sixty-day siege of Nantes, at the mouth of the Loire, by the Franks led by Clovis himself; he was put to flight by the Visigoths. The latter also regained control of Tours, on the south bank of the Loire, and Bordeaux – the capital city of Aquitaine – by 505; these cities had been captured by the Franks in the previous decade in what seems to historians to have been more of a raid than a campaign of conquest.

Around 500, Clovis made the unwise decision to be drawn into the Burgundian civil war on the side of the Burgundian king Godegisel. The latter's defeat was a political and diplomatic setback for Clovis, with Frankish captives sent 'in exile, to Toulouse, to King Alaric', while the Visigoths, who had supported Godegisel's rival Gundobad, even gained control over Avignon for their troubles. Nevertheless, Clovis continued to have designs on Aquitania. He planned to improve his standing in western Europe by strengthening his alliance with other Germanic leaders; thus he married his sister Audefleda to the ambitious Ostrogothic king Theoderic.

It has been argued that the Battle of Vouillé was the opening military encounter of a campaign to destroy the Visigothic kingdom in Aquitaine and to conquer the south-western region of Gaul. Bachrach, however, has raised serious doubts as to whether this military campaign was the initiative of the Frankish king. He speculates that:

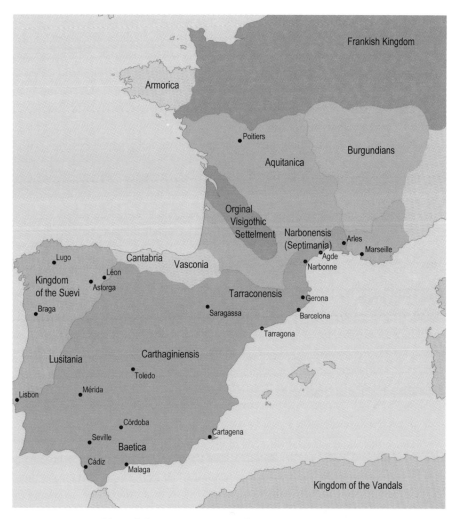

Ethnic and administrative organization of Western Europe around AD500.

… an imperial policy intended to strengthen the position of the Franks, now Nicene Christians with the support of the episcopal hierarchy in the north against the Arian Visigoths and Ostrogoths, surely would have been attractive to [Byzantine] Emperor Anastasius.[1]

In fact, the primary sources report of Emperor Anastasius' envoys who met with Clovis, probably at his capital in Paris, and promises were made by both sides.[2] The role of the Nicene bishops in Aquitaine, who worked as mediators between Paris and Constantinople to support the cause of the Roman-Christian king of the Franks against the Arian Visigoths, should also be considered a strong possibility, although the sources are silent on this issue.[3]

In 506, the year before the battle, Clovis agreed a non-aggression pact with the Visigoth king Alaric, after a meeting on an island in the middle of the River Loire – the symbolic border between the two kingdoms.[4] And it is probably at this time that Alaric handed over to Clovis the fortress cities of Nantes, Angers, Tours and Orléans, which controlled the lower Loire valley with its immense agricultural and commercial importance; people in the aforementioned cities were Roman-Catholic Christians who despised, or even hated, the Arian Visigoths.

However, we will never know whether the two leaders negotiated in good faith, or if this was a ruse perpetrated by Clovis to throw off the Visigoth king from his real intention of invading Aquitaine. Finally, the Frankish king arranged for a military alliance with the Burgundian king, Gundobad, which involved Burgundian troops mounting operations against various Visigoth cities and strongholds in the south-east, perhaps acting as a 'shield' army to intercept a possible Ostrogoth invasion by Theoderic to support his son-in-law, Alaric.

THE PRELUDE TO THE BATTLE

In February or early March 507, Clovis issued orders throughout the *regnum Francorum* for the mobilization of the army. Shortly after, in early spring, he crossed the Loire into Aquitaine. Clovis' campaign strategy was to invade Visigoth-controlled Aquitaine and move south as fast as possible, hoping, no doubt, that he would be welcomed by the Catholic Gallo-Roman socio-political élite of the region, who opposed Visigoth domination. Some historians have added that Clovis probably believed that he could integrate the militia levies of the fortified cities of Aquitaine into his army.

On the other hand, it is clear from the *History* of Gregory of Tours that Alaric's strategy was reactive, ordering his troops to concentrate at Poitiers to intercept the invading Franks.[5] It also points out the fact that the Visigoth king had intelligence about the invasion early enough to allow him to order his units drawn from the civitates of Aquitaine and Auvergne, to concentrate at the strongly fortified city of Poitiers, some 100km (60 miles) south of the Loire.

Poitier's importance lay in its strategic location at the junction of old Roman roads going north to south, and the crossing of a navigable river. As would be the case twenty-two centuries later, when Charles Martel invaded Aquitaine to intercept a Muslim campaigning army, the River Vienne was a major obstacle to overcome – especially in April, a period when the early spring rains and the melting snows had swollen the river. Poitiers was also the site of an important religious centre, the late Roman basilica of St-Hilaire, which would be restored and adorned with golden mosaics and precious relics by Clovis shortly after his victory.

After fording the Vienne where wild animals were seen crossing it, Clovis placed his encampment in the environs of Vouillé to the north-west of Poitiers, at a place where the distance between his army and the city of Poitiers was about 15 kilometres (9 miles). He had sent his scouts the day before the battle to find out about the whereabouts of the

Visigoth army, thus having ample time to position his soldiers on a field of battle of his own choice.

THE OPPOSING FORCES

Weapons

There is very little evidence of what might be thought of as typically 'barbarian' equipment, because there was very little standardization among, or even within, the various tribal armies that had infiltrated the empire in the fourth and fifth centuries. The only exception is the *francisca*, a Frankish throwing axe that had an average weight of 1 to 2kg, the wooden handle measuring some 40cm in length, and the iron head some 18cm.

Similarities between 'barbarian' and Roman weapons in post-Roman Europe came as a direct result not only of the enormous cultural and economic influence of the empire beyond its frontiers for many centuries, but also because of the vast quantities of manufactured arms and armour in the local *fabricae* that supplied the 'barbarians' who fought with/for the Romans. In fact, the arms utilized by the late Roman army remained the basic weapons of fighting men in the period up to and through the rule of Charlemagne (ruled 768–814).

Soldiers fighting on foot largely used the short sword and the spear. As it is to be expected for this early period, there was no standardization in spear design, and archaeological findings point to the conclusion that each smith produced his own style and size of spearhead, with no official guidelines. A possible exception was the Frankish *angon*, a throwing spear that resembled a Roman *pilum* and was modified (in the seventh century) by three points attached at the end of the shaft where the iron staff was fixed, and were turned backwards like hooks to get stuck on an enemy warrior's shield and put it out of use.

Numerous 'barbarian' gravesites point to the assumption that the Germanic peoples in pre-Carolingian Europe were carrying both long swords (75–100cm long, 6cm in width) and short ones (40cm long, 4cm in width), both straight and two-edged, and the *scramasax* – a long (20cm) dagger used by peoples in northern Europe (Vikings, Saxons, Franks), either as a primary edged weapon or as a side arm. Probably the most common weapon of the period, however, was the spear, which varied enormously in shape and size. Mounted troops carried the lance and long sword, although most mounted fighting men had short swords as well.

The most basic defensive armament would have been the wooden shield, either round or convex, and some 80–90cm in diameter. Manuscript illuminations support the idea that helmets between the late fifth to seventh centuries were commonly of a type called *Spangenhelme*, where the bowl of the helmet was made of several parts, held together by reinforcing clasps, which covered the joins. Contemporary written sources imply that metallic armour (both mail and lamellar) was also common, though far from universal.

Where metallic armour was not available, warriors probably made use of boiled leather or padded protection. Nobles also owned a helmet, usually produced from a single sheet of iron, and chain mail body armour, both lavishly decorated and similar in construction to late Roman military equipment.

Military Forces

Alaric's military forces were composed of an unknown number of both Visigoths and Gallo-Romans. The former were the descendants of the victorious armies that had defeated Attila and the Huns fifty-six years earlier; the more affluent who were able to support a horse and armour were fighting as cavalry, while the poorer levies were conscripted to fight on foot, with either a spear or a bow.

The majority of the campaigning army, however, was largely composed of the local Gallo-Roman levies, who lacked both horses and sophisticated military equipment because of the low level of the minimum wealth requirement. Finally, there was a rather small élite of well armed and well trained mounted troops among the men serving in these armies, who were the household troops of the Gallo-Roman aristocrats.

Clovis' forces were also drawn from a wide variety of sources, although again, their exact numbers are not known. These were mainly troops from the military household of the king and his aristocrats, a group of élite warriors of either Frankish or Gallo-Roman descent, or foreign mercenaries from neighbouring countries. Other sources that contributed to the early Merovingian army were the landholders of military lands who owed military service, and the regular troops from the late Roman institution of the *laeti* – defeated enemy troops who were settled in Roman territory and owed hereditary military service to the late Roman state.

THE BATTLE

There are no surviving eyewitness accounts of the battle, hence there is no way to ascertain the battle deployment of either of the armies, or the ratio between mounted and foot soldiers. Nevertheless, Gregory of Tours recounts that the battle promptly opened with the ordinary exchanges of missiles – arrows and probably lances as well, thus firmly conforming to the Roman battle practices that had been in place for many centuries.[6] This was followed by a mounted charge by the Visigoths against the Frankish phalanx of foot soldiers, who held their ground despite the ferocity of the attack, reminiscent of the Visigoth mounted charge at Châlons fifty years earlier.

Our sources do not give any more details on the course of the battle, or the tactics employed by the two opposing armies. However, there is a reference in Gregory of Tour's *History* of a possible feigned retreat conducted by the Visigoth cavalry in the face of the Frankish phalanx, apparently in an attempt to break their solid formation. This effort failed. Regrettably, Gregory is silent about what followed the Visigoths' retreat, and he notes simply that 'king Clovis won the victory by God's aid'. This comment could very well mean that Clovis counter-attacked with a cavalry unit he may have kept in reserve, but this is mere speculation.

The end result was a complete victory for the Franks after Alaric was killed in the final stage of the battle; tradition has it that Clovis was directly responsible for Alaric's death.

CONCLUSIONS

Following the successful outcome of the battle, the Frankish king swept south to take the Gothic-ruled cities of the northern, central and western Aquitaine (*Gallia Aquitania*), including the fortress city of Bordeaux. The Visigoth capital at Toulouse in south-eastern Aquitaine (*Gallia Narbonensis*) was also captured, along with the royal treasure, while Clovis' Burgundian allies took Narbonne. Further Frankish advances to the south and east, both along Carcassonne and Arles, failed because of the intervention of the Ostrogothic king, Theodoric, who shortly thereafter captured both Narbonne and Toulouse. It would be another two centuries before the Franks gained access to the Mediterranean Sea.

When Clovis returned to Tours in spring 508 to celebrate his triumph, he received both the patriciate and the honorary consulate by Emperor Anastasius. These honours qualified Clovis to serve as an imperial governor in southern Gaul, while recognizing his *de facto* status as βασιλεύς (king) in the northern half of Gaul. He had won a decisive victory at Vouillé against another emerging superpower of the age, a victory that settled once and for all the future of continental Gaul. King Alaric was killed, and his army was in tatters and unable to withstand the further conquest of Aquitaine. The future history of Gaul was to be written not by the Goths but by the Franks, who also gave it a new name: France.

4 THE BATTLE OF ONGAL

The Establishment of the First Bulgarian State

Date Summer AD680
Location The Ongal area in the Danube delta (present-day Tulcea County, Romania)

THE HISTORICAL BACKGROUND

THE BULGARS WERE a Turkic people who had been living in scattered tribes north of the Black Sea and the Sea of Azov, and along the lower Don, already since the late fifth century AD.[1] They held their origins to lie in the fifth-century Hunnic confederation, and considered Attila (434–453) to be their first ruler.

Historians have identified two major groups: the Kutrigurs, who had moved west of the Black Sea in the 490s, and the Utigurs to their east. Before and during the reign of Emperor Justinian (reigned 527–65), contemporary sources note that both groups raided the empire from time to time, and the government was fairly effective at either buying them off with tributes, or playing off one group against the other.[2] In the late sixth century, both of these groups became clients of other nomads that dominated the northern shores of the Black Sea: the Avars and the West Turks.

Around the 630s, several contemporary sources refer to a group of Onogur Bulgars living in the region between the Caucasus and the Sea of Azov. Their ruler was mentioned by the name Kuvrat, and it is known that he had already established good relations with the empire, as Theophanes and Nicephorus – both ninth-century historians but probably drawing from a common source – report of an Onogur Bulgar prince named Orhan and his nephew Kuvrat arriving at Constantinople in 619 to agree on a treaty with the empire, and who accepted Christianity and the Byzantine title of patrician (*patrikios*).[3] Kuvrat became the ruler of the Onogurs, and in 635 he threw off Avar rule. He also succeeded in uniting all the eastern Bulgar groups who were living north of the Black Sea, the Sea of Azov and the Caucasus.

Kuvrat died in 642, after which date one of his five sons, Asparukh, moved into what is now Bessarabia in modern-day Moldova. The reason behind the mass migration of this Bulgar tribe was the pressure applied by another Turkic nation that had migrated westwards – the Khazars, who were soon to establish a great Steppe empire centred on the lower Volga. Then in the 670s, Asparukh's Bulgars crossed the Danube into Byzantine territory and began conquering the Slavic tribes who had been living in the eastern Balkans since the second half of the fifth century. These Slavs had not formed a state but were living as tribes, and since the 670s primary sources talk about the 'Seven Tribes' being subjugated by the Bulgars, perhaps a kind of Slavic proto-federation.

The Byzantine government was slow to react to this growing threat by Asparukh and his tribesmen because of troubles with their arch enemy – the Arabs.[4] The Empire was confronted with the first Arab siege of Constantinople between 674 and 678, a major conflict that broke out between the two superpowers during which the Arabs, led by Caliph Mu'awiya I (ruled 661–680), used the peninsula of Cyzicus near the city as a base to spend the winter, and returned every spring to launch attacks against the city's fortifications.

Even before the launching of the Arab campaign against the Byzantine capital, Arab forces under the Caliph's son Yazid had been harrying Anatolia with land and sea raids, capturing Amorion in the heart of the Anatolian theme, while Arab fleets were attacking both Sicily and Africa. In 672 the Caliph had dispatched three fleets that paralysed the naval theme of the Carabisiani on the southern Anatolian coast, and the following year an Arab army took most of Cilicia in south-eastern Asia Minor, including its chief city Tarsus.

Small wonder, therefore, that the Byzantine government considered the Danube invasions by the Bulgars as a mere side show. Perhaps the Emperor and his advisers also

Bulgarian settlement and territorial expansion along the River Danube in the seventh and eighth centuries.

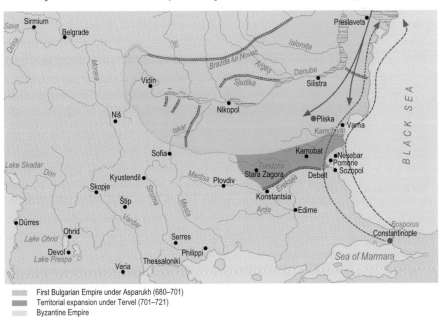

First Bulgarian Empire under Asparukh (680–701)
Territorial expansion under Tervel (701–721)
Byzantine Empire
Bulgarians of Asparukh
Campain of Constantine IV against Asparukh (680)
Earthen fortifications

considered they could use the Bulgars, with whom they had developed good relations until then, in the same way that the Romans had been using 'barbarians' for centuries: (a) as *dediticii*, 'barbarians' who had surrendered themselves to the Empire and been received into the state for settlement; (b) as *laeti*, 'barbarians' captured by the Romans and settled on the land; and (c) as *foederati*, 'barbarians' held in a treaty (*foedus*) relationship with the Empire and compelled to settle in imperial land and serve the Empire.[5] Whatever the case, Emperor Constantine IV (reigned 668–85) was able to pay attention to the Balkans only after the pressure by the Arabs had been relieved, following the truce and the subsequent peace treaty agreed – probably – in 679.

The Emperor launched a campaign in Macedonia and Greece against the Slavs, who had been raiding Thessalonica since 677, apparently taking advantage of the Arab siege of the capital; he invaded Slav territory through the valley of the Strymon river, which cuts through the Rhodope mountains in eastern Macedonia, and he reoccupied the Slavic enclaves in northern and central Greece (theme of Hellas). Yet the Byzantines were still unaware of the danger posed by the crossing of the Danube by Asparukh and his tribesmen and women.

THE PRELUDE TO THE BATTLE

Sometime in the middle of the 670s, Asparukh built a fortified camp to serve as a fortress and base for raiding expeditions south of the Danube and into Dobruja – the area between the lower Danube river and the Black Sea – and the eastern Danubian Plain. This fortified position was carefully selected because it was situated in a naturally defended region, bordered by rivers and marshes near the Peuce Island, called the Ongal (Greek: Onglos), north of the Danube in southern Moldavia.[6] In the summer of 680, the Byzantines launched an attack against the Bulgars in the Ongal, aspiring to a quick victory and a show of force that would push the Bulgars to accept imperial suzerainty. They were oblivious to the fact that the Bulgar wooden ramparts and the swampy terrain would pose a serious threat to the imperial forces.

THE OPPOSING FORCES

The primary sources offer absolutely no indication about the numbers for the opposing armies that clashed in the swampy area of the Ongal. Theophanes mentions that the emperor assembled an army from 'all the themata', which he ordered to cross into Thrace to face the growing menace from the Bulgars. Although Nicephorus does not corroborate Theophanes' information, the latter's comment could have been an oversimplification rather than an exaggeration; in spite of the peace with the Arabs in the East, it would have been inconceivable for Constantine to have stripped his eastern borders of troops for his upcoming campaign in the Lower Danube.

What Theophanes could have meant with the aforementioned comment is that the Byzantines had mustered a strong army, with units from all five themes of the Empire, to march into north-eastern Thrace against the invaders. According to Treadgold's meticulous calculations, the total number of troops from all five themes in Asia Minor and the Balkans (Opsician, Thracesian, Anatolian, Armeniac and Carabisiani) could have amounted to anything between 90,000 to 150,000 combat troops.[7] On top of that, the sources also do not offer any hints about the Bulgarian army's numbers; the only thing we know is that the Bulgars would have been greatly outnumbered.

Historians have very little evidence about the structure of the Bulgarian army during the first two centuries of the state's expansion south of the Danube. Since the Bulgars were originally steppe people, it can be assumed they fought mostly as nomadic cavalry, while the subjugated Slavs generally fought as infantry. The Bulgar cavalry was organized within a decimal system, exactly like the rest of the steppe people such as the Huns, the Mongols and other north Asian peoples, in units of 10, 100, 1,000 and 10,000.

Weapons and Fighting Tactics

The majority of the Bulgar warriors were lightly armed horsemen whose main weapon was the composite bow – a weapon with an effective range of over 250m (880ft). Nevertheless, they were also very well equipped for hand-to-hand combat, and they carried weapons for *mêlée* conflict such as the sword and the lasso. These kinds of troops were weighed down with little or no body armour or helmets, making them ideal for conducting military operations in the mountainous, wooded and broken terrain of the Balkans, while their lack of heavy armour allowed them to move fast and surprise their enemies. The Bulgars also fielded a body of noble cavalry who could afford metallic armour and who carried a lance in addition to bow, sword and lasso.

Because steppe nations such as the Bulgars were initially lacking in arms and armour compared to their sedentary neighbours, they relied on taking full advantage of the potential of two key components of nomadic life: first, the horse, which had always been an important animal for the peoples who lived on the grasslands of Eurasia for millennia. Its taming had a profound impact on the life of the steppe peoples because it allowed them to range over a much wider distance and outpace their enemies in the battlefield. But the full potential of the horse as a tactical system was only realized when it was combined with another steppe innovation: the composite bow, which brought both mobility and firepower. Therefore the steppe peoples gained the edge on the battlefield when they kept their distance from the enemy and harassed them by repeated attacks and withdrawals that would frustrate and disorganize them.

Regarding the Slavs and their fighting tactics in this period, the best descriptions come from Procopius of Caesarea's *History of the Wars* (Book VII, written around AD550), and the military handbook known as the *Strategikon* (written around AD600).[8] We read in the *Strategikon*:

> They are armed with short javelins, two to each man. Some also have nice-looking but unwieldy shields. In addition, they use wooden bows with short arrows smeared

with a poisonous drug which is very effective. They live like bandits and love to carry out attacks against their enemies in densely wooded, narrow, and steep places ... They are also not prepared to fight a battle standing in close order, or to present themselves on open and level ground.

This last comment provided crucial information about their battle tactics. They could be viewed as typically unconventional warriors who could cause troubles to the imperial armies.

Evidence from historical texts and pictorial representations shows that many swords of the Byzantine period fall into the category of the straight-bladed, round-tipped, double-edged weapon, capable of inflicting both a cutting and a thrusting blow. In fact, sources such as Procopius and the *Strategikon* suggest that the influence of the Avars was particularly powerful in the Byzantine armies of the sixth century. According to Procopius, the best armed horseman was equipped with a lance and a 'Herul' sword that was hung from a baldric or a shoulder strap on his left shoulder.

The spear was the paramount weapon for the infantry of the period as well, with the *Strategikon* instructing the general to fill the first two lines of the infantry formation and the last one with spearmen (κοντάτους). Finally, the Byzantine archer was armed with the same composite bow introduced during the fourth century by the Huns.

For the Byzantines, torso armour would have varied between chain mail, scale, lamellar, quilted or leather corselet worn over a thick or padded undergarment, depending on the financial standing of the wearer. For infantry, this corselet generally resembled a cuirass in form, although elbow-length sleeves or hanging strips were common, while for cavalry it extended down to protect much of the thighs by being split up the front and back. This kind of protection was supplemented by helmets and felt caps. Rectangular and oval shields, averaging some 1.2m (4ft) in height and 77cm (2.5ft) in width, were mostly carried by infantry, with the cavalry being armed with smaller round ones.

THE BATTLE

Regrettably there is very little information available on this all-important battle, which resulted in the first serious setback for the Byzantine empire in the Balkans since the Battle of Adrianople in AD378. Strategically speaking, the Byzantines made the serious mistake of fighting in a battlefield chosen by the enemy. Vegetius, the late Roman author of the famous *Epitome of Military Science*, noted that 'the good general should know that a large part of a victory depends on the actual place in which the battle is fought'; fourteen centuries later, Clausewitz wrote that 'in these ways the relationship between warfare and terrain determines the peculiar character of military action'.

Therefore, as in every conflict, the outcome of a campaign relies on how well a military leader can grasp and take advantage of both the physical landscape (the diversity of terrain features, weather patterns and so on) and the human landscape (political

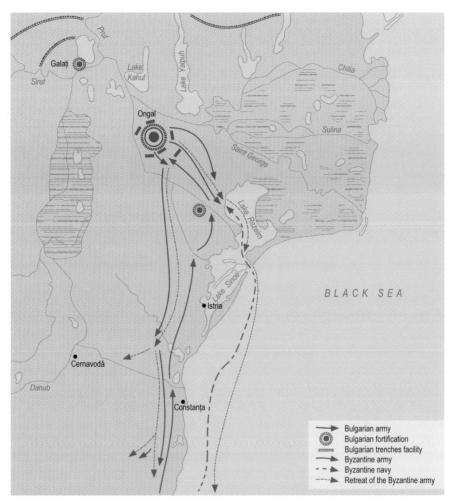

Emperor Constantine IV's summer campaign of 680 against the Bulgarian fortified position near Peuce Island, called the Ongal (Greek: Onglos), north of the Danube in southern Moldavia.

structures, population distribution and settlement, road networks), both of which affect a military operation. Constantine and his advisers made the grave mistake of planning a piecemeal attack against the Bulgar fortifications through the wet and boggy terrain that covered the entire area. The marshes and the river channels not only blocked the view of the enemy units, but turned the regular marching of heavily armed units – especially the cavalry – into an ordeal.

Instead of attacking in a solid front, with units supporting each other and being able to bring their siege machines close to the base of the wooden ramparts, the marshes forced the Byzantines to attack in smaller groups, and literally bogged down their attack. The Byzantines would also have lost the advantage of their cavalry, which would have been rendered useless in a siege operation anyway; after all, we read in the *Strategikon*:

Aerial view of Lake Razelm, a large freshwater lagoon on the shores of the Black Sea in Romania, south of the Danube Delta. It formed the point of entry into the Danube Delta of the Byzantine naval squadron dispatched to support the 680 campaign. An indication of the boggy and marshy ground of the region.

'Select open, smooth, and level terrain, if you can do so, without any swamps, ditches, or brush which could break up the formation.'

With the attacks against the wooden ramparts failing miserably for the Byzantines, the sources note that the Bulgars 'became bolder', and probably launched a series of counter attacks against the disorganized imperial units, thus forcing the latter into a retreat. They may also have been working their way around to outflank the main Byzantine army. Whatever the case, the retreat quickly broke down into a rout, with many Byzantine soldiers losing their lives in the surrounding area.

According to popular belief, the emperor was struck by gout and decided to withdraw to Mesembria, a major port further south along the Black Sea coast, to seek treatment. The troops thought that he had fled the battlefield, and in turn began fleeing. But this is nothing more than a well thought attempt to conceal Constantine's defeat by 'that foul and unclean tribe', as Theophanes calls the Bulgars.

CONCLUSIONS

The Byzantine debacle at Ongal enabled the Bulgars to overrun Dobruja and the eastern Danubian Plain, a fertile region that offered more socio-economic advantages to the newcomers than the featureless and sparsely populated steppes of Ukraine and the lower Don river. Asparukh spent a year consolidating his control over the region, subjugating or reducing to tributaries their Slavic inhabitants. In order to prevent Byzantine territories south of the Balkan Mountains from being raided by Asparukh's tribesmen, Emperor Constantine was reduced to negotiating a peace agreement.

The treaty concluded in autumn 681 was the first in which the Byzantines officially surrendered Balkan imperial lands by recognizing the existence of a foreign state controlling the peninsula's lower Danubian territories. Asparukh was also granted annual tribute, and ruled a huge Bulgar state that stretched from the Dniester river on the steppes to the Balkan mountains, organizing his state's defences and consolidating his authority by establishing a centralized Bulgar governmental infrastructure with himself as the head of state and supreme commander (*khan*). He transplanted subject Slavs *en masse* from their original homes on the plains to frontier regions to serve as border guards, with limited local autonomy under their local leaders (*župans*). These Slavic population transfers rendered the heartlands of the state – Dobruja and the eastern Danubian Plain – exclusive Bulgar preserves, settled and worked by Bulgars, who soon became mixed pastoralists-agriculturalists.

The Byzantine Empire had just won another arch enemy, this time in a different operational theatre – the Balkans. Following the outcome of the Battle of Ongal, regional antagonism and feelings of (pre-modern) nationalism in the region south of the Danube ran high until the Ottoman conquest unified the region politically and economically under the *millet system*, only to re-emerge in the first decades of the twentieth century when the entire Balkan Peninsula was being reshaped both politically, ethnically and linguistically.

5 THE BATTLE OF GUADALETE

The Beginning of the Muslim Conquest of Spain

Date Between 19 and 26 July 711
Location Between the ancient city of Medina Sidonia, in modern Andalucía, and
the River Guadalete, in southern Spain

THE HISTORICAL BACKGROUND

THE EXPANSION OF Islam has been portrayed as one of the most dramatic geo-political events in the last two millennia of human history – an explosion of Semitic people out of the Arabian Peninsula that incorporated all the southern coast of the Mediterranean Sea, from the Middle East and Egypt to Morocco and the Iberian Peninsula in a short space of time (the seventh century). There was no attack upon – or forced conversion of – the 'People of the Book', and the Islamic expansion could be interpreted as a takeover of territory where the established ruling class was simply replaced by another, while the administrative mechanisms remained largely unaffected.

Therefore, the Islamic overthrow of the seemingly powerful Visigoth Kingdom of Spain in five years in the early eighth century AD should be appreciated as one of the most decisive events in the history of Europe for a thousand years, from the collapse of Roman power in Spain in the fifth century to the Spanish conquest of the last Muslim *bastion* in Granada in 1492.

Within a generation after the death of the Prophet Muhammad in 632, Muslim armies had inflicted decisive defeats over the two superpowers of the time, the Byzantines (in the Battle of Yarmouk, AD636) and the Sassanid Persians (in the Battle of al-Qadisiya, AD636), destroying the latter and taking a huge chunk from the former's possessions in the Middle East, in Mesopotamia and in Egypt. By the middle of the seventh century, Muslim generals were launching sporadic raiding expeditions into Cyrenaica (modern Libya). Byzantine rule in north-west Africa at the time was largely confined to the coastal plains, while autonomous Berber polities controlled the rest.

In 670, the Muslims founded a forward base in northern Tunisia, the settlement of Kairouan, from where to launch further attacks westwards. They eventually captured Carthage in 698, and Tangiers sometime between 705 and 710. Crucially, after the fall of Tangiers, many Berbers joined the Muslim army, providing the Muslim generals with a huge stock of highly skilled mounted troops for their expansionist campaigns.

The Visigoths had settled in southern France in 418 and established their capital at Toulouse. The advance of the Vandals from Iberia into North Africa in 429, combined with the Suevic annexation of the Roman provinces of Lusitania, Baetica and Carthaginensis in the west and central regions of the peninsula between AD438 and 446, provided the Visigoths with the opportunity to expand into Spain, while the southward expansion of the Franks under Clovis (especially after his defeat of the Visigoths at Vouillé in 507) made it necessary.

The Visigoths first arrived in Spain in 446 as *foederati* in the service of the *magister utriusque militiae* Vitus, who failed to subdue the Suevi and restore Roman administration in Hispania. They eventually defeated the Suevi in 456, pushing them into the north-west corner of the peninsula, and clearing the way for their follow-up expansion as far south as Gibraltar by 584.

The Visigoth state was an ethnically stratified society where relations between the new socio-political élite and the Hispano-Romans were strained, as about 200,000 Goths ruled an indigenous population of almost eight million. The ethnic rift between German-speaking suzerains and Latin-speaking subjects was heightened even further by religious difference: the Visigoths were nominally Arian Christians, while the Hispano-Romans were, for the most part, Catholic. The Spanish territories also had a significant Jewish population, which further muddled the religious map of the Hispanic society, especially in the cities. The need to acculturate to the majority population was self-evident, leading to the church council held at Toledo in 589, which formally enacted this conversion to Catholicism for the entire kingdom.

The small numbers the Visigoths had to contend with to rule Iberia restricted them to residing in special urban quarters, largely staying away from the Spanish countryside. Until 652, the Goths promoted both an institutional and legal separation of the two ethnic groups: each province had both a Roman governor, who administered Roman law to the Hispano-Roman population, and Gothic officials who dealt with infractions committed by Visigoths. Therefore, King Recceswinth's (reigned AD649–672) abolition of the Roman law – and of the dual system as a consequence – was viewed as an act that served only to heighten ethnic tensions.

Furthermore the religious and legal merger of the two peoples proved only fictive, as the Romans now had to play according to rules set by the Gothic élite, who had the military and economic power. Hence the intense stratification of the society along ethnic lines was reinforced rather than diminished, to the point where distinctions between Romans and Goths persisted even after the Islamic conquest.[1]

Economic division of labour further separated the two peoples: the Goths were largely herders, while the Hispano-Romans farmed the land and grew wheat and barley, grapes and vegetables. On top of this, the entire economy was in a state of disarray, and agriculture was ruined as a result of a series of natural disasters that began in the seventh century, with contemporary chronicles reporting devastating famine and plagues in the reign of Erwig (680–686).[2] Therefore the growing political instability of late seventh-century and early eighth-century Spain has to be looked at from the perspective of the worsening harvests, droughts, famine, ethnic tensions, urban decline and depopulation that preceded the Muslim conquest of 711.

The ending of King Wittiza's reign plunged the Visigoth kingdom into the deepest political crisis. Wittiza was the Visigoth King of Spain from 694 until his death, co-ruling with his father, Egica, until 702 or 703. It was during the joint reign of Egica and Wittiza that a Byzantine fleet raided the coasts of southern Spain, probably as part of a failed Byzantine expedition to relieve Carthage from the Muslims in 697.

In 710 (or 711) Wittiza was overthrown, and most probably murdered, in a military coup mounted by Roderic, the *dux* of Baetica (modern Andalusia). Following the military coup, the kingdom was divided into two factions: the south-west faction (Lusitania and western Carthaginiensis) remained in Roderic's hands, while the north-east (Tarraconensis and Narbonensis) went to a certain Achilla, whose relationship to Roderic is unknown – his rule is confirmed solely by numismatic evidence.

THE PRELUDE TO THE BATTLE

The campaign that culminated in the Battle of Guadalete was not a raid or an isolated Muslim attack across the Straits of Gibraltar, but rather, the logical outcome of the Muslim expansionist strategy in western Mediterranean to date. After the Muslim conquest of Tangiers (between 705 and 710), the new governor of Ifriqiya (Africa), called Mūsā ibn Nuṣayr, appointed Ṭāriq ibn Ziyād as governor of the city of Tangiers, the commander who was to lead the Muslim armies to victory at Guadalete.

On or around 28 April 711, Ṭāriq launched his campaign from Ceuta and disembarked at Jabal-al-Ṭāriq ('Rock of Ṭāriq') on the southern tip of the Iberian Peninsula. From there, he pushed north to Caetaria (modern Algeciras), and then followed the Roman road that led north-west to Seville. At the time, Roderic was fighting the Basques in the vicinity of Pamplona, when he was recalled to deal with the Muslim invasion. What happened next is obscure, but we think that between 19 and 23 July, the week before the battle, there were numerous inconclusive skirmishes near the La Janda lake, in the plain stretching from the Río Barbate to the Río Guadalete (modern province of Cádiz, Andalucía).[3]

The *Mozarabic Chronicle* of 754 talks about the battle that took place in the 'Transductine mountains', which is impossible to identify on its own, unless we combine it with the first Arabic narrative of the conquest of al-Andalus by Ibn 'Abd al-Hakam (c. 803–71), where the author mentions a battle in a place called 'Shedunia, in a valley which is called this day the valley of Umm-Hakim'. Taking this into consideration, we can then identify the place of the battle as somewhere between the ancient city of Medina Sidonia, in modern Andalucía, and the River Guadalete, some 20km (12 miles) to the north of the city.[4]

THE OPPOSING FORCES

Sadly, it is almost impossible to ascertain either the exact numbers or the composition of the armies that clashed near the La Janda lake in late July of 711. Neither Christian nor Muslim accounts of the eighth and ninth centuries provide us with numbers for the opposing armies. Some modern historians have put their trust in much later Muslim sources, which speak of an invading force of 7,000 to 12,000 men, facing a Visigothic army of over 100,000 strong. Although Roderic's numbers certainly look outrageously high, Collins believes that even the number 7,000 is also likely to be too high for the size of the Berber invading forces. Otherwise, Glick has determined that the three-month delay between Ṭāriq's landing in April, and the clash with the Goths in July, could be attributed to the Muslim leader's request for some 5,000 men as reinforcements from Mūsā ibn Nuṣayr – hence the number of 12,000 may be viewed as plausible.[5]

However, to me it seems highly unlikely that Roderic would have been able to muster more than a couple of thousand troops to counter the threat in the south, bearing in mind not just the political upheaval of the previous year, but that he was also fighting a Basque insurrection to the north of the country. Furthermore, after the sixth century, and definitely in the seventh, paid regular armies had ceased to exist, and we can no longer talk about a standing army in Visigothic Spain. Both kings Wamba (reigned 672–680) and Erwing (reigned 680–687) had issued military laws according to which all landowners were liable for military service, although what this – practically – meant was that a stratum of reasonably significant landowners with their retinues would have appeared for military service after they were summoned.

For some historians,[6] the decline of the Visigoth kingdom owes much to this shift, from an army whose mobilization was carried out by royally appointed officers, to one where military forces were composed essentially of the followings of greater landholders. The latter had to be rewarded with lands and booty to maintain their allegiance to the king, but when the Visigothic expansion ceased after the unification of the kingdom in the early seventh century, the relationship between a king and his magnates would have deteriorated, and it would have been very difficult to raise a substantial field force. Therefore Roderic would probably have had to rely on only a small number of élite landowners and their warrior followings, including his personal following, to face the Muslim invading army.

Military Equipment and Armour

Since I have dealt with the equipment and armour of the Visigoths and the early Muslim soldiers in the studies of the battles of Vouillé and Poitiers, respectively, it will suffice here to give a brief outlook of the two types of soldier that would have faced each other in 711. Depending on his financial standing, the military equipment of an early medieval Visigoth warrior would have included two main offensive weapons, the sword and the spear. Pre-Carolingian Germanic warriors would have carried a variety of long, straight, two-edged swords and spears that also varied enormously in shape and size.

Visigothic law also implies that archery was important, and retainers brought to the army were to be equipped with bows. For defence against the weapons just described, Visigoth warriors relied upon a round, or perhaps oval, wooden shield, while ownership of metallic helmets and armour (both mail and lamellar) was common, though far from universal.

Historians surmise that Ṭāriq ibn Ziyād's army was predominantly non-Arab Berber cavalry that would have fought as mounted infantry. Berber troops very often accompanied the regular (multi-ethnic) Muslim armies of the Umayyads, the Abbasids of Baghdad, and the Fatimids of Egypt. This lightly armed cavalry wore little or no armour, and were armed with a short lance. A Byzantine military treatise from the tenth century confirms that the Berbers were using enveloping tactics against their enemies:

> If the enemy proceeds in close order with their forces in proper formation, bringing along a vast host of cavalry and infantry, and their forces move in against one side of our units, the *Arabitai* will encircle our four-sided [infantry] formation in a swarm, as they usually do, confident in their horses.[7]

THE BATTLE

The amount of information available to scholars about the Battle of Guadalete is frustratingly meagre. The only thing that is indisputable is that the Visigoths were completely defeated, and their king, Roderic, was killed in the field of battle. One of the two main Christian primary sources for the battle is the *Mozarabic Chronicle*, compiled shortly after 754. It was written by a Christian ecclesiastic who seems to have had an intimate knowledge of events in Muslim Spain, while his derogatory description of the Berbers mirrors the contemporary Arab contempt for the native peoples of Morocco. He probably had access to written or oral sources in Arabic, and it has even been suggested that he may have been some sort of a minister of the Arab government that followed the conquest of the 710s.

Nevertheless, the *Chronicle*'s account for the battle is surprisingly short, and lacks any battle details besides the outcome. What the author does emphasize, however, are the internal rivalries in the Visigoth army that led to the disastrous outcome for Roderic after his 'allies' abandoned him. He writes:

> Roderic headed for the Transductine mountains to fight them [Muslims], and in that battle the entire army of the Goths, which had come with him fraudulently and in rivalry out of ambition for the kingship, fled and he was killed.

The aforementioned information is corroborated by the *Chronicle of Alfonso III*, an account written by Alfonso III of Asturias in the 880s. The author of the chronicle confirms that the Visigoths were in the midst of a civil war at the time of the invasion, and there is the overhanging suspicion of a treacherous alliance between Wittiza's sons (Olmund, Romulus and Ardabast), or some other disaffected Visigothic noblemen or relatives of Wittiza, and the Muslims that led to a substantial part of the Gothic army to flee the battlefield. We read in the *Chronicle*:

> But, weighed down by the quantity of their sins, and exposed by the treachery of the sons of Witiza, the Goths were put to flight. The army, fleeing to its destruction, was almost annihilated.

Perhaps Roderic's enemies intended to abandon him on the field, to be defeated and killed by the Muslims, and possibly replace him with a puppet king; however, nothing of this can be verified by the primary sources.

Sadly, similar problems with regard to details about the course of the battle exist with the Arabic sources. Most of them are much later than the Christian ones in date, but come increasingly under heavy criticism.[8] Crucially, none of them predates the account by Ibn 'Abd al-Hakam (c. 803–71). The latter simply reports that 'they [Ṭāriq and Roderic] fought a severe battle; but God, mighty and great, killed Roderic and his companions.'

CONCLUSIONS

The Gothic rout and the death of King Roderic, the 'last of the Goths', at the Battle of Guadalete in July 711, eclipsed the Visigothic kingdom and radically changed the course of the history of Spain and Europe for the next five centuries. The conquest of Spain appears to have been a dry run, and after this first decisive battle, few more challenges got in the way of the Muslim columns that followed the old Roman roads in their conquest of Iberia. By 718, the captured territory was organized as a province of the Umayyad caliphate of Damascus. Nevertheless, the Umayyads did not permanently occupy large stretches of the northern mountainous zones, and this allowed for the gradual establishment of small independent Christian states such as Asturias, Leon, Castile, Navarre, Aragon and Catalonia, which remained on the defensive against the Muslim encroachment on their lands for more than three centuries.

After the middle of the eighth century, there began a period in the history of medieval Spain that modern historians have called the *Reconquista* (the 'Reconquest'). First finding expression in the mid-ninth-century chronicles from Asturias, such as the *Prophetic Chronicle* and the *Chronicle of Alfonso III*, this idea of the Reconquista has been portrayed – both in medieval *and* modern accounts – as a holy war to expel the Muslims, who were regarded as interlopers wrongfully occupying territory that belonged to Christians. According to the *Chronicle of Alfonso III*, Divine Providence led Pelayo (719–737), son of Duke Fafila of royal blood, to come to Asturias and be elected as king by the people who had fled the Muslim flood. Therefore the concept of a unified and indivisible (Christian) kingdom embracing the whole of Iberia was the most significant element in the Visigothic legacy of the kings of the Asturias (later Asturias-León-Castile), and which endured all the way until the conquest of Granada in 1492.

The Iberian Peninsula, AD750–1030.

By the middle of the eleventh century and on the eve of the First Crusade, the idea of the Reconquest of Iberia was coupled with the notion of *holy war*, promoted by the propaganda language used by the Popes of the period, who wished to transform Christian attitudes towards violence and the shedding of blood. In that sense, war was made sacred when crusading ideology permeated Iberia as a consequence of the opening of the peninsula to French and papal influences on the eve of the launching of the First Crusade to the Holy Land, in the second half of the eleventh century.

Papal interest in the war against the Spanish Muslims was also beginning to manifest itself, when Alexander II (papacy, 1062–73) and Gregory VII (papacy, 1073–85) encouraged French knights to carry out expeditions into Spain by offering relief from penance and the remission of sins. The major French and Spanish expedition to capture Barbastro, north-east of Zaragoza, in 1064, and the conquest of Toledo by Alfonso VI of León and Castile, in 1085, were both hailed all over Catholic Europe as much for the loot as for the financial and spiritual support that Rome and the Abbey of Cluny had invested in Iberia. It was becoming all the clearer that by the end of the eleventh century the Spanish Reconquest had assumed a different character as the Christian rulers intensified their pressure on the Iberian Muslims, while Pope Urban II (papacy, 1088–99) reiterated the theme of Christian restoration in the peninsula.

Christian success led to the involvement of the Almoravids in Spain, a Sunni Muslim sect that had seized control of North Africa and the Maghreb. They kept the Christian expansion in check for half a century, while they absorbed the Muslim-Iberian polities into their north African empire. At the same time, both Urban II and Paschal II (papacy, 1099–1118) were convinced about the importance of the Spanish knights to the struggle against Islam in Iberia, to the point of conceding to those who fought there the same remission of sins granted to the crusaders in the Orient. Hence by 1118, Alfonso I of Aragon (1104–34), with the aid of French and Norman nobles, was threatening Zaragoza, while in 1125 he led a great expedition to Granada, the heart of Muslim power.

Then again, the break-up of Spanish unity put Christian expansion on hold, which coincided with the Almohad expansion in the region, a Berber dynasty that had replaced the Almoravids, who managed to push back the frontiers to the River Tagus. Despite the danger, a legacy of Christian distrust remained, until the victory of the Almohads over the Castilian Alfonso VIII at the Battle of Alarcos, in 1195. This signalled a period of Almohad dominance that would last for some twenty years, until the victory of Alfonso VIII of Castile and Peter II of Aragon at Las Navas de Tolosa on 16 July 1212, a battle that seriously undermined the Almohad empire, and tipped the balance of power in Iberia decisively in favour of the Christians.

6 THE SECOND SIEGE OF CONSTANTINOPLE

Turning Back the Arab Expansion

Date 15 July/August 717–15 August 718
Location Constantinople and its European and Asian suburbs

THE HISTORICAL BACKGROUND

THE BYZANTINE EMPIRE experienced one of the most decisive periods in its history immediately after the disastrous defeat by the Arab armies at the Battle of Yarmuk in 636, followed by the imperial succession crisis triggered by the death of Heraclius (reigned 610–41) in 641.

Following the withdrawal of the imperial armies from Syria and Upper Mesopotamia, by the late 630s and early 640s the Byzantine government had managed to regroup and redeploy the imperial troops, and establish new lines of defence in depth in Anatolia, taking advantage of the mountains of south-eastern Asia Minor and key fortified points in the interior. However, no 'hard border' was ever established; rather, a sort of 'no man's land' (or 'zone of devastation') would gradually develop after the 650s. This zone came to be known in Arabic as *al-Ḍawāḥī* (the 'outer lands') and in Greek as τὰ ἄκρα ('the extremities'), and it emerged in Cilicia, along the southern approaches of the Taurus mountain range.

During the third quarter of the seventh century Arab generals made further significant territorial conquests in central and western Mediterranean at Byzantium's expense. But these territories would come to be seen as the periphery of the Byzantine Empire's extended land mass. Political, topographical and logistical impediments combined with Byzantine military resilience to halt major Arab advances into the core of the Empire – Anatolia.

The Arabs initially used a combination of force and diplomacy to overcome the Byzantine defences, being prepared to engage in fierce and decisive pitched battles, while also negotiating separate terms with both local civilians and military commanders.[1] Nevertheless, these tactics would prove largely ineffective once their armies tried to penetrate and establish permanent control into Asia Minor proper, as the Byzantine commanders would tend to avoid the risk of major land battles, preferring to seek refuge in fortified positions instead.

The earliest reports of Muslim expeditions into the Anatolian Plateau came in the mid-640s, when an important city of the Anatolic theme, the metropolis of Amorion, was targeted in 644 (AH23), during a period when the Emperor Constans II (reigned 642–668) was too young to take any defensive action. This, and subsequent campaigns, were led by the governor of Syria – later to become Caliph – Muawiya (602–680). He was the driving force of the Muslim effort against Byzantium, especially at sea where the newly built fleet would soon challenge the Byzantine navy (the Battle of the Masts, in 655) and devastate the Byzantine islands and coasts of the Aegean Sea.

Inland, Muawiya's strategy began to take shape in the late 640s, focusing on summer (sometimes even winter) raids launched from Mesopotamian and Syrian towns, with the raiders penetrating Anatolia and campaigning deep into hostile territory, looting and destroying in their path, before returning to their bases several weeks later. Byzantium's response was to fortify key positions along the invasion routes, and to develop a coherent military response based on localized defence, reinforced by troops from the interior.

Nevertheless, Muawiya's aggressive strategy against Byzantium did not result in any lasting Muslim conquests in Anatolia between 643 and his death in 680. The climax of his strategy was the first Arab siege of Constantinople, which lasted between 674 and 678, when the Muslim army used the peninsula of Cyzicus near the city as a base to spend the winter, and returned every spring to launch attacks against the city.

Eventually, the Muslim expansion into Anatolia and the Aegean Sea was halted, and the Islamic expansion into Europe was prevented for another thirty years, although this should not only be attributed to the Byzantine successful defence of their city. A combination of the harsh Anatolian climate, the logistical difficulty in supplying armies invading the Plateau, the ethnical and religious homogeneity of the Anatolian populations, and the general rivalry and envy among Arab leaders that led to the Second

The themes and major cities of Asia Minor, around AD750.

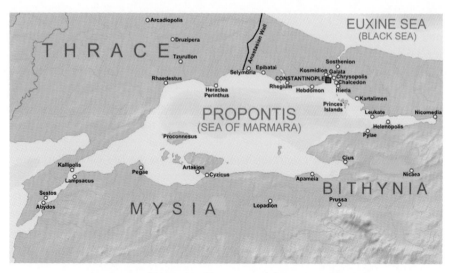

The main towns in the suburbs of Constantinople and around the Marmara Sea.

Fitna, a period of general political and military disorder that afflicted the Umayyad empire between 680 and 692, all contributed in stemming the Muslim expansion, but only temporarily.

Emboldened by military victories against the Bulgars and the Slavs in Thrace and in Macedonia in the late 680s, and by the significant increase in the numbers of the imperial army following his 'mandatory' recruitment of 30,000 Slavs in 688, Emperor Justinian II (reigned 685–695 and 705–711) decided to renew the war against the Arabs, until he was comprehensively defeated at the Battle of Sebastopolis (692), in the Armeniac theme. Following their victory at Sebastopolis, the Muslims under Abd al-Malik (reigned 685–705) now had the upper hand in the war that had flared up again between the two superpowers. The strategic region of Armenia was quickly absorbed by the Arabs without a fight, and in 694 the Caliph began sending new armies to invade Anatolia through the 'Cilician Gates'.

Taking advantage of the political instability in Constantinople that stemmed from the dethronement and imprisonment of Justinian II by his senior general, Leontius, Abd al-Malik's strategy between 695 and 697 developed into a two-pronged attack against Byzantine possessions in both North Africa and Asia Minor – Leontius wisely prioritized the defence of the richest province of Africa. But the loss of Carthage in 698 sparked another revolt, which prompted the second regime change in Constantinople in two years. The conflict with the Arabs in Anatolia continued unabated after 699, with heavy and humiliating defeats for the Byzantine armies, especially in Armenia and Pontic Lazica on the Black Sea.

Justinian II was restored to the throne is 705, and this may have given a glimpse of hope to the people of Anatolia, that the Arab campaigns would be curbed. But the new Caliph, al-Walid (reigned 705–15), was determined to pursue his father's aggressive

expansionist strategy in Armenia and Anatolia, and in 707 his armies crushed an imperial army sent to relieve the siege of the strategic Cappadocian city of Tyana, in the
heart of Anatolia. The following year, Arab armies defeated another Byzantine army at
Amorion, while western Anatolia was now laid open to Muslim raiding parties.

By 712, Maslama ibn Abd al-Malik (d. 738), the uncle of al-Walid and, after 708,
the Umayyad military governor of Syria, Armenia and Azerbaijan, had completed
the conquest of Cilicia, the south-eastern region of Asia Minor, and of all the lands
in Byzantine hands east of the River Euphrates. Between 712 and 714 Maslama also
launched several campaigns that devastated Galatia (north-western Asia Minor),
sacking Amaseia and Melitene.

In 714 a Byzantine embassy visited the court of al-Walid in Damascus to discuss a
truce, but returned to report that the Caliph was preparing for a siege of Constantinople
by land and sea. And while the Umayyad fleet was sailing to Phoenix (across the island
of Rhodes, in the south-western Anatolian coast) with the intention of gathering wood
to build more warships, the Byzantine government in Constantinople was plunged into
yet another civil conflict: Anastasius II (reigned 713–15) was deposed and replaced by a
minor tax collector, who took the name of Theodosius III (reigned 715–17).

Meanwhile, following the death of al-Walid in 715, his brother and successor
Suleyman (reigned 715–17) took up the challenge of conquering Constantinople with
increased vigour, because according to a Muslim prophecy, a Caliph bearing the name
of a prophet would capture Constantinople, and Suleyman (Solomon) was the only
member of the Umayyad family to bear such a name.

Carte postale (postcard) from the end of the nineteenth century: the land walls of Constantinople. The photo is
taken just to the south of the dried Lycus Valley, and close to the Gate of St Romanus. Old photos like this one
provide a much better idea of the three-layered Byzantine fortification system (inner wall, outer wall, moat),
before these were irreversibly damaged by modern construction works and botched restoration attempts.

THE PRELUDE TO THE BATTLE

The Invasion of Anatolia

The Caliph entrusted the command of the land forces to Maslama ibn Abd al-Malik, and the expeditionary army began assembling at the plain of Doliche (Dabiq), north of Aleppo, in the spring and summer of 715. The sea forces were handed over to one of Maslama's proteges, Umar b. Hubayra. In September, the vanguard, under general Suleyman, marched into Cilicia and took the strategic fortress of Loulon on its way.[2] They wintered at Afik, an unidentified location somewhere in the western exit of the 'Cilician Gates', the narrow mountain passes leading through the Taurus Mountains of south-eastern Asia Minor. In early spring of 716, Suleyman's army marched into central Anatolia, and the Umayyad fleet cruised along the Pamphylian and Lycian coastline, while Maslama and the main army waited for news in Syria.

Modern historians have assumed that Suleyman's plan of invasion of central Anatolia would have led him to the strategic city of Amorion, in the Anatolic theme; this city had been the obvious target of Muslim invading armies for many decades, and it was a base where Maslama's army could spend the winter of 716/17. The general of the Anatolic theme was Konon (later, he took the name Leo), who had been appointed by the previous emperor Anastasius in 713.

Upon Anastasius' deposition by the troops of the Opsicion theme in spring 715, Konon joined with his colleague Artabasdos, the general of the Armeniac theme, in conspiring to overthrow the new emperor Theodosius III. Because Konon was born in Germanikeia (modern Maraş) in south-eastern Asia Minor in 675, it is highly likely that he not only spoke Arabic, but that he also knew the Arabs and Islam very well. Therefore there must have been some sort of communication between himself and Suleyman, between the summer of 715 and the summer of 716, for an agreement that could serve the ambitions of both parties against the current emperor in Constantinople – Theodosius III.[3]

When he arrived outside Amorion, Suleyman offered the defenders of the city the opportunity to save their lives if they acknowledged Konon/Leo as their emperor. Soon after, the general of the Anatolic arrived in the vicinity of the city with a small army and tried to install his own garrison in the fortress of Amorion. But negotiations between the two parties eventually broke down,[4] although this might have been nothing less than a skilful diplomatic manoeuvre by Leo.

Eventually, Leo retreated to Pisidia (south of Amorion), and in the summer of 716, supported by Artabasdos, he was proclaimed emperor, thus openly challenging Theodosius' legitimacy for the imperial crown. Suleyman also had to withdraw from Amorion, taking instead the westerly road to Constantinople via the Aegean coast and the Thrakesion theme, where he spent the winter of 716/17. In the meantime, Maslama had already crossed the Taurus Mountains with the main invading army, and was heading towards Constantinople.

Impatient to end the civil war against Theodosius and his supporters, Leo marched with his army to the capital in the early months of 717, and after short negotiations with Theodosius that guaranteed the latter's life, he entered the city on the Feast of the Annunciation (25 March 717), thus becoming emperor as Leo III (reigned 717–41).

THE OPPOSING FORCES

The twelfth-century Syriac chronicler Michael the Syrian provides an exaggerated number for the Arab expeditionary army – some 200,000 men and 5,000 war and transport ships. The tenth-century Arab historian and geographer al-Mas'udi mentions 120,000 troops, while the chronicle of Theophanes the Confessor reports of 1,800 ships. According to the thirteenth-century historian Bar Hebraeus, the troops totalled some 30,000 volunteers (*muttawi'ah*) for the *Jihad*.[5] Sadly, next to nothing is known about the numbers and composition of the city's defenders.

Infantry would form the vast majority of the Muslim armies in the first centuries of the expansion out of the Arabian Peninsula, and it would serve in every Muslim army from the seventh to the eleventh centuries. The most significant weapon of the early Muslim infantry was, surprisingly, the humble camel, because it enabled the early Muslim armies to outmanoeuvre their enemies. In the early eighth century, foot soldiers would largely come from the Arab tribes, including local volunteers (*muttawi'ah*) of the frontier regions, and city militias (*ahdaths*) that were used mainly for defensive campaigns because they primarily served on a local basis and only for a limited period.

Professional infantry were recruited mainly on an ethnic basis, and for the armies of the Umayyads this meant Arab tribesmen, Black Africans and Iranian *Daylami* from the Elburz Mountains of northern Iran. Although armour was not rare in the early Muslim armies, it was not universal. Therefore, it was only reasonable for the well armoured foot soldiers to be deployed in the front ranks of a formation, to protect the less well armoured men behind them.

Soon after their expansion out of Arabia, the Arabs acquired the horse-breeding territories in the Fertile Crescent, especially in Syria. Heavy cavalry was rather slow in developing in the first centuries of Islam, and during the Umayyad era it was divided into armoured and unarmoured; the former was usually deployed in small 'shock' units, waiting for the right chance to deliver the 'coup de grâce' at the enemy's flanks, while the latter would usually hover around en masse in an attempt to harass and encircle the enemy formations. The unarmoured (or lightly armoured) cavalry would be relegated to reconnaissance and/or skirmishing roles only after Caliph Marwan II's military reforms in c. 750.[6] But even until the early ninth century, heavy cavalry was prepared to dismount and fight on foot and at close quarters if the need arose.

Arms and Armour

The coat of mail, either lamellar or scale, was the standard form of protective body armour for an Umayyad soldier, but only the relatively well-off soldiers would have been able to afford it.[7] The helmet was another important piece of equipment, and the most common word for helmet was *bayḍa*, which can be translated as an 'egg' or 'egg-shaped'. There was also the *mighfar*, a kind of mail hood for the protection of the neck. Round wooden shields complemented the armour of both mounted and infantry soldiers.

The main offensive weapon of a soldier for the Umayyad period was the straight-bladed, double-edged sword (*sayf*), capable of inflicting both a cutting and a thrusting blow. Curved sabre swords arrived a few centuries later with the Seljuk Turks. Along with the sword came the spear (*rumh*), a thrusting weapon with an iron point, which was accompanied by the *harba*, a shorter javelin with a long blade. Iron maces are also well reported, with the *amud* denoting a mace with three, four, or more metallic spikes fitted in a wooden shaft.

I have examined the arms and armour of the Byzantine soldier of the period in the chapter on the Battle of Ongal, so a brief outline would be sufficient here. A Byzantine soldier around 700 would have carried a straight-bladed, round-tipped, double-edged sword of Avar influence, and a spear, while the best-armed horseman was equipped with a cavalry lance and a 'herul' sword. Foot and mounted archers would also have carried the typical short bow introduced by the Huns some three centuries earlier. For protection, they would have worn either a chain mail, scale, lamellar, quilted, or leather corselet worn over a thick or padded undergarment. They would also, of course, have worn helmets or felt caps, and would have carried rectangular or oval shields.

THE SIEGE

In the early summer of 717 Maslama crossed the Dardanelle Straits with his army at Abydos, and marched into Thrace, devastating the countryside, gathering supplies, and sacking the towns they encountered on the way. Sometime before the middle of August (the Feast of the Assumption), the Arab army enforced a full land and sea blockade of Constantinople by erecting a double siege wall of 'drystone', one facing the city and one facing the Thracian countryside, with their camp positioned between them. The Arab fleet first laid anchor in the southern suburb district of Hebdomon (modern Bakırköy) on the Marmara Sea, before proceeding to enforce a naval blockade by anchoring on the European and Asian suburbs of the city, including Chalcedon (modern Kadıköy), Galata (modern Beyoğlu) and Kleidion (modern Defterdarburnu, in Ortaköy).

At this early stage of the siege the first Arab debacle is reported by Theophanes, when a rear-guard squadron of their fleet, mostly consisting of transport vessels that were slow-moving and difficult to manoeuvre, was caught by a strong current and a southerly wind and was thrown against the sea walls of the city. Leo then ordered a squadron of the imperial navy, anchored on the Golden Horn, to attack them using the dreaded 'Greek fire'. According to Theophanes:

> Some of them [Arab ships] were cast up burning by the sea walls, others sank to the bottom with their crews, and others were swept down flaming as far as the islands Oxeia and Plateia [modern Princes' Islands].

That proved to be an unexpected boost to the Byzantine morale, especially since the Arabs were planning, according to Theophanes, a night attack against the sea walls, with the intention of scaling them using the ships' steering paddles; however, they quickly abandoned their plans!

Soon after, Leo ordered a chain to be strung between the city and Galata, thus sealing the mouth of the Golden Horn where the imperial navy was at anchor. Eventually the Arab fleet became reluctant to engage the Byzantine squadrons, and withdrew to the harbour of Sosthenion, further north on the European shore of the Bosporus.[8]

Early autumn quickly gave way to early winter, with both armies preparing feverishly as bitter weather drew ever closer. It seems that the Arab army was relatively well supplied for the winter of 717/18, as they had already devastated the Thracian countryside, and had even brought along wheat to sow and harvest the following year. But the failure of the Arab navy to impose an effective blockade on the city meant that the Byzantines could also bring in supplies.

At this stage of the siege Leo and Maslama resumed negotiations, although it is surprising that only the Muslim sources make any mention of these taking place.[9] According to one Muslim chronicler, Leo offered to ransom the city by paying a gold coin for every inhabitant, but Maslama replied that there could not be peace, and that the Arab garrison of Constantinople had already been selected.

Both the Byzantine and the Muslim sources agree that the winter of 717/18 was extremely harsh and bitterly cold. The effects on the besieging soldiers who had to spend these months in the Thracian countryside must have been horrendous. The primary sources paint a vivid description of the evils that afflicted the Arab army that winter; Theophanes reports that:

> The Arabs, on the other hand, suffered from a severe famine, so that they ate all of their dead animals, namely horses, asses, and camels. It is said that they even cooked in ovens and ate dead men and their own dung, which they leavened. A pestilence fell upon them also and killed an infinite number of them.[10]

And the anonymous author of the *Khitab Al 'Uyun* (*Book of Springs*) gives a similar description of the dreadful situation in the Arab camp:

> And the winter came upon them: and Maslama gave orders to his followers, and they made houses of wood and dug caves ... and the Moslems met with hardships such as no one had ever met with before, till a man was afraid to go out of his camp alone; and the Moslems ate draught-animals and skins and the dung of their draught-animals, and roots and leaves of trees and dead bodies.[11]

It is remarkable to see how quickly an army of several thousands of combat soldiers and men on a military operation thousands of miles from friendly territory could so easily run out of supplies and be devastated by disease, even though, as I mentioned before, they had apparently come to Thrace relatively well prepared and determined to hold their siege as long as necessary. This serves to illustrate the enormous difficulties in supplying such a vast army in pre-industrial times, far away from its bases and for a prolonged (or indefinite) period of time.

The situation in the Arab camp looked set to improve in spring when the new Caliph, Umar II (reigned 717–720), planned to send some relief to the besiegers; indeed, two fleets arrived carrying supplies and arms in 400 ships from Egypt, and another 360 ships came from Africa. At the same time, a relief army began marching through Anatolia to reinforce the blockade of the city and boost the plummeting morale of Maslama's army.

The newly arrived fleets would no doubt have kept a safe distance from the city walls, bearing in mind the last debacle with the transport vessels that were set on fire or captured when they got too close to the fortifications. Most likely they dropped anchor at the southern (Marmara) coast of the Asian suburbs of the city, and in fact Theophanes reports that the Egyptians were in the north of the Gulf of Nicomedia, near modern Tuzla, and the Africans south of Chalcedon. The majority of the crew of the Egyptian fleet would have comprised Christian Egyptians, but Theophanes writes about massive desertions that almost immediately affected the Arab fleet upon their arrival.[12]

At that crucial moment of the siege, and probably informed by Christian Egyptian intelligence as to the disposition of the Arab reinforcements, Leo launched a naval attack against the Arab fleets. The outcome was a crushing defeat for the Arab naval force, which, crippled by the defection of their crews and helpless against Greek fire, was destroyed or captured along with the weapons and supplies they carried. So Constantinople was now safe from a seaborne attack! The relief army dispatched by the Caliph Umar through Anatolia was also intercepted and destroyed in the hills south of Nicomedia.

The 'coup de grâce' to the Arab besieging army was delivered by the Bulgars rather than the Byzantines. Now that the capital could easily be resupplied by sea, as the Arab fleet abandoned the partially enforced naval blockade of the city, the Arabs reportedly lost a major battle against the Bulgars, who killed, according to Theophanes, some 22,000 men. The sources are not clear, however, whether the Bulgars became

Byzantine cavalry charging against Arab cavalry – illustrated manuscript of Skylitzes, Biblioteca Nacional de España in Madrid, twelfth century.

involved in the conflict as a result of the treaty that Leo had renewed with Khan Tervel (ruled 700–21) in the early summer of 717 – because the Bulgars were also fearful of a strong Arab caliphate in their southern borders – or whether the Arabs had strayed into Bulgar territory in their desperate search for supplies.

In fact I think that Tervel had realized, long before the arrival of Maslama's army in Thrace, that he would be much better advantaged by conducting political and diplomatic negotiations with the Byzantine emperors than with anyone else, and especially with the powerful Umayyad caliph. After all, it was Tervel who, in 705, had assisted the deposed Byzantine Emperor Justinian II in regaining his throne in return for the area of Zagore in northern Thrace – this was the first expansion of Bulgaria to the south of the Balkan mountains, and he was honoured with the high-ranking title of 'Caesar' and with numerous gifts given by Leo's predecessors.[13] Therefore by 717 it would have looked crystal clear to him where his interests lay.

By the high summer of 718 the siege of Constantinople had clearly failed, and Caliph Umar sent orders to Maslama to withdraw his armies and retreat. After thirteen months of siege, the Arabs raised the siege on 15 August 718 (the Feast of the Assumption), and it was to the Virgin Mary that the Byzantines ascribed their victory. The retreating Arabs lost more ships in a storm in the Marmara Sea, and other ships were set alight by ashes from the volcano of Santorini in the southern Aegean Sea; furthermore numerous survivors were captured by the Byzantines.

CONCLUSIONS

In the short term, the outcome of the second siege of Constantinople brought much needed relief to the city and its defenders, as the great Arab conquest operation had ended in a fiasco. This allowed Leo to recover territory in the strategic frontier zone of western Armenia, while in 719, the Byzantine fleet raided the Syrian coast and burned down the port of Laodicea. However, historians have underlined Leo's reluctance (or, more likely, inability) to take the war to the Arabs. In fact, in the south-eastern region of Cilicia, Mopsuestia and other strategic towns remained in Arab hands as a defensive bulwark to protect Antioch.

Thus the decades that followed the successful defence of the Byzantine capital were a period of stabilization of the frontiers, rather than of reconquest of lands lost. But once the theme system was fully operational, it provided substantial strength, and this would help Leo win significant victories against Arab armies, specifically Nicaea in 726, and Akroinon in 740. Eventually, by the end of Leo's reign in 741, western Asia Minor would be relatively secure against Arab incursions.

In the longer term, the Arabs retained the military initiative during the caliphate of Yazid II (720–4) and Hisham (724–43), penetrating more effectively into Anatolia than they would manage to do again in the remaining years of the Umayyad dynasty. Nevertheless, historians have emphasized a ground-breaking change in the Arab strategy of expansion into Asia Minor, which can be discerned in the period that immediately followed Maslama's failed campaign of 717/18. The caliphate had finally come to terms with the existence of the Byzantine empire in its northern borders, and, while long-term Byzantine counter attacks would only occur some two hundred years later, in the middle of the tenth century, the Arab strategic objectives were now taking a much different shape.

From the 750s onwards, the main strategic aim of the Arab expeditionary armies would be to loot, destroy, besiege key economic and strategic centres, take prisoners and return to their homelands laden with booty, rather than bogging themselves down in any sort of permanent conquests in Asia Minor. Facing the Byzantine forces in pitched battle was contemplated only as a desperate solution – which is the reason for the relatively low number of major pitched battles between Arab and Byzantine forces between the 750s and the 950s.

And it is exactly this sort of defensive strategy of avoiding battle that was adopted by the Byzantines in Anatolia as a response, and is vividly reflected in the mid-tenth-century Byzantine military treatise *On Skirmishing*. The most important aspect of this frontier strategy for the Byzantines was the 'shadowing' of the enemy forces, the basic idea being to wear down the invading army, which would give the Byzantines time to concentrate a significant number of reinforcements from neighbouring themes, in order to attack the enemy on their way back to their bases.

Therefore it appears that Byzantine strategic planning in Asia Minor had developed into a sort of defence-in-depth, which included three main zones: (a) the frontier zone of eastern Asia Minor, which was, usually, a 'zone of devastation'; (b) the territories of

The formidable Taurus Mountains, separating Anatolia from Upper Mesopotamia and Syria – Peak Demirkazik (3,756m) of the Aladaglar Mountains, Niğde Province, Turkey.

the Anatolian plateau, where the local forces would garrison key fortresses and towns – though if an invading army seemed undeterred in its march through the Anatolian plateau and continued further west, an imperial army would then be mobilized to protect the (c) third zone: the fertile coastal plains of Bithynia, western Asia Minor, and, of course, the capital! This is why it is no coincidence that all major battles where the emperor himself took to the field between 750 and 950 were fought in the second zone of defence, in the heart of Anatolia.

Finally, the outcome of the second siege of Constantinople should also be acknowledged for its considerable macro-historical importance for the history of Europe. The Byzantine capital's survival preserved the Byzantine empire as a bulwark against Islamic expansion into Europe until the fifteenth century and the conquests of the Ottoman Turks. Had a victorious caliph made Constantinople, already at the beginning of the Middle Ages, into the political capital of Islam, as happened at the end of the Middle Ages by the Ottomans, the consequences for Christian Europe would have been incalculable.

7 THE BATTLE OF TOURS

Stemming the Muslim Tide

Also called the Battle of Poitiers, and in Arabic 'Ma'arakat Balât ash-Shuhadâ'
(Battle of the Court of the Martyrs)

Date Several dates have been suggested – probably 25 October 732
Location Near Moussais-la-Bataille (modern Vouneuil-sur-Vienne), 20km (12 miles) north of Poitiers

THE HISTORICAL BACKGROUND

THE BATTLE OF Tours followed two decades of Umayyad conquests in Europe, which had begun with the invasion of the Visigoth Christian Kingdom of the Iberian Peninsula in 711. Islam had erupted out of the Arabian Peninsula in the decades following the death of the Prophet Muhammad in 632, and within a generation Muslim armies had destroyed the Sassanid Persian Empire at the Battle of al-Qadisiya (636), and taken away a huge chunk of the Byzantine Empire's possessions after the Battle of Yarmouk (636). By 661 the new ruling Muslim dynasty, the Umayyads, continued to push eastwards towards the Indus river and westwards across northern Africa, conquering Egypt in the 640s and Morocco in the early eighth century.

The conquest of Iberia was achieved by a force of some 15,000 men, mostly Mozarab Berbers from northern Africa under Arab pay and command, and the sources report that the subjugation of the Visigoth kingdom was rapid and effective; indeed, the Arabs simply replaced the established ruling class as the dominant socio-political and military élite. The increasing rivalry between the Arabs and the Berbers eventually led to a political deadlock in the region, because no *wali* (governor) who was left to govern the new province survived for more than five years before being assassinated. Nevertheless, every *wali* between 716 – the year of the assassination of the first governor after the conquest – and the campaign of al-Ghafiqi in southern France that culminated in the Battle of Poitiers in 732, strove to consolidate Muslim control in the north of the peninsula, including the lands of the restless Basques, Catalunya and the Ebro valley, and Septimania in the Pyrenees.

The Muslims further took control of the still Visigoth region of Narbonne in 719.

This fertile, urbanized province in the Occitan region in the south of France, with flourishing trade links with the rest of the Mediterranean Sea, was a treasured prize for the expansionist Muslims, who eventually succeeded in conquering the entire region up to the borders with Provence, after taking the city of Carcassonne in 725.

The next target for the Muslims seemed to be the south-west Frankish region of Aquitaine that bordered both Septimania and the Basque country to the south of the Pyrenees. Campaigns beyond such frontiers were commonplace in the form of *razzias* – raiding campaigns of a few thousand troops launched over the border to loot and weaken the enemy.[1] Muslim attacks on Avignon and Lyon in the Rhone valley fitted this pattern well, but the attack on the city of Toulouse in 721 bore the hallmarks of a campaign to conquer. The failure to take Toulouse by storm, and the death of the Andalusian governor al-Samn in battle, was seen as a significant setback for the expansionist strategy of the Muslims in the region, and a victory of prestige for Prince Eudes of Aquitaine.

The setback outside Toulouse may have been the reason why the Muslim invasions concentrated north-east along the Rhone valley, instead of north-west, in the following decade. The Muslims seem to have found a formidable enemy in Prince Eudes, who, already since 714 – the year when Charles Martel's father, Pepin Herstal, died – had proclaimed his independence from the Merovingian authority. The loss of this rich and fertile region was a significant blow to the Merovingian kings and their Pepinid mayordoms, especially when a feared alliance between Aquitaine and Burgundy against the Muslims was not far from becoming a reality after the successful defence of Toulouse in 721: Charles had to act!

In 730–31, Martel and Eudes seem to have developed completely different plans on how to deal with the Muslim incursions in Aquitaine and the Rhone Valley. Eudes had decided on a more realistic approach to the almost annual *razzias* launched by the Muslim *wali* north of the Pyrenees; these were either directed east through Septimania and then followed the Rhone valley north and into Provence and Burgundy, or they were launched west directly against the major bastions of southern Aquitaine. Hence, military logic dictated a defensive and reactive strategy focusing around the region of Toulouse.

On the other hand, Charles was making plans for an offensive campaign south of the River Loire, aiming to intercept the Muslims while operating within another state, the former Merovingian principality of Aquitaine. Threatened by both the Umayyads in the south and by the Franks in the north, in 730 Eudes allied himself with the Berber commander Uthman ibn Naissa, called 'Munuza' by the Franks, the deputy governor of what would later become Catalunya. Sources also report secret negotiations between the Duke and an ex-mayordom of Neustria (western Francia), an action that increased Martel's hostility towards Eudes.

Abd al-Rahman al Ghafiqi's intention in 731-32 was not to overrun France or conquer Europe in the name of Islam. This was another typical *razzia* that fell within the well-established strategy that was applied for decades in the border regions of Islam, from southern France to eastern Anatolia. Al-Ghafiqi had been preparing for this expedition for almost two years, and his aims went beyond a mere raid to acquire loot and display the banner of Islam in the Christian lands. The Andalusian governor would have been afraid of Eudes' overtures with Munuza, thus setting out to re-establish control over this strategically vital border region.

THE PRELUDE TO THE BATTLE

Opposing Plans

Al-Ghafiqi would have recognized the alliance between Eudes and Munusa as a threat to his control over the border region between Al-Andalus and Aquitaine, more specifically Septimania; he would also have been worried about possible restlessness within the superficially Muslim Mozarab Berbers who had been settled in the region by previous awliya (sing. wali: the governor or 'custodian'). Thus in the spring of 731, al-Ghafiqi ordered the local governor of Septimania to send a raiding expedition in and around the Rhone valley, targeting Lyon, Macon and Chalons, all of which they reportedly burned, while a party reached as far north as Dijon. Later that summer, a Muslim force also raided the region around Arles.

Once al-Ghafiqi felt strong enough to deal with Munusa, he launched a surprise attack against his strongpoint in the Cerdagne region on the eastern Pyrenees, defeating him in battle and forcing him to commit suicide. That year also saw Charles Martel twice attacking the north-eastern region of Aquitaine, a move intended as a warning against a pact between Eudes and the ex-mayor of Neustria. The pressure was mounting on the Prince of Aquitaine!

In the early summer of 732, al-Ghafiqi launched his invasion of Aquitaine through Pamplona and the Basque country, targeting the heartland of Eudes' power – the south-western region of Gascony. After crossing the Roncesvalles Pass into enemy territory, they began the devastation of the region around Bayonne – the main port in the area. It seems that Eudes' main concern was to defend his capital, especially after the Muslim army was advancing north in separate columns that would have been almost impossible to block. The *Chronicle of 754* reports that Eudes collected his army at Bordeaux and prepared to face his enemy, but was defeated in June.[2]

With his capital plundered, Eudes and large numbers from his army managed to escape the carnage, only to be decisively defeated shortly after on the northern side of the River Dordogne. Eventually he was forced to appeal to the Franks for assistance, which Martel only granted after Eudes agreed to submit to his authority.

Charles immediately chose to march with his army south of the Loire river, the official border between Neustria and Aquitaine, and towards the strategically important city of Tours. The city would have to be protected from the Muslim advancing parties, and the Franks pitched their camp on its southern approaches. For the next three months following the sack of Bordeaux, the Muslim raiding parties looted and burned numerous Frankish cities in the province of Aquitaine, including Saintes, Perigueux and Angoulême. They marched north via the old Roman road, bypassing the strong fortifications of Poitiers that dated from the Visigoth rule – but not before sacking the rich abbey of Saint Hilaire on the city's suburbs.

A possible motive for al-Ghafiqi, according to the second continuator of the *Chronicle of Fredegar*, seems to have been the riches of the Abbey of Saint Martin of Tours, the holiest and most prestigious shrine in Western Europe at the time.[3] The Muslim leader would then probably have followed the old Roman road north from Poitiers to Tours, along the valley of the rivers Clain and the Vienne.

And that was exactly where Charles Martel was waiting for him in the second week of October 732, marching 20 kilometres (12 miles) south to block the Muslims from crossing the River Creuse. Clashes were reported between parties from both sides during the week from the 11 to the 15 October on the river valley west of the Vienne, while on or before the 18 October al-Ghafriqi ordered his forces to be redeployed on the south bank of the river. The campaign was about to reach its climax on the rolling ground between the rivers Clain and Vienne.

THE OPPOSING FORCES

Charles Martel's Army

Charles Martel's military power consisted mainly of his Austrasian (eastern Frankish) forces commanded by *leudes* – military governors – installed by Charles during his expansionist campaigns to the east, west and south since the 720s. It also included allies from Neustria (western Francia), Brittany, Burgundy, Swabia, Aquitaine, the Lombards from northern Italy and pagan mercenaries from the River Rhine. Estimates regarding the total number under the mayordom's command vary greatly from 30,000 to 80,000, but only 15,000 to 20,000 would have been mounted and able to ride against the Arab forces, thus giving Martel the strategic mobility required to move his forces from Austrasia to the area near Tours in early October 732.[4]

It would be misleading to consider that the army commanded by Charles Martel against the Muslims in 732 bore any great similarities to the one led by Charlemagne some fifty years later. Rather, it is more appropriate to say that the Frankish army of the first half of the eighth century was in the process of evolution. Warriors in the Frankish armies of the period were expected to equip themselves according to wealth and status. Aristocrats were required to bring along their retainers, the number of which was fixed according to the productivity of the land, and abbeys and monasteries – they were significant landholders – were also obliged to provide a specific number of troops, with senior clergymen leading their own troops into a campaign despite being exempted from military service. All able-bodied men were legally required to perform military service in defence of their territories for a period of up to three months a year, although money payments in return for military service were already widespread by the time of Martel's rule over the kingdom.

Charles would have commanded a few thousand of heavy cavalry as shock troops, made up largely from the wealthiest of the landholders of the kingdom. Nevertheless, the Frankish armies of the period were primarily a force of mounted infantry that dismounted to fight, but campaigned on horseback for speed and strategic mobility; they could also have been used for search-and-destroy missions against small groups of relatively untrained enemies.

We can only be relatively sure about the composition of the armies of the Basques, the Spanish Visigoths and – probably – the Bretons, who would have fought on horseback, mainly because of the long tradition of mounted warfare in these regions on the Frankish periphery.

Arms and Armour

The wealthier noblemen serving as cavalry would have worn mail hauberks and conical helmets, and they would have carried round or concave wooden shields with a metallic boss. They would also have made use of their long swords and their lances against enemy infantry. On the other hand, lesser vassals would have worn little or no protection, usually just a conical helmet and a wooden shield, while they would have been armed with a light lance, and – often – a javelin and the *scramasax* (a long dagger used by peoples in northern Europe, either as a primary edged weapon or as a side arm). Stirrups would still not have been a common feature on Frankish cavalry in the first half of the eighth century.

The Umayyad Army

Modern historians have estimated the strength of the Umayyad army at Tours at between 20,000 and 80,000, although these numbers seem logistically to be improbably high since we know that medieval armies largely had to live off the land while campaigning in hostile territory. Hence any attempt to be more accurate would be futile. Adding to this, there was no one 'Umayyad army', but rather a number of different armies at different times and in different regions of the empire. However, the armies of the westernmost provinces of the Umayyad empire would have consisted of two main groups of soldiers: the first category included the Berbers of northern Africa, those highly mobile, camel-riding nomads from the deserts who were renowned for raids and lightning attacks, for their light equipment and their lust for loot.

A significant part of the armies that conquered Al-Andalus and would later invade France were Arab and non-Arab volunteers enlisted in the regional regiments (*jund*; pl. *ajnad*), and largely fighting as mounted infantry with swords and spears. We need to bear in mind that until the mid-eleventh century there was very little Arab migration into *Ifriqiya*, and the Berbers remained the largest element of the population and the army, although they lived under the new Arab socio-political élite.

Arms and Armour

Early Muslim sources consider the coat of mail, either lamellar or scale, as the standard form of protective body armour, which would often be worn under a cloak to disguise it. Because the coat of mail was expensive to procure – especially in the Arab world – only the well-off soldiers would have been able to afford it.[5] We must also bear in mind that the wearing of protective armour was by no means universal, and sometimes men chose to fight without it.

Along with body armour, the helmet was the most important piece of protective equipment, and the most common word for helmet is *bayḍa*, which can be translated as an 'egg', or 'egg-shaped'. There was also the *mighfar*, a kind of mail hood for the protection of the neck. Round wooden shields complemented the armour of both mounted and infantry soldiers.

The main offensive weapon of a soldier for the Umayyad period was the straight-bladed, double-edged sword (*sayf*), capable of inflicting both a cutting and a thrusting blow. Curved sabre swords arrived a few centuries later with the Seljuk Turks. Along with the sword came the spear (*rumh*), a thrusting weapon with an iron point that was accompanied by the *harba*, a shorter javelin with a long blade. Iron maces are also well reported, with the *amud* denoting a mace with three, four, or more metallic spikes fitted in a wooden shaft.

THE BATTLE

A key point of the battle was the crossing of the River Vienne at Cenon. At some time between the 18 and the 25 October, the Frankish forces crossed the river and deployed in a defensive formation on its southern bank, close to modern Moussais-le-Bataille. Charles Martel had deployed his largely dismounted cavalry into a number of large battle squares, which from afar would have resembled a long defensive 'shield wall' – which is exactly how the sources of the period describe it. His flanks would also have been covered by the dense woods in the region, thus preventing any encircling manoeuvres from the Berber light cavalry. Charles did, however, maintain a small contingent of cavalry behind one of the flanks of the infantry in order to counter attack when needed, and this separate force would probably have been under the command of Prince Eudes. Regrettably, no sources describe the battle formation of the Muslim army that morning.

Historians agree that on the dawn of the 25 October it was the Muslims who made the first move and attacked the Franks in their defensive position on the south bank of the river.[6] The Muslim leader ordered repeated attacks with his cavalry all along the lines, but their piecemeal nature made little impression on the Frankish shield walls. Indeed, the well-trained Frankish soldiers accomplished what was thought almost impossible at that time: infantry withstanding a cavalry charge! The *Chronicle of 754* comments:

> The northern peoples remained as immobile as a wall, holding together like a glacier in the cold regions. In the blink of an eye, they annihilated the Arabs with the sword.[7]

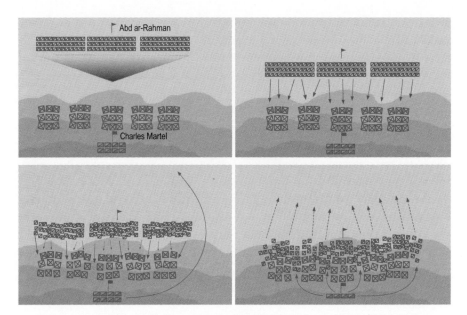

The four main stages of The Battle of Tours, 25 October 732 – Charles Martel's army in blue, and Abd al-Rahman al-Ghafiqi's army in red. Notice in the third stage of the battle the small contingent of mounted troops under the command of Eudes, which took advantage of their superior knowledge of the terrain and performed a wide flanking manoeuvre against the Muslim camp.

It was only in the evening of the first day that breaches started to appear in the front ranks of the Frankish foot soldiers, where the exhausted troops were beginning to give way to the repeated, though uncoordinated and piecemeal attacks by the Berbers, who were already cutting their way into the vulnerable centre of the Frankish formation.

The battle was still in flux when – according to Christian sources – a rumour went through the Umayyad army attacking the centre of the Franks that enemy scouting parties were threatening the families and the booty they had been carrying with them after the sack of Bordeaux in June. Many units of the Umayyad troops at once broke off the battle and returned to camp to secure their loot. Although it seems highly unlikely that a professional army such as the Umayyad one would have left their camp undefended, we will never know whether the withdrawal was a spontaneous reaction to a rumour, or if al-Ghafiqi ordered it.

Nicolle has suggested that it was the small contingent of mounted troops under the command of Eudes that took advantage of their superior knowledge of the terrain and performed a wide flanking manoeuvre against the Muslim camp.[8] Although this may sound perfectly plausible, it cannot be corroborated by any of the primary sources. And with the Muslim army pulling back to defend their camp, it was the turn of the Frankish army to take advantage of the situation and move forwards to the attack, although not necessarily in pursuit of the retreating Muslims.

At this crucial point in the evening of the first day the leader of the Muslim army, al-Ghafiqi, was mortally wounded while defending the camp from the cavalry commanded by Eudes and the advancing units of the Frankish army. Nevertheless, the attack was repulsed.

The Franks returned to the protection of their own camp, and spent an uneasy night on constant alert. However, what they discovered the following morning (26 October) was that the Muslims had fled during the night, abandoning all their plunder, which promptly fell into the hands of the Frankish soldiers. This seems reasonable enough, because the Muslims had lost their leader in the heat of battle, and any loot or prisoners would have hindered their speed and mobility while they were attempting a strategic retreat.

After retiring past the – still Christian-held – city of Poitiers with its formidable fortifications, the Muslim army struck camp somewhere to the south of the city. Charles also retired northwards to Orleans via the Loire river, leaving Eudes the task of clearing the Muslims out of central and northern Aquitaine.

Charles Martel's victory over the Muslim invaders was a near-run thing. Still, the Umayyad army had performed a remarkable feat of strategic retreat in good order from the heart of an enemy territory, far from its lines of communication and logistics, back to the relative safety of Septimania in November. One part of the force retreated south through the route the invaders had taken earlier in the summer via Bordeaux and the valley of the River Garonne. Another force linked with the Muslim forces operating in the Rhone valley, and looted their way south to Provence and Septimania.

No casualty numbers are reported by any of the Christian or Muslim sources that deal with the Battle of Poitiers, hence any attempt by modern historians to give an estimate of the number of troops that fell on the 25 and 26 October is pure speculation. Nevertheless, the reports on the aftermath of the battle suggest that the Muslim armies performed an orderly strategic retreat back to their bases, which could be an indication that they were not written off as an effective fighting force; furthermore for that reason they should not have suffered great losses in the battlefield.

CONCLUSIONS

Contemporary chroniclers interpreted the outcome of the Battle of Poitiers as divine judgment in favour of Charles Martel, and gave him the nickname *Martellus* ('the Hammer'). Other Christian chroniclers praised Charles Martel as the champion of Christianity, characterizing the battle as the decisive turning point in the struggle against Islam. On the other hand, the reticence of the Muslim sources in reporting the events related to the battle, and especially its aftermath and casualties, point to a defeat better to be left forgotten. The great nineteenth-century German historian Leopold von Ranke felt that 'Poitiers was the turning point of one of the most important epochs in the history of the world'.

The Frankish victory at Tours was certainly a great strategic victory for Christian Europe, but in no way did it form the bulwark of Christianity against 'the tide' of Islam as very often it has been portrayed. Al-Ghafiqi's expedition in Aquitaine was no campaign

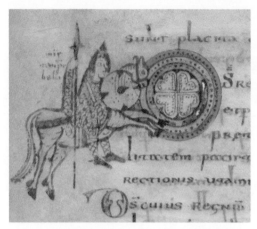

One of the earliest representations of a Carolingian cavalryman – the 'Gellone Sacramentary', c. 790–95.

Ms. Lat. 12048, National Library of France, Paris.

of conquest as, for example, the thwarted attempt to conquer Toulouse in 721, which had resulted in appalling losses on both sides and left a more enduring impression on the Muslim world than the Battle of Tours eleven years later. The *wali's* invasion north of the Pyrenees was just another large-scale *razzia*, very similar to the ones encountered by the Byzantines in Asia Minor throughout the eighth, ninth and tenth centuries. The Byzantines had to endure the Muslim attacks deep into Anatolia for more than two and a half centuries, until a massive counter attack was launched to conquer key border regions between the two empires.

Charles Martel would face other Muslim raiders in southern France almost immediately after the news of the defeat at Poitiers reached the *wali* of Tunisia in 733, and the presence of the Muslims north of the Pyrenees would not be vanquished until his heir, Pepin III ('the Short'), would force them out of Septimania in 759. Nevertheless, the Arab prestige in the Iberian Peninsula took a heavy blow, with Berber revolts flaring up in the following decade, a development that undermined caliphal control of the region and enabled Alfonso I of Asturias to claim large chunks of the region south of the Pyrenees. But for the Muslims of Al-Andalus, the defeat at Poitiers was merely a setback rather than a decisive defeat.

More importantly, the Battle of Poitiers was a great political victory for Charles Martel, who secured his position as the most powerful man in France through diplomacy and sheer force of arms. Charles now controlled one of the richest and most powerful regions of France, the Duchy of Aquitaine, and he replaced many of the local bishops in Aquitaine and Burgundy with his own candidates. Furthermore, he showed diplomatic moderation in courting with the Burgundian aristocrats as he tried to extend his power down the Rhone valley.

More importantly it was Martel's heir, rather than the dukes of Aquitaine, who would reap the fruits of victory over the Muslims of Septimania in the second half of the century. This would bring the Carolingians huge international prestige, which they would use in their dealings with the papacy and their eventual interference in Italian affairs. Thus it was the aftermath of Poitiers that propelled Charles and his dynasty to the pinnacle of European politics, and opened the gateway for his son Pepin to be crowned by the Pope of Rome as the new Frankish king, ushering in a dynastical change that would see the Carolingians changing the face of France and Europe until 987.

8 THE BATTLE OF LECHFELD

The Final Defeat of the Magyars

Date 10 August 955
Location Lechfeld plain, near Augsburg, Bavaria, Germany

THE HISTORICAL BACKGROUND

THE MAGYARS WERE a tribe of Finno-Ugrian[1] origin that first appeared in the eastern borders of the Eastern Carolingian realm in the year 862; they came from the region between the Ural Mountains and the River Volga. During the second half of the ninth century, the Magyars often served as mercenaries in the rapidly declining empire/ khanate of the Khazars who dominated the northern shores of the Black Sea, while a number of incursions were reported in the Byzantine theme of Cherson, in modern Crimea.

The reason why the Magyars were enticed to cross the Carpathian Mountains in 862 was probably because they were hired as mercenaries by Carloman (reigned 876–79), the eldest son of Louis II the German (reigned 843–76) and King of East Francia/Germany, when the former rebelled against his father between 861 and 863; this fact could explain the appearance of the Bulgars, the Magyars' most hated enemy, on the side of Louis. The Magyars only managed to establish themselves in the south-eastern marches of the German kingdom after 896, following their involvement in the Byzantine-Bulgar war of 894–96 on the side of the Byzantines, which led to their disastrous defeat at Boulgarofygon in 896, and their forceful eviction to the Upper Danube plain.

The Magyars managed to take full advantage of the political instability in central Europe in the decades that followed the overthrow of Charles III 'the Fat' (reigned 881–87) in 887; this led to his empire falling apart, and a thirty-six-year interregnum by Berengar I of Friuli (d. 924), who ruled as King of Italy from 887 and as the East-Frankish/ German king after 915. The Magyars defeated no fewer than three large German armies between 907 and 910, victories that forced open the gates of Great Moravia (modern Czechoslovakia), Germany and Italy for further raids. Furthermore, we should note the defeat of Louis IV's German army at the first Battle of Lechfeld in 910, which resulted not only in the annihilation of the royal army, but also in the Swabian, Franconian, Bavarian and Saxon princes agreeing to pay a humiliating tribute to the Magyars.

In northern Italy, Berengar I was preoccupied with his southern neighbours, the Duchy of Spoleto, and with the Muslim raids in Tuscany and Latium. This political turmoil was one of the reasons that could explain the success of the Magyar raids in the first three decades of the 900s. Another reason was the paucity of urban fortifications in Bavaria, Saxony, and along the eastern Alpine passes, which could have impeded the Magyar raids, in the same fashion as the Anglo-Saxon system of fortified towns, known as *burghs*, was used in England in the same period against the Vikings. Only later, in the second quarter of the tenth century, would the founder of the Ottonian dynasty and father of Otto the Great, Duke Henry I of Saxony (ruled 876–936; King of Germany, 919–36), carry out his ambitious plans to fortify the southern marches of his realm.

The most devastating Magyar raids of the tenth century were those that took place in 924, 926 and 954. The second was the continuation of the first raid, which targeted a vast geographical area of southern Germany, and eastern and southern France, and it even reached as far south as the Frankish-Spanish marches. The raid of 954 was the precursor to their final offensive to break through the defences of the German realm, which inevitably led to the Battle of Lechfeld a year later.

After completely ravaging Bavaria and Franconia, meeting almost no resistance, the Magyars advanced west and crossed the River Rhine at Worms. They proceeded to invade eastern France after agreeing an alliance with Duke Conrad 'the Peaceful' of Burgundy and Provence (925–93), who directed them against his personal enemy, Duke Reginald of Lorraine. The nomads entered eastern France through the valley of the Meuse and followed the river south towards Burgundy, only to return to their lands through the eastern Alpine passes and Lombard Italy, completing a raid that covered vast expanses of Christian Europe.

Even though the Battle of Lechfeld is considered by most modern historians as the decisive event when the 'wings' of the Magyar invaders were clipped by the German army of Otto the Great, the tipping point in the German-Magyar struggle for supremacy in central Europe was at the Battle of Riade in 933.[2] The battle was fought between the armies of Henry I and the Magyars at an unidentified location close to the German city of Erfurt and along the River Unstrut on 15 March 933. Earlier, the Synod of Erfurt had decided not to renew the peace treaty with the Magyars, which had been bought some ten years before, and this had resulted in an immediate renewal of the Magyar raids.

The Magyars poured into Thuringia following their usual nomadic tactics of sending small bands of mounted troops into neighbouring areas to pillage and spread terror. These small bands of raiders were cut to pieces by the local militia who confronted them outside their towns, while the main body of the Magyar forces were attacked by an army led by Henry I. The latter applied a trick that was used by the nomads themselves: he only deployed for battle the levies from Thurringia, while keeping the élite cavalry from Franconia, Saxony and Bavaria concealed behind some hills. The Magyars took the bait and attacked the Thurringian infantry head on, only to be trapped and eventually crushed after the German cavalry launched an attack against both the nomad wings.

This victory boosted the morale of the Germans, and brought to a halt the Magyar raids for the next two decades.

THE PRELUDE TO THE BATTLE

The political situation in Germany on the eve of the Magyar invasion of 954 was very unstable, due to internal strife between Otto I (Duke of Saxony and King of Germany, 936–73) and two of his dukes. Since the year before, Liudolf of Italy, the son of the heiress of the Lombard kingdom of Italy, Adelaide, and an heir to the throne of the German kingdom, had allied himself with Duke Conrad of Lorraine and the Archbishop of Mainz (in western Germany) against his father Otto. While the latter was initially successful in suppressing the rebellion in Lorraine, the rebels made the fatal move of allying themselves with the Magyars, giving them the pretext they needed to mount one of their most devastating raids to date.

After dealing with the rebels in the winter of 954/55, Otto received a number of disturbing reports in June of the following year about the Magyars raiding his territories: they had crossed into Bavaria, south of the Danube, and they were besieging the border city of Augsburg-on-Lech. Otto put an army into the field to deal with these raiders once and for all.

THE OPPOSING FORCES

Otto's Army

The relief army that Otto assembled to go to the rescue of the town of Augsburg consisted of eight divisions – the chronicler Widukind calls them *legiones* – each one composed of troops from different parts of the east Francian/German realm (Bavaria, Saxony, Franconia, Swabia and Bohemia) according to nationality and personal relationship with the leading lord.[3]

The strongest and ablest unit making up the king's royal retinue was Otto's *legio regia* (royal legion), probably of Saxon and Franconian cavalrymen under his direct service. On this crucial day, however, Otto's army would miss the services of the troops from Saxony, Lotharingia and Thuringia because of the aggressive movements of the Slavs in the lower River Elbe, where the river originates in the borders between the modern Czech Republic and Germany. This would inevitably have caused some unnecessary distraction and diversion of forces far from the operational theatre around Augsburg in the south of the country.

Estimates put the German army at around 7,000 to 8,000 men, with each division numbering around 1,000 strong, highly trained and experienced veterans of previous conflicts.[4] Although the forces that garrisoned Augsburg would probably have been local levies, like those intended to be deployed in defence of the wide range of fortifications that were constructed along the frontiers and within the interior of the East-Frankish/

German kingdom, this would not have been the case for the troops that clashed with the Magyars on the banks of the River Lech.

Judging by their relatively small numbers and by the campaigning tactics of their enemies, the German troops would have been recruited from two main sources: the smaller element would have been the military households of the king and his aristocrats, who served in return for a stipend (whether land or pay and remuneration), and would have been in a permanent war footing; while the second source would have come from the 'ancient' legal requirement of those who owed military service to their senior lord in return for their lands. Additional élite troops would have come from professionals hired for a specific campaign or series of military operations, and/or armies hired from neighbouring kingdoms, and who served the king or lord as allies or vassals.

Otto's army was a purposefully small but heavily equipped mounted force capable of strategic surprise and great tactical mobility. Because most nomad warriors found sieges very difficult to undertake, experience would have taught the king that any kind of infantry levies would prove utterly useless against such an enemy, except to garrison a strategic town. Rather, he needed to deploy an expeditionary force that could match the mobility of the nomads whose campaigning strategy focused, primarily, on fast-moving overland raids deep into enemy territory.

The Magyar Military Forces

As the Magyar military forces typically consisted of light cavalry armed with bows, their primary objective in battle was to outflank or encircle the main body of the enemy units. Being expert mounted archers, they were able to apply the tactic of 'feigned retreat' by releasing constant showers of arrows from a distance, and falling back when their enemies charged forwards to neutralize them – but when pretending to retreat, they would then make a sudden turn and come back to harass them.

Arms and Armour

Because the Magyars were not particularly well armed and armoured compared to the German *milites*, if they could be brought to battle soon enough, they could be defeated – the problem was, they could not be easily pinned down.[5] Most scholars believe that beyond a composite bow, their main weapon, most of the Magyar equipment was acquired by looting the battlefield, and only in the following centuries did the Magyars establish a professional system of equipping their armies.

The composite bow was made from layers of horn, wood, sinew and glue, and they would have carried two quivers with around forty to sixty arrows in each one. The bow possessed a maximum range of 300m (although the effective range would have been much shorter, at around 100m), and a well-trained horse-archer could discharge up to five arrows in just three seconds.

Although the Magyars served primarily as light cavalry, their élite warriors often wore lamellar armour that provided adequate protection against arrows. The majority of them, however, would have worn a knee-length armour made from quilted cowhide, or no armour at all.

In complete contrast to the nomadic cavalry of the Magyars, the heavy Ottonian cavalry comprised office holders able to possess horses and expensive arms and armour. These men were heavy cavalry because they were fully armed, and in particular, because they had the expensive mail coat. Latin sources of the period call such men *armati* – 'armoured men' – or *loricati* – 'men with mail coats'. Earlier ninth-century pictorial sources occasionally mention the wearing of a conical-shaped helmet with a mail curtain forming a neck guard.

The cheapest piece of military gear was the wooden shield, and contemporary sources show that both foot soldiers and horsemen carried them. These would have been both round and concave at around 0.8m in diameter, protecting the soldier from the neck down to his thighs. Richer vassals called for service were required to wear a *brunia*, an expensive mail reaching down to the hips, while poorer soldiers would have had to make do with different kinds of padded armour for protection.

Because swords were expensive items of military equipment, only the cavalry were required to possess them, and archaeological finds confirm the use of the *spatha*, a long double-edged weapon (90–100cm in length), ideal for downward slashing blows. The lance, or *lancea*, was the cheapest weapon in medieval armies and was carried by the infantry and cavalry alike; contemporary sources indicate that the soldiers of the period primarily used their lances as thrusting weapons, rather than as missiles. Both infantry and cavalry of the Ottonian armies also regularly used the shorter, D-shaped wooden bow (about 1m long).

THE BATTLE

When the Magyars were informed of Otto's approach, they raised the siege of Augsburg and moved to the north-east of the city in order to cross the Lech. This tactical move can be explained on the basis of the terrain on the right side of the river being more suitable for the steppe tactics of the Magyar horsemen, as it was wide enough to allow the cavalry to manoeuvre unimpeded by any natural obstacles.

Otto drew his forces in a single column, putting his *royal legia* in the centre, with the three Bavarian corps and the one from Franconia on its right, and the two Swabian divisions on the left. He placed the Bohemian cavalry in the rear, charged with escorting the army's baggage train, probably because he had doubts about their loyalty. The Magyars, on the other hand, appeared on the battlefield as a solid but very much confused and disorganized mass of horsemen, with no effective leadership, rather operating in small bands as they did during their raids.

The Magyars opened the battle, using their usual steppe tactics, threatening the German centre by releasing volleys of arrows to thin down the front ranks of the heavy cavalry, while another unit of unknown numbers managed to slip away unnoticed

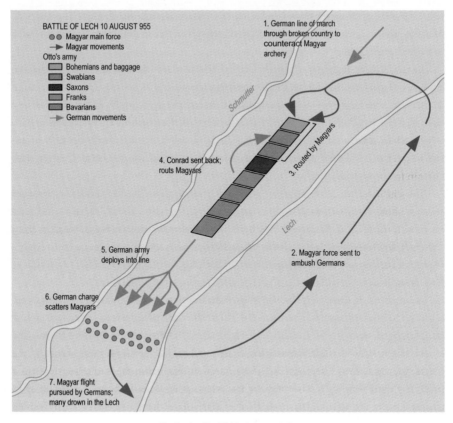

The Battle of Lechfeld, 10 August 955.

because of the overgrown foliage on the banks of the river to attack Otto's camp that was
guarded by the Bohemians. It is difficult to say whether this tactical move was ordered
by the Magyar nobility (the leaders of the nomadic clans) who were in command of the
army units, or if it was an independent move by a group that simply targeted the German
camp for the loot. Nevertheless, the Bohemians on guard duty were unable to resist the
Magyar attack and melted away quite quickly, with the rout spreading to the two Swabian
divisions that fell back to the *royal legia* in the centre of the German formation.

    In this critical moment Otto did not lose heart, and sent for the Franconians under
Duke Conrad on the right wing for some much needed help. The latter quickly ran down
the Magyars who, at that stage of the battle, had dismounted and were pillaging the
German camp. While the Franconians had managed to turn the tables in their favour
on the left wing, the rest of the units were under attack by the main body of the Magyar
army. With his rear now protected, Otto's next move was to reorganize his units and
order a general attack of his entire line. Crucially, he rearranged his army from a column
into a line of battle, trusting that the weight of a heavy cavalry charge would overwhelm
his lightly equipped opponents.

The River Lech at Augsburg.
© THORSTEN HARTMANN

The sources report that the Magyars attempted to mirror the German formation in battle-line, and in fact, they even over-reached the enemy line due to the size of their force and their numbers.[6] They attacked in what appeared to be two lines of mounted troops, and the leaders of the nomads would no doubt have placed the more heavily equipped and experienced ones in the vanguard of the first attacking formation. Otto's heavy cavalry kept good order as they closed with the enemy, shifting from a trot to a gallop to a full charge just before contact with the Magyar cavalry.

At this decisive moment of the battle Otto is said to have shouted: 'They surpass us, I know, in numbers, but neither in weapons nor in courage. We know also that they are quite without the help of God, which is the greatest comfort to us!'

Despite the repeated arrow shots released by the Magyar cavalry while charging against the Germans in an attempt to thin down their numbers and break up their morale and cohesion, the German ranks held firm until the inevitable clash with the Magyar vanguard. The sources report that a section of the Magyars applied their usual battle tactic of the 'feigned retreat' to entice the Germans to break ranks and give chase in order to be lured into a trap. As the Crusader armies of the First Crusade were to discover to their cost at Doryleum, in north-western Anatolia in 1097, it was essential for a heavier army facing lightly armed and manoeuvrable nomadic forces, to come into contact with the enemy as soon as possible in order to minimize the losses inflicted by the repeated release of arrows from the powerful nomadic composite bows. In this case, after the initial clash between the two armies, the Germans did not take the bait, and shied away from following the Magyars in their feigned flight.

After an onslaught that lasted for about ten hours, the units of the Magyars that did

The illustrated 'Prudentius manuscript', created around AD900 in the region of Lake Constance, is counted among the outstanding examples of Carolingian book art. Here is a depiction of Carolingian foot soldiers in action.

© BERN, BURGERBIBLIOTHEK, cod. 264, p.81 – PRUDENTIUS, CARMINA (https://www.e-codices.ch/en/list/one/bbb/0264)

not retreat westwards and away from the attacking German army were killed to the last man, while large numbers of nomads were also drowned while trying to cross the Lech. Inevitably, it was the heavier equipment and discipline in battle that made all the difference between a typical European 'feudal' army such as the Ottonian one, and the predominantly nomadic army of the Magyar raiders.

Casualty figures are not given for either side, though probably the German rear-guard suffered heavily in the first stage of the battle, and it is known that Duke Conrad was slain by a Magyar arrow piercing his throat. The rest of the German divisions in the centre and right of Otto's army would have stayed relatively intact.

Concerning the Magyars, it is certainly futile to try and give an account of their casualties, because the slaughter did not simply end that day. For the next two days the nomads were pursued by the Germans, who cut down every one of them they could find. This proved to be, no doubt, a glorious victory for the Christian nobles.

CONCLUSIONS

As the contemporary chronicler Widukind remarks, the victory at Lechfeld was the greatest victory that Christendom had won over the heathen for two hundred years, reminiscent of the battle at Poitiers in 732 and Charles Martel's rout of the Spanish Muslims. Indeed, it is no exaggeration to assert the opinion that the German victory on the banks of the River Lech was of paramount significance for the future and stability of the Holy Roman Empire.

This was the last time that the Magyars invaded German or Italian territories, and the danger had now passed. However, it is only fair to say that it was Henry I's organization of the German marches, and his long-term building plan of fortifications, along with his victory at Riade in 933, which enabled his son to put a check on the Magyar invasions into German lands.

About half a century later, the Magyars had converted to Roman Catholicism and settled down to establish the kingdom of Hungary, which grew into a powerful Christian kingdom, one that would bear the brunt of other nomadic invasions from the East, most notably the Mongols and Ottoman Turks.

9 THE BATTLE OF CIVITATE

The Establishment of the Normans in Italy

Date 17 June 1053
Location Civitella del Fortore, Foggia, Apulia, Italy (north-west of modern San Severo and Torremaggiore)

THE HISTORICAL BACKGROUND

THE NORMANS ARE first attested to have been in southern Italy as early as 999, when a group of Norman pilgrims came to the support of the local population in Salerno, who were being attacked by marauding Arab raiders from the emirate of Sicily. Italy was the crossing point of every major pilgrimage route leading to the Holy Land. Furthermore, a religious visitor could perform his pious duty at the Sanctuary of Monte Sant'Angelo sul Gargano in northern Apulia, and the Normans appear as pilgrims in two of the three relatively different versions mentioning the coming of the Normans to Italy around the turn of the millennium.

Several Normans became involved in the revolt of Melus of Bari against Byzantine rule in Apulia in the years 1017–18. As a direct result of this *impromptu* military involvement, other Normans arrived in Italy, no longer as pilgrims, but as mercenaries recruited by local Lombard princes. At this initial stage of Norman expansion, the Norman troops that were employed by the rebellious Lombards numbered only 250, with their role being therefore undoubtedly auxiliary.

In the aftermath of the Battle of Cannae in 1018, many Normans under Rainulf, the future (after 1030) Count of Aversa, were employed by the Lombard dukes Gaimar III of Salerno and Pandulf IV for siege operations. By the end of the 1020s, the number of men under Rainulf's command swelled following the death of Duke Robert of Normandy in 1035 and the minority years of his son William. Yet they were still not the main players in the political insurrection against Byzantine authority in Apulia – rather, they were taking the side of the highest bidder.

The Norman establishment in Aversa, north of Naples, in 1030, and in Melfi, in the Apulian-Campanian borders in 1041, were events with profound long-term socio-political consequences for the area. Geoffrey Malaterra, one of the three main primary chroniclers of the period, recorded that the Normans were only 500 strong when they established themselves in Melfi. In the short term, however, the Byzantines reacted sharply and confronted the united Lombard-Norman forces in two pitched battles at Olivento (17 March 1041) and Ofanto (4 May 1041), followed by a third at Montepeloso in early autumn. We only know the outcome of the battles in favour of the Lombard-Norman forces.[1]

At this early stage of the Norman infiltration into Italy, these newcomers had not yet established a coherent political identity. They were still divided, with the two most powerful groups being those in Aversa and Melfi, while other smaller bands were operating independently in Capitanata and northern Campania, and where they systematically annexed large areas in Apulia from the Byzantines, who seemed powerless to respond.

The greatest opportunity the Byzantines and the papacy had to stop this systematic erosion of their territories by the Normans presented itself in 1053, when three years of

Map of southern Italy and Sicily around AD1050.

diplomatic negotiations between Pope Leo IX and the Lombard principalities, Germany and Byzantium, ended in one of the most crucial confrontations in medieval Italian history at the Battle of Civitate, in the Capitanata region north of Lucera.

THE PRELUDE TO THE BATTLE

The Norman advances in southern Italy had alarmed the papacy for many years, while many of the Italian-Lombard locals did not take kindly to the Normans raiding their lands and wished to respond in kind, regarding them as little better than brigands.

Even though the Normans had managed to acquire a permanent base in Italy since the 1030s, they were still working as mercenaries, and there must have been other independent groups living off the land in Campania and Apulia – in fact, the chronicles of the monasteries of Montecassino and St Vincent on Volturno in central and northern Campania make frequent note of their raids and depredations. This anti-Norman feeling was exacerbated by the murder in unclear circumstances of Drogo de Hauteville, in August 1051, who up to that time had been the nominal war leader of the Normans of Apulia.

Another reason that led to the formation of an anti-Norman coalition in the summer of 1053 was the conflicting interests of the major parties in Italy. These included not just the Pope of Rome, but also the Byzantine Emperor as overlord of the regions of Apulia and Calabria, who had aspirations to reconquer Sicily from the Muslims (there would be an imperial expedition between 1038 and 1041); then there was the Holy Roman Emperor who had been marching to Italy to press his imperial claims to large parts of the peninsula since Otto I's (912–73) 'Italian expeditions' in the middle of the tenth century.

In 1052, Pope Leo IX met with his relative Holy Roman Emperor Henry III, in Saxony, and asked for aid in curbing the growing Norman power. Leo returned to Rome in March 1053 with only 700 Swabian infantry under Adalbert II, Count of Winterthur (in modern-day Switzerland). The Prince of Benevento, Rudolf, the Duke of Gaeta, the Counts of Aquino and Teano, the Archbishop and the citizens of Amalfi – together with Lombards from Apulia, Molise, Campania, Abruzzo and Latium – also answered the call of the Pope, who had 'resolved to destroy the name of the Frankish race'.

The Pope found another friendly power in the shape of the Byzantine Emperor; in the years that followed the Lombard-Norman victories against the Byzantines in the 1040s, the Byzantine governor in the region, Argyros, had been ordered to buy off the Normans as mercenaries, following the long-established Byzantine practice of hiring élite mercenaries from regions far and wide in Europe. The Normans, however, rejected the proposal, thus spurning Argyrus to contact the Pope. The plan was for a pincer movement against the Norman armies, with Leo moving his forces from Rome to Apulia to engage the Normans in battle, while a Byzantine army personally led by Argyrus would move from Apulia with the same plan. This plan was never to materialize.

THE OPPOSING FORCES

The army that Pope Leo had managed to gather after his trip to Germany in March 1053 and his descent to southern Italy in May was substantial. It was made up of troops from Capua, the Abruzzi and the Lombard areas of northern Capitanata, with some troops also arriving from Benevento and Spoleto. Their overall numbers, however, are almost impossible to estimate. This force was augmented with reinforcements from Germany, probably freebooters who made up an infantry force of several hundred (seven, according to William of Apulia, who is our most detailed source for this battle, but probably not more than three) from Swabia.[2]

Faced with this threat, the Normans were also forced to reconcile their differences. Humphrey de Hauteville, who had succeeded his brother Drogo as leader of the one of the main bands of Normans two years earlier, had the overall command of the army, along with the Normans from Benevento, Count Richard of Aversa and Robert Guiscard, his famous brother from Calabria who would become the Duke of Apulia by the end of the decade. Estimates put their numbers at 3,000 cavalry.[3]

The typical Italian-Lombard soldiers of the tenth and eleventh centuries were the *contarati* (κονταράτοι), with the most likely derivation of the term coming from the Greek κοντάρι (*spear*), meaning that these soldiers were probably armed with short spears. These were locally raised militiamen of Lombard origin who were lightly armed, poorly trained, and rather undisciplined. They were fighting mostly on foot, which can explain the élite role that the Norman cavalry played in the first four decades of their infiltration into the south.

Arms and Armour

Fortunately we know far more about the arms and armour of the Norman knights of the eleventh century than we do about the Lombards who clashed with them at Civitate. The basic body defence of the Norman knight was the mail coat that was pulled on over the head to form a kind of protective hood – usually leather – called a *coif*. Mail consisted of numerous small iron rings each interlinked with four others to form a flexible defence. However, many of the first Normans would not have possessed any mail at all, or may have simply worn a coat of hide. Those who did, would have had a coat that reached to the hip only – only later, in the twelth century, did it reach down to the knees. It is possible that some form of padded garment was worn under the mail.

The helmet of the time was conical and almost invariably made with a nose-guard. An indispensable item of armour for the Norman knight was his shield. He would have carried a circular wooden shield, probably faced and perhaps lined with leather. Around the middle of the eleventh century such shields were supplemented by the introduction of the so-called kite-shaped shield. This form was ideal for horsemen, since the longer shape guarded the rider's left side and his vulnerable leg.

The most celebrated weapon of the mounted knight in the Middle Ages was his sword. The type in use in the tenth century and into the eleventh century was a double-edged

Engraving of Normans fighting on foot – Church of St Nicolas, Bari, Italy (built between AD1087 and 1197).
© RAFFAELE D'AMATO

cutting or slashing sword with a blade about 80cm in length. The other main weapon of the Norman knight was his spear, a plain ash shaft fitted with an iron head of leaf or lozenge shape and with a long socket. In the eleventh century the lance was also being carried under the armpit, so that the full force of the rider and galloping horse was imparted to the tip. Maces were far less commonly used than the sword, and appear to have consisted of a wooden haft fitted with an iron or bronze head.

THE BATTLE

The two armies were divided by a small hill, somewhere to the north-west of modern San Paolo di Civitate and the River Fortore. The Normans divided their forces into three main divisions: the centre was commanded by Humphrey de Hauteville, the right wing by Richard Count of Aversa, and the left was entrusted to Robert 'Guiscard' (the Cunning) de Hauteville and his troops from Calabria.

The Norman forces in the centre of the formation under Humphrey may have dismounted to fight, in the same fashion as in England and Normandy in the following century.[4] In fact William of Apulia, one of the main sources of the period, confirms in his chronicle account that the Normans had already used the tactic of dismounting part of their heavy cavalry before battle some twelve years earlier, when they fought against a Byzantine army at the Battle of Olivento (17 March 1041), not very far from Civitate.

The dismounting of heavy cavalry troops made the army as a whole more effective, and stiffened the resolve of the knights themselves and of the less experienced masses

Engraving of Norman knights charging on horseback – Church of St Nicolas, Bari, Italy.

© RAFFAELE D'AMATO

who may have been fighting alongside them, for it effectively removed flight as a safe alternative. Furthermore, the dismounting of the cavalry changed their tactical use from a unit that was deployed for an attack mainly against enemy infantry, to a defensive formation used to receive a heavy enemy attack; in the latter case, the knights formed a shield and lance wall in the centre of the line, and a cavalry attack stood little chance against such a formidable force.

It is possible that the Normans at Civitate would have considered dismounting their heavy cavalry in the centre of their three-division formation, the one that was directly opposite the élite and heavily armed Swabian foot soldiers, counting on their centre holding firm while their wings closed in and encircled the papal force. Regrettably, none of the primary sources for the battle indicate whether the Normans decided to fight dismounted or not.

Humphrey had the Swabian infantry opposite him, 'proud people of great courage, but not versed in horsemanship, who fought rather with the sword than with the lance' as suggested by William of Apulia, who emphasizes that these Germans were, truly, formidable warriors. The heavy Swabian infantry was deployed on a thin and long line from the centre extending to the right, while the Italian levies were amassed in a mob on the left.

The Battle of Civitate opened with the mounted troops on the Norman right under Richard of Aversa directly attacking the Italians in the opposite left wing, who melted away almost immediately and were pursued by the advancing Norman horsemen. While this pursuit was under way, the rest of the Norman army had already crossed the plain and had engaged the enemy who, according to William, chose to retreat, apart from the

Swabians who put up a vigorous resistance and refused to leave their position. At this crucial point, we are aware of Richard's return from the pursuit of the Italians to attack the Swabian infantry from behind and complete their encirclement. His manoeuvre culminated in a massacre, and one of the most decisive victories of the eleventh century.[5]

No doubt the mere sight of a Norman cavalry charge must have been terrifying to the poorly armed Italian militia, which would have comprised the bulk of the papal army. But we must also point out that despite the Norman inferiority in numbers, the key to their victory lay in their use of the traditional heavy cavalry charge against a heterogeneous infantry army such as the papal one. It also proves beyond doubt that even a heavily armed, well-trained and disciplined unit fighting on foot could not withstand/repel a sustained heavy cavalry attack unless it was itself supported by units of archers and cavalry.

In this case, the Swabians could stand their ground and deny the Normans their advantage in mobility and numbers, but as their flanks became exposed because of the retreat of their Italian allies, and since they lacked any archer or cavalry support, their encirclement and eventual annihilation became inevitable.

CONCLUSIONS

The Battle of Civitate was a turning point in the future of the Normans in Italy, who, following the outcome of the battle, were able to solidify their legitimacy in the process of expanding further south into the heel of Otranto, in Calabria and, soon enough, to the Muslim-held island of Sicily. Not only that, it was the first major victory for Robert Guiscard, the half-brother of Humphrey de Hauteville, who would eventually rise to prominence as the leader of the Normans in Italy and Sicily.

In terms of its implications, the Battle of Civitate had the same long-term political ramifications as had the Battle of Hastings in England and Northern Europe. It turned on its head the political and diplomatic balance in the region, with the influence of the Byzantine emperor rapidly fading away, while the Normans gained a prominent ally in the Pope of Rome.

Six years after the battle, in 1059, Robert Guiscard made peace with Pope Nicholas II, to whom he and Richard of Aversa swore oaths of fealty. Robert was invested as Duke of Apulia and Calabria and 'future' Duke of Sicily, while Richard, Count of Aversa, was acknowledged as Prince of Capua, having captured that city in the previous year (1058). An alliance between the Norman rulers, sealed with marriages, marked the beginning of Lombard and papal acceptance of Norman supremacy in southern Italy.

Finally, Robert Guiscard's crowning achievement in the mainland of Italy was the conquest of the Byzantine capital Bari after a three-year siege. The Battle of Civitate transformed a peripheral region of the Mediterranean and a frontier area between the Byzantine East, the Muslim South and the Latin West, into a dominant political structure that encompassed the entire southern Italian peninsula and the island of Sicily, and which was to endure for some seven centuries, until 1816.

10 THE BATTLE OF HASTINGS

Conquering a Kingdom

Date 14 October 1066
Location Battle, Rother, East Sussex, England

THE HISTORICAL BACKGROUND

The 'Norman Phenomenon'

THE SECOND HALF of the eleventh century was the period of so-called Norman expansion, when the power of the Norman chivalry became known from England to Italy, Sicily, the Balkans and the Middle East. Many scholars would agree that, while the Anglo-Saxons created England, it was the Normans coming from France that set the foundations of what we now know as the United Kingdom of England, Wales, Scotland and Northern Ireland. The same could be said about the state the Normans established in Italy and Sicily, which survived, in the same form, until the unification of the country in the nineteenth century.

The 'Norman phenomenon' began in northern Europe with a small fleet of Scandinavian ships and their miscellaneous crews cruising into the Seine estuary at the beginning of the second decade of the tenth century. It continued in Italy a century later with a band of mercenaries who offered their services to the highest bidder. It culminated in England with the conquest of one of the most developed kingdoms in northern Europe.

Writing in the 1090s, Geoffrey Malaterra's vivid depiction of the military expansion of the Vikings from Scandinavia into Normandy is portrayed more like the 'conquest' of a woman than territorial aggrandizement – *Normannia* is depicted as a beautiful and fertile woman who stood defenceless and ready to be grabbed by her powerful new masters: the famous Rollo and his followers. To complete this picture of sexual conquest, the Norman chroniclers of the period described the Normans as quintessential warriors – the definition of bravery and manliness, while epitomising their natural inclination to dominate over other peoples and lands.

Many historians of the Norman expansion in England and the Mediterranean – such as Geoffrey Malaterra, William of Apulia, Orderic Vitalis, William of Poitiers or William of Jumièges – ascribe the Norman success to a series of psychological characteristics: first, their energy (*strenuitas*), which Malaterra contrasts to their 'effeminate' enemies. As well as being vigorous, the Normans were also courageous, always fighting bravely to gain their fame in the battlefield. But they were also resourceful, and they were particularly distinguished for their craftiness and cunning spirit. Savagery was another important character aspect, with images of cruelty, bloodthirstiness and destruction preceding their advance – especially in the Mediterranean – against their enemies, an image they carefully and meticulously cultivated and promoted.

Political Developments Across the Seas

In 1002, the English King Æthelred II 'the Unræd' – meaning the 'ill-advised' or 'poorly counselled' – married Emma, the sister of Richard II, Duke of Normandy (d. 1026). Following the Battle of Maldon in 991, Æthelred had been paying tribute, or *Danegeld*, to the Danish king, but in 1013 King Swein Forkbeard (986–1014) set sail for England, having decided to put an end to the kingdom of Wessex and all of non-Danish England. As a result of the Danish invasion, Æthelred fled to the safety of his father-in-law in Normandy, surrendering his kingdom to Swein.

When the latter unexpectedly died early the following year, his seventeen-year old son Cnute returned to Denmark to secure his throne, thus giving the chance to Æthelred and his eldest son Edmund Ironside to sail back to England to organize the English resistance. But Cnute quickly defeated the English in 1015, had Edmund killed, and after Æthelred's death, married his widow Emma, thus becoming the undisputed overlord of the united kingdom of Denmark and England (1016–1035) with rights to Normandy through his wife.

Following Cnute's death in 1035, his two sons, who possessed none of their father's talents, bickered over the Danish throne for seven years. Meanwhile the Anglo-Saxon *witan* (or nobles' council) recalled Æthelred's second son Edward the Confessor (1042–1066) from Normandy, and placed him on the throne. Edward had spent many years in exile in Normandy, which led to the establishment of a powerful Norman interest in English politics, as Edward drew heavily on his former hosts for political and military support. Nevertheless, there were many leading English prelates who opposed the growing influence of the Norman nobles in England, one of the leading contenders being Edward's father-in-law, Godwin Earl of Wessex, who had managed to marry his daughter Edith to the new king in 1045.

By the early 1060s Edward appeared likely to die childless, and realizing that the English crown would be up for grabs, the leading barons of England began to prepare openly for the forthcoming struggle. By the time of Edward's death in 1066 there were three main contenders, first and foremost being Harold Godwinson, the richest and most powerful of the English aristocrats and son of Godwin – he was elected king by the *witenagemot* ('meeting of wise men') of England, and crowned by the Archbishop of York.

However, Harold was soon challenged by his two most powerful neighbouring rulers: Duke William of Normandy claimed that he had been promised the throne by

Edward the Confessor, and that Harold had conceded to this; and Harald III of Norway – Harald Hardrada – also challenged the succession. His claim to the throne was based on an agreement between his predecessor Magnus I of Norway and the earlier King of England, Harthacnute. Both William and Harald therefore set about assembling troops for separate invasions of England.

THE PRELUDE TO THE BATTLE

Harald Hardrada was the first to challenge the political *status quo* in England. He had found a potential ally in Tostig Godwinson, Harold's disgruntled exiled brother who was raiding south-eastern England with a fleet he had recruited in Flanders and from Orkney. Hardrada was intrigued by this Anglo-Saxon contender, thinking that he could reinstate Tostig in northern England and establish a foothold for further conquest. Hardrada therefore launched an invasion fleet of 300 ships in mid-September 1066, sailing into the Humber river and disembarking a force of 9,000 men 16 kilometres (10 miles) south-east of their target, the northern city of York. On 20 September, Hardrada met and defeated an Anglo-Saxon army of perhaps 4,000 men at Fulford Gate, leading to the surrender of York to the Norwegians.

The news reached Harold Godwinson in London. Harald's landing in the Humber estuary and his conquest of York prompted an immediate reaction from the English king, who gathered a force of 8,000 men and marched north. Harold's army was made up of 2,000 of his personal bodyguard, the housecarls, and perhaps another 6,000 from the *fyrds* of the north of England. Godwinson's army traversed 300km (190 miles) from London to Yorkshire in just five days and took the Norwegians by surprise, defeating them at the Battle of Stamford Bridge on 25 September.[1]

The deaths of Harald and Tostig at Stamford Bridge quashed any threat of invasion from the north, leaving the battered Anglo-Saxon army to limp back to York. But here, on 1 October while resting and enjoying a victory feast, news arrived that William had landed on the Sussex coast at Pevensey on 28 September. William had spent almost nine months on his preparations, mainly in constructing an invasion fleet that would carry his forces across the English Channel. According to some Norman chronicles, he also secured diplomatic support, the most famous of which is Pope Alexander II's endorse-ment of a papal banner. William mustered his forces at Saint Valéry-sur-Somme, and was ready to cross the English Channel around the 12 August, but the weather delayed his operation for the next month and a half.

THE OPPOSING FORCES

The Norman Army

The sources for the Hastings campaign offer several figures to modern historians, ranging from William of Poitiers' 50,000 to the *Carmen de Hastingae Proelio*'s 150,000.[2]

Historians have reached some sort of consensus, with a number between 7,000 and 8,000 effectives being considered as the most likely one, bearing in mind that William would certainly have left troops to guard the fortifications and the ships at Pevensey.[3] This force was accompanied by some 2,000–2,500 horses, transported from St Valéry to Pevensey on a number of vessels, which chroniclers put between 696 (Wace) to 3,000 (William of Jumièges), although it is unlikely that they exceeded 800.[4]

Therefore, with the cavalry numbering no more than 2,500, the rest of the force consisted probably of 4,000 foot soldiers of various sorts, and around 1,500 archers, and probably crossbowmen as well.

The Saxon Army

The main difference between the two opposing armies at Hastings was that, while the Normans had a proportion of mounted troops that constituted their élite unit, the English army consisted almost entirely of combatants who either fought on foot, or travelled on horseback but rather chose to dismount and fight on foot. Theirs was a core force of around 800–1,000 housecarls – élite fighters, some of whom lived at the court or hall of the king or earls and received a wage – supplemented by some 6,500 men of the selected *fyrd* – men performing military service in return for the land they held – of several counties of the south and central England, and men from the great *fyrd* – every able-bodied man called for service by the king in case of emergency – of Sussex and perhaps Kent.

We have no clear idea about their numbers, but bearing in mind that Harold did not have time to replenish his losses after Stamford Bridge or wait for the *fyrds* from the west and north, historians put the Saxon army's numbers to around a total slightly higher than that of the Normans, some 8,000 in all.[5]

Arms and Armour

As the arms and armour of the Norman knight were examined in the previous chapter on the Battle of Civitate, suffice it to say here that the Saxon and Norman armies were comparable in many respects. The Saxon housecarls and thegns were deployed for battle wearing a kind of mail coat similar to the Norman of the period, although poorer soldiers would have had to make do with different kinds of padded armour – if any. The Bayeux Tapestry also confirms the use of wooden kite-shaped and round shields by the Saxons, spears of different lengths, and conical helmets, although it is possible that the iron helmets of leading housecarls would have included an iron mask.

The main difference between the soldiers on both sides was the use of the battle-axe. The Tapestry shows two different kinds of axe wielded by Saxon troops: first the Danish axe, which, despite the numerous typologies identified by experts in the field, can be described as a weapon with a single wide, thin blade, with pronounced 'horns' at both the toe and heel, and a cutting surface that varied between 20 and 30cm (8 and 12in). It

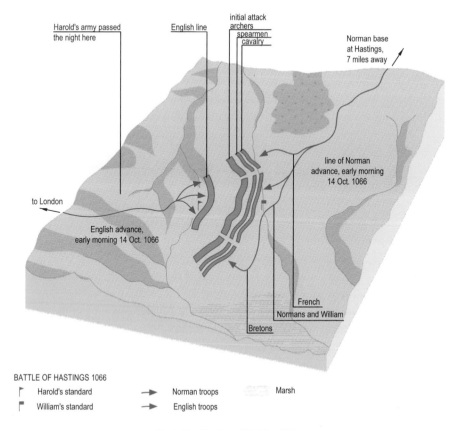

Harold's army passed the night here

English line

initial attack
archers
spearmen
cavalry

Norman base
at Hastings,
7 miles away

line of Norman
advance, early morning
14 Oct. 1066

to London

English advance,
early morning 14 Oct. 1066

French

Normans and William

Bretons

BATTLE OF HASTINGS 1066

Harold's standard   → Norman troops   Marsh

William's standard   → English troops

The Battle of Hastings, 14 October 1066.

was mounted on a light shaft and could be swung with one hand. The second and most popular type was the broad axe, with a cutting blade of more than 30cm (12in) long, and mounted on a thick shaft about 0.9m (3ft) long, to be wielded with both hands.

The Normans were superior to the Saxons in terms of another weapon, the bow, the use of which required a high degree of professional training and skill. Harold's army included a very small number of archers and slingers, probably because the survivors from Stamford Bridge lacked the horses to keep up with the rapid advance of the Saxon army south after their victory over the Viking invaders; there is just a solitary figure depicted in the Bayeux Tapestry.

According to William of Poitiers, the hail of arrows launched against the Saxons in the first stage of the battle had some effect in 'killing and maiming many', with the tightly massed housecarls and thegns providing a good target for the Norman bowmen. But the Saxon shield-wall and the elevated ground would have protected the ranks of the English from heavy casualties, and the counter attack by the latter with all kinds of missile weapons – if William of Poitiers is to be believed – swept back the Norman archers!

THE TERRAIN

The terrain at Hastings offered several advantages to an army that was on the defensive while fighting on foot. Harold deployed his forces at a place called Senlac, identified by Orderic Vitalis as a Norman-French adaptation of the Old English word 'Sandlacu', which means 'sandy water'. This location consists of a hill called Caldbec, some 1,000m (1,100yd) long, 140m (150yd) broad, with the greater part of the ridge being 76m (250ft) high. The south slope facing the Normans was quite gentle, while the north side was very steep, which prevented the Norman cavalry giving chase in the event of a Saxon retreat. Also, the dense vegetation on the west edge of the hill would have offered significant protection to the Saxon army's right flank from cavalry attacks.

The hill sinks to a marshy bottom, from where the opposite hill of Telham climbs up again to 135m (441ft); the Normans had descended Telham to deploy their forces. The topography of the battlefield offered William no alternative except a frontal uphill attack with his cavalry.

This location seemed ideal for an army such as the Saxon one, consisting almost entirely of foot soldiers, and whose tactics compelled it to stand on the defensive and in a tight formation. It was the latter, along with the elevated ground and the marshy bottom of the hill, which matched the Saxon lack of heavy horse – their army would have been easily overrun by the Norman cavalry if they had deployed on the plain.

But was a defensive battle Harold's original plan? Following the chronicler accounts of Florence of Worcester and the *Anglo-Saxon Chronicle*, it was Harold who had the intention to surprise William – but instead it was the latter who turned the tables on Harold and seized the initiative.[6]

THE BATTLE FORMATIONS

William deployed his forces at Hastings in three lines: archers and, if we believe William of Poitiers, crossbowmen as well; infantry, with only a small number of them having mail coats; and finally the heavy cavalry, which was kept back to deliver the knock-out blow. Less clear is the composition of each of the corps; we assume from William of Poitiers' writing that the centre division, by far the largest of the three, was composed of Norman contingents with, presumably, William in command, while on the left flank were the units from Anjou, Poitou and Maine, with the French and the Flemings on the right. Since William placed the bulk of his élite cavalry in the centre of his formation, and not in the flanks as was recommended by Vegetius – the early fifth-century Roman author of a famous military treatise – it is clear that the Norman Duke considered an attack on the well-protected Saxon wings as futile, preferring instead a coordinated infantry-cavalry charge at the centre, where he could see Harold's banner.

The troops that William was about to face at Hastings consisted of both heavily armed housecarls and thegns, packed together with the militia from the *fyrd*, in what seemed, from a distance, as a single shield-wall between eight to ten shields deep – although it is

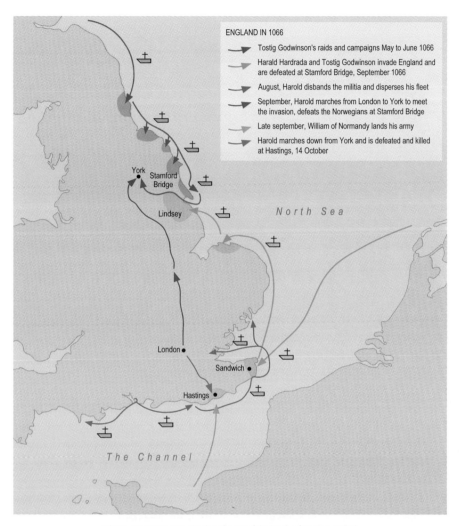

ENGLAND IN 1066

➤ Tostig Godwinson's raids and campaigns May to June 1066

➤ Harald Hardrada and Tostig Godwinson invade England and are defeated at Stamford Bridge, September 1066

➤ August, Harold disbands the militia and disperses his fleet

➤ September, Harold marches from London to York to meet the invasion, defeats the Norwegians at Stamford Bridge

➤ Late september, William of Normandy lands his army

➤ Harold marches down from York and is defeated and killed at Hastings, 14 October

York
Stamford Bridge
Lindsey
North Sea
London
Sandwich
Hastings
The Channel

Military operations in England on the eve of the Battle of Hastings (1066).

likely it would have comprised ten sub-units, with only small gaps between them. Harold placed the best armed and armoured of his warriors in the front lines, while the lesser thegns and the militia stood right behind them. It has been suggested that the wings of the Saxon army were bent back in order to deploy more men on the lower ground.

THE BATTLE

The Battle of Hastings was opened by the skirmishers, who moved forwards to shoot at the enemy – but falling short from what was expected of them, their attack produced poor results due to the fact that they had to shoot uphill: their arrows were easily repulsed by the housecarls, whose shield-wall must have served its purpose quite well!

Saxon shield-wall, Bayeux Tapestry.

Then William ordered his archers to withdraw, and called his heavy infantry into the attack – but they were met with a heavy shower of arrows, javelins, lances and other 'primitive casting weapons'. Fierce fighting ensued after the Norman infantry crashed into the English shield-wall, so the duke ordered his heavy cavalry of knights into the attack.

In this crucial stage of the battle, and while the Norman cavalry also failed to break the solid Saxon shield-wall, sources report of the panicky retirement of the Norman left wing, which affected the entire Norman army. It is possible that the Bretons on William's left, who met the English line first, became confused and disengaged in order to regroup at the bottom of the hill. Or the toll of dead and wounded might have forced a retreat in order to regroup – it is impossible to know with certainty. Nevertheless, the apparent flight of the Bretons forced William to disengage his centre and right to cover his exposed left flank. Rumours had also spread that William had been killed, so he was obliged to ride among his comrades lifting his conical helm, to reassure them that he was still alive.

If the Norman sources are to be believed, then the English were greatly weakened by the fact that many of their comrades abandoned their position to pursue the Normans downhill.[7] Hence, what happened at the second stage of the battle proves one significant point: no tactical body of infantry can go after a retreating enemy when lacking the necessary training and discipline, and without adequate support from cavalry units.

Engraving of a Norman knight on horseback charging against an archer and a foot soldier – Church of St Nicolas, Bari, Italy.

© RAFFAELE D'AMATO

Furthermore, if any unit of heavy infantry is projected forwards from the main army, its flanks are left exposed to enemy attack, thus significantly increasing the chance of encirclement by the enemy cavalry. Whether, however, this move came simply as a result of indiscipline, or the Saxon officers decided that this was the right moment to counter attack, we will never know with certainty. The Duke of Normandy, however, reacted sharply by ordering his centre to wheel left and pursue the Anglo-Saxon counter attack, cutting it off from any support from the ridge. The crisis seemed to have passed!

At this moment there seems to have been a lull in the battle, allowing for units to be re-deployed, and food and water to be brought to the front ranks. By this time it was early afternoon, and William must have been starting to get really worried by the fact that his cavalry still could not dislodge the Saxon housecarls from the top of the hill. After the lull, the fighting resumed, with the Duke ordering his cavalry and infantry to try once again to dislodge the Saxons from the ridge by putting all their efforts into creating gaps in their solid formation. After this attempt also failed, we reach the second of the well-known incidents of the battle that decided its outcome: the 'feigned retreat' of the Norman cavalry.

The debate as to whether there was indeed a feigned retreat of William's cavalry in the second stage of the battle has been fought as hard as did the two enemy armies at Hastings. Personally I am ready to believe that there was, indeed, a feigned flight

Field of the Battle of Hastings 1066, Battle Abbey, East Sussex.

© TIMOTHY NORTON

Field of the Battle of Hastings 1066, Battle Abbey, East Sussex.

© TIMOTHY NORTON

of the Norman cavalry, and the fact that the men under William would have been trained to attack the enemy in this manner for many years, as many sources from the eleventh century confirm, meant that they were perfectly capable of enacting this challenging battle manoeuvre. With units of the English being enticed to leave their defensive formation and march down the slope to chase the 'retreating' Normans, the latter got exactly what they wanted: a chance to turn their horses (*regiratis equis*)[8] and ride them down.

The number of housecarls and thegns holding the ridge was therefore greatly reduced because so many left their ranks to pursue the Norman knights; furthermore their place was taken by the less experienced and poorly armed and armoured men of the great *fyrd*. Also the Saxon position was becoming increasingly untenable because of the growing numbers of dead and wounded men and horses sprawled in front of their line. But without light infantry and a cavalry arm, Harold had no choice but to remain on the defensive and receive the Norman attacks, in the hope that the invaders would attack themselves to exhaustion.

The role of the Norman archers in this last-ditch attempt by William to win the battlefield was crucial – the Tapestry gives no real hint, but does suggest their importance at this stage by showing the large number of quivers standing next to the small figures of the archers, whose barrage would have had a much more devastating effect than in the opening stages of the battle.

And it was at this point in the battle that King Harold was killed. Unfortunately, William of Poitiers' short description of the incident shows that he lacked the necessary details of what exactly happened, confining himself to a brief statement. Nevertheless, the famous depiction in the Tapestry has created a myth about the death of King Harold by an arrow-shot through the eye, which has been discounted by many modern historians.[9] Rather, the king would probably have been lying wounded by an arrow-shot when the Norman knights broke through the Saxon lines and into the inner circle where the royal banner would have been flown, and finished him off.

No doubt Wace's elaborate description of a king struck by an arrow above the right eye, and then vainly trying to pull it out before being hacked down by an enemy knight, provides a more heroic end to a rather inglorious but more realistic death in battle – one that sealed the future of an entire kingdom! News of the king's death spread quickly through the Anglo-Saxon ranks, and this broke the defenders' morale. Soon a general rout ensued towards the safety of the forest that loomed beyond Caldbec hill, and the Normans finally overran the ridge.

CONCLUSIONS

The conquest of England was the most remarkable and well planned of all enterprises conducted by a Norman leader in history. Good fortune may have played a large part in William's success, as William of Poitiers may have hinted when he compared the Norman Duke – and now King – to Julius Caesar, who left too much to chance. In fact the death

The famous scene of Harold's death by an arrow – Bayeux Tapestry.

of Harold proved to be the catalyst that tipped the scale in favour of the Normans and led to the Saxon resistance crumbling rapidly after that.

This was undoubtedly a development of tremendous importance for the future of the Anglo-Saxon kingdom. At Dyrrachium (modern Durres in Albania) in October 1081, a battle of equal significance for the future of the Byzantine Empire took place, when the imperial armies of the recently crowned emperor Alexius Comnenus were put to shame by the invading army of the Norman Duke of Apulia and Calabria, Robert Guiscard. Alexius Comnenus was hotly pursued and surrounded by the Norman knights, but managed to escape almost unscathed, and established a rallying point at Thessaloniki, in Macedonia. Alexius' death would have brought the state to the brink of a renewed civil war, just like the aftermath of the Battle of Manzikert ten years before, and the future of the Byzantine Empire would have been very different. In a period when a leader fought in the front ranks with the rest of the army, and not in some headquarters many kilometres to the rear, his death could potentially have catastrophic ramifications.

William's rule over his new realm got off to a shaky start since the newcomers were not only despised by the native Anglo-Saxons, but were also greatly outnumbered by them. The new king spent several years subduing pockets of resistance, of which there were many, especially in the north of England. He also initiated a building programme that would see the face of the southern, western and northern marches of his realm changed for ever: a Norman motte-and-bailey castle was built in every important borough – perhaps 550 of these were built between 1066 and 1087 – and a Norman vassal was appointed to serve in each as a royal sheriff.

William was careful to claim the entire kingdom of England as his own by the right of conquest, and made his vassals swear an oath of personal loyalty to him in return for their fiefs. The old English estates were transformed into European fiefs, held by the crown and given to its vassals – the lords – in return for military service. This new system spread aggressively, endorsed by the rapid building of the motte-and-bailey castles that quickly dotted the English countryside (both royal and baronial). He also extended his control to southern Scotland in 1072, initiating centuries of border wars with the Scots. And because he and his heirs retained the title of the Duke of Normandy, at his death in 1087, William left an Anglo-Norman empire that would be a source of contention between England and France for the next four centuries.

As a final note, I would like to emphasize that combined arms tactics (infantry, cavalry and archers) almost always had an advantage over tactics that relied on one type of soldier alone (infantry). The Normans widely applied combined cavalry and infantry tactics in both England and southern Italy in the second half of the eleventh century, where the cavalry played the leading role in deciding the battle in their favour. At the turn of the twelfth century, however, the change in Anglo-Norman attitudes regarding the effectiveness of the cavalry charge, and the move towards the dismounting of knights to a dense phalanx formation, supported by archers and smaller units of heavy cavalry, indicated a minor revolution in the approach to battle.

11 THE BATTLE OF LAS NAVAS DE TOLOSA

A Turning Point in the Dynamics of Iberian Politics

Also known in Arab history as the Battle of Al-Uqab.

Date 16 July 1212
Location Near Las Navas de Tolosa, Jaén, Andalucía

THE HISTORICAL BACKGROUND

DESPITE THE SUCCESSES in Spain and Portugal, the failure of the Second Crusade in its primary objective to take Damascus dampened enthusiasm for crusading throughout Catholic Europe. Indicative of this anti-crusade atmosphere during the period between the Second and Third Crusades is the vain attempt by Alfonso VII of León and Castile (reigned 1126–57) to recruit Louis VII of France for a crusade in Spain while the latter was on his way to Santiago de Compostela, in Galicia, to complete a pilgrimage. Louis VII had been discouraged from undertaking such an ambitious expedition by Pope Adrian IV (papacy, 1154–59) who, contrary to his many predecessors, had proved reluctant to authorize – or encourage – another Spanish crusade without an endorsement by the local princes.

Following Alfonso VII's death in 1157, his lands were divided between his two sons: Sancho III (1157–58) took Castile, while Fernando II (1157–88) established himself in Léon. But Sancho's early death ushered in the regency of the under-aged Alfonso VIII (1158–1214), which happened to coincide with that of Alfonso II of Aragon (1162–96), the leader of another emerging political power in the peninsula, now united with the county of Barcelona. Both regencies precipitated aristocratic rebellions that seriously jeopardized the past victories against the Muslims by enabling a new North African dynasty, that of the Almohads, to gradually wrest control from the Almoravids of Spain in the 1160s, until 1173.

At the Council of Segovia in 1166, the new kings of Castile and Léon rushed to condemn anyone entering the service of the Muslim princes, while – once again – the war against Islam in the peninsula was equated with the oriental crusade. When the Almohad caliph Abu Ya'qub Yusuf I (1163–84) planned a massive campaign to besiege the Christian outpost of Huete, about 50 kilometres (30 miles) west of Cuenca, in July 1172,

Alfonso VIII and his Christians were offered remission of sins (*grandes solturas*) in their effort to stem the forthcoming Muslim tide. They eventually succeeded in compelling the Almohads to abandon the siege within two weeks, but despite the uncoordinated and largely reactive attitude of the Christian kings in this period, in ensuing years the Almohads would force the Spanish frontier back to the River Tagus.

On 23 March 1175, Pope Alexander III (papacy, 1159–81) was persuaded to summon the Spanish people to a crusade against the Almohads, a bull that included full remission of sins to anyone who enlisted for a year at his own expense. The capture of Cuenca in September 1178, about 180 kilometres (110 miles) east of Toledo, by the kings of Castile and Aragon, was a key to further Christian expansion in the south-east and into the kingdoms of Valencia and Murcia. Between 1179 and 1184, sporadic warfare between the Christian kingdoms (in 1183 Castile and León agreed an alliance) and the Almohads carried on unabated, while the Christian powers could often count on the naval support of the Almoravid Kingdom of Majorca.

Following the disaster of the Third Crusade and the fall of Jerusalem in 1187, the crusader spirit was kept alive by Pope Clement III's (papacy, 1187–91) guarantee of remission of sins to those who campaigned in Spain. Furthermore, the Pope authorized for the first time the collection of ecclesiastical revenues to support the Iberian crusade.

The most important response to the papal appeal for a crusade came from northern Europeans. Two fleets sailed south to Portuguese waters in the spring and summer of 1189, the first comprising ships from Denmark and Frisia, which stopped at Lisbon where they were joined by many Portuguese, while the other bore crusaders from England, France and Germany, and also reached Lisbon in July. Both fleets coordinated with Sancho I of Portugal (reigned 1185–1211) for a joint attack on Silves. Although the city was starved into submission on the 1 September, the Christian success was short-lived, as Abu Yusuf Ya'qub (1184–99) took back the city in July 1191.

Following the surrender of Silves to Abu Ya'qub, the Christian kings concluded a series of truces with the Almohad caliph, allowing them to resume their bitter territorial rivalries. These truces lasted until 1194, after which year Archbishop Martin of Toledo and the Knights of Calatrava ravaged the Guadalquivir, in central Andalucía. Abu Ya'qub was provoked even further by the building of the fortress of Alarcos, north of the strategic Despeñaperros Pass that connects Andalucía and Castile, by Alfonso VIII of Castile in 1194. The Christian aggression resulted in the Almohad invasion of Castile, culminating in the Battle of Alarcos (19 July 1195) fought between Abu Yusuf Ya'qub and King Alfonso VIII of Castile. It resulted in the defeat of the Castilian forces and their subsequent retreat to Toledo.

After the defeat at Alarcos, the Christian kings continued to quarrel, and were prepared to agree on alliance treaties with the enemy, to the dismay of the Popes. A period of Almohad dominance would last for some twenty years after the Battle of Alarcos. In the spring of 1196, the Almohads ravaged the Tagus valley, while Alfonso IX of León (reigned 1188–1230) was plundering western Castile with Almohad money. This action led to Alfonso's excommunication by Pope Celestine III (papacy, 1191–98), who also

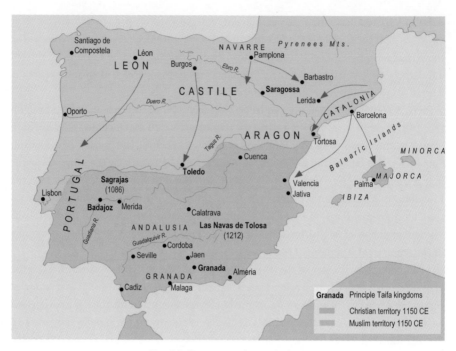

Map of the Iberian peninsula around AD1150.

instructed the archbishops of Toledo and Compostela to rouse the people to take up arms against their king. A plundering expedition in the Tagus valley, led by Abu Ya'qub, ended in a ten-year truce with Alfonso VIII of Castile, once again enabling the Christian kings to continue their quarrels.

Nevertheless, the crusading spirit had been growing steadily in Aragon and Castile following the Christian disaster at Alarcos. Pedro II of Aragon, probably late in 1203, notified Pope Innocent III (papacy, 1198–1214) of his aspiration to make war against the Almohads. He went as far as to offer his kingdom to the papacy, and agreed to hold it in vassalage to Rome. After the truce with the Almohads expired, the new caliph Abu 'Abd Allah al-Nasir (reigned 1199–1213) crossed the Straits of Gibraltar in May 1211, intent on making war against the king of Castile. In July he marched north through the Despeñaperros Pass, invading Castile and besieging the headquarters of the Order of Calatrava, the castle of Salvatierra, some 40km (25 miles) north of the pass.

The castle surrendered in early September, while in the following winter months the word spread around the Catholic core of Europe for a crusade to be launched against the Almohads. Innocent III appealed to the bishops of France and Provence, and offered remission of sins to everyone who would participate in the crusade or provide financial support. Then Archbishop Rodrigo of Toledo was sent to southern France to request urgent military assistance from the French aristocrats.

On Palm Sunday in April 1212, Innocent III exhorted the kings in Spain to remain united against the Muslim tide threatening to sweep the Christians out of Iberia. The

Catholic core of Europe was already bracing itself for the forthcoming crusade of 1212, the so-called Crusade of Las Navas de Tolosa.

THE PRELUDE TO THE BATTLE

Modern historians have adequate information about the Crusade of Las Navas de Tolosa to be able to piece together the events that unfolded in the summer of 1212. In a report sent by Alfonso VIII of Castile to the Pope, just days after the battle, we read about the impact of the call for a crusade that had been preached by Innocent a few months before:

> Hence it was that, when people heard of the remission of sins which you [Innocent] granted to those coming to join us, there arrived a vast number of knights from the regions beyond the Pyrenees, including the Archbishops of Narbonne and Bordeaux and the Bishop of Nantes. Those who came numbered up to 2,000 knights with their squires, and up to 10,000 of their serving-men on horseback, with up to 50,000 serving-men on foot, for all of whom we had to provide food. There came also our illustrious friends and relatives the Kings of Aragon and of Navarre in support of the Catholic cause, with all their forces.[1]

The Christian army that gathered in Toledo in the spring of 1212 was a multinational army, and it included Alfonso VIII of Castile, Pedro II of Aragon, archbishops Arnald Amaury of Narbonne and Guillaume of Bordeaux, the Bishop of Nantes, several counts and viscounts from southern France, the knights of the Military Orders of Calatrava, Santiago, the Temple and the Hospital, as well as Castilian nobles and urban militias. The kings of León and Portugal did not participate in the crusade, but many of their subjects went regardless.

On 20 June, the Crusader army left Toledo and marched south, heading towards the Despeñaperros Pass, which would lead them into Andalucía. As the Christian army was marching south, part of the French contingent broke off and, apparently seeking plunder, sacked the town of Malagon on 24 June, some 90km (55 miles) south of Toledo, and slaughtered its defenders. They followed this early success by besieging the castle of Calatrava, which capitulated after just four days of siege and was restored to the Order on 1 July.

Crucially, however, Alfonso forbade the plunder of the city, a decision that did not go down well with a large number of French knights, who eventually decided to abandon their leaders and return to France; according to Alfonso VIII, 'scarcely 150' of them remained with the rest of the crusaders.

After the French desertion, the Crusader army was more homogenous and 'Spanish', with the author of the anonymous *Latin Chronicle of the Kings of Castile* thanking God, with the assurance that the glory of victory in battle would be attributed 'to the famous Spaniards and not to the northerners'.[2] It was at this point that Sancho VII of Navarre, with some 200 knights, joined the Crusader army, marching to Andalucía via the Despeñaperros Pass.

Meanwhile, Abu 'Abd Allah al-Nasir had already moved his headquarters from Seville to Jaen, some 240km (150 miles) east of Seville and 80km (50 miles) south of the Despeñaperros Pass. The Almohad caliph was clearly aware of the Christian plan, and it is likely that he had detailed and accurate intelligence about their movements. Further encouraged by the French desertion, al-Nasir left his base at Jaen on 7 July and moved to the foot of the canyon leading south through the Despeñaperros Pass, while the Crusaders entrusted their fate to a mysterious shepherd who led them through the pass and down the plain of the Mesa del Rey, some 20km (12 miles) north of Las Navas de Tolosa. The two enemies met each other on 13 July.

THE OPPOSING FORCES

The Spanish Armies

The Christian Spanish kingdoms that were struggling for dominance on the northern part of the Iberian peninsula also adopted the lord-vassal relations (anachronistically called 'feudalism') that were known to the north of the Pyrenees, although these were not so rigidly defined or institutionalized as in France. The Spanish rulers in Aragon, Navarre, Castile and León maintained the right to summon armies in times of need, making effective use of two main pools of mounted soldiers: the *caballeros hidalgos* (full-time soldiers armed with lance and sword), who were either landed or household stipendiary troops (the equivalent of the English *familiae*, called the *mesnadas*); and the *caballeros villanos* (non-noble knights supported by termed benefices). The *peones* were the lower class urban militia, poorly equipped with bows and arrows, spears and short swords, and they were mainly used as mounted or infantry auxiliary troops.[3] The Spanish kings could also hire the services of mercenaries and the Spanish orders such as the Calatrava, the Santiago and the Alcantara.

Arms, Armour and Tactics

The Spanish Militias

In terms of arms, armour and tactics, French influence south of the Pyrenees was already becoming palpable from the second half of the eleventh century.[4] After that period, Iberian cavalry tactics involved knights approaching the enemy in closed formation, carrying their couched lances, designed to break enemy formation by their sheer momentum. The Iberian élite also adopted the mail *hauberk* and the *coif* around the same period, although the earlier scale-armour (of both Arab and Gothic influence) remained in use until well into the thirteenth century, when it was gradually replaced by the coat-of-plates. The wearing of padded and quilted armour over the *hauberk* was widespread in Iberia, indicating Arab-Islamic influence.

The eleventh century brought another change in the shape and size of the shields, from the smaller, round bucklers to the larger round (but sometimes even kite-shaped) shields that covered a substantial part of the torso and groin area. A Spanish knight would also have worn a conical *bascinet* over the *coif*, with a *visor* to cover the face. His arms would have included a straight-bladed sword, with a wide and flat blade and a narrow tip, and a long lance. The mace seems to have been more of a status symbol than a real weapon to be used in battle.

Finally, both the tactical role and equipment of the Spanish urban militias were more rigidly regulated around the end of the twelfth century. If mounted, the horses had to be of minimum quality, but otherwise the militia had to carry shields, wear metallic helmets, be armed with spears and swords, while their body armour would have included a mail *hauberk* and a padded overcoat.[5]

The Almohad Armies

The second half of the twelfth century was a period of socio-political transition for Muslim Spain, marking the gradual expansion of the Muslim sect of the Almohads of Morocco in southern Spain. The Almohads had developed their social structure in the urbanized areas of the mountains of Morocco, thus they had a more sophisticated military organization based on their Berber tribes. They soon absorbed many élite Almoravid units into their new structure, especially the élite black mounted regiments from Senegal and other black units that would come to form the caliph's guard.

On the battlefield, the Almohads formed hollow infantry squares where they placed the heavily armed spearmen in the front ranks, followed by other spearmen and javeliners, while the slingers and archers were deployed in the rear ranks of the formation to provide support with their bows. The Almohad cavalry would let the infantry phalanx receive the enemy attack, before charging between the infantry lines to break and pursue the enemy. Still, it was the infantry armies that bore the brunt of the fighting in Andalus, and although they travelled on camels, they nevertheless dismounted before the battle to fight in a dense phalanx formation.

The Almohad warriors in Iberia would quickly become virtually identical to their Christian counterparts in terms of arms and armour; the main things that distinguished them in battle were superficial elements, such as the Saharan face-veil (*litham*) of the Berbers, or the cotton tunics distinguished by their bright colours.[6] They would have carried long heavy lances, circular ('adarga' type, the circle shape evolved to become more heart-shaped) or kite-shaped wooden shields, a straight-bladed sword, and a dagger. A mail *hauberk* would have protected their body, usually supplemented by a mail *coif*, although scale armour is more commonly associated with Muslim infantry. Finally, a conical *bascinet*-type of helmet, with either a nasal or a full-face visor, would have completed their armour. An Andalucían infantryman of the period would have carried a single-edged sword with a typical wooden sword-pommel, and he would have been protected by padded and/or quilted armour.

THE BATTLE

Apparently, the Christian crossing of the Mesa del Rey with the help of the famous shepherd caught the Muslims at camp by surprise. They would probably have been unaware that there was a defile leading behind their camp and down to the valley, thus their camp would have been facing north towards the main passage-way south via the Despeñaperros Pass. Hence on 13 July, the Almohad caliph had to re-orientate his forces from north to west to meet this threat, placing his army in a strong defensive position on the foothills of a nearby hill.

Although the primary sources are not clear about this point, Al-Nasir would probably have deployed his foot soldiers into a strong defensive formation, placing his élite and heavier infantry in the first rank. Behind them would have come the lighter foot soldiers with their spears, javelins and slings, thus leaving the archers to the rear to provide missile support. The caliph would have placed his heavy Andalucían cavalry and the Berber light horsemen on the wings[7] while he held the rearguard, surrounded by his bodyguard of black Africans.

Following the writings of al-Turtushi,[8] a Muslim from al-Andalus who was writing in Egypt in the mid-twelfth century, we are able to reconstruct the marshalling of the infantry units in a typical Muslim battlefield deployment of the period:

> The infantry, armed with large shields, long pikes and sharp tipped javelins, form the first ranks, taking their positions with their pikes thrust into the ground behind them and the points aimed at the enemy, each man kneeling on the ground on his left knee with his shield in front of him … When the enemy draws near, the archers [behind the infantry] loose their arrows and the infantry throw their javelins and take up their pikes. They then go to the right and left and the Muslim cavalry charges between the archers and the infantry.[9]

What we see here is a significant similarity in the tactical formation of the infantry in Muslim armies with those in Byzantine armies of the same period.[10] Both armies place their heavy infantry armed with long pikes in the front ranks of the formation, while after them came the archers, who were supposed to weaken the enemy attack by releasing volleys of arrows against the charging enemy cavalry. The cavalry kept the 'élite' role of counter attacking and delivering the final charge, usually deployed behind the main infantry force or at its flanks.

Alfonso of Castile also organized his army in a typical medieval fashion, deploying them into three divisions, including a reserve. According to the *Latin Chronicle of the Kings of Castile*, the Crusader centre was made up of men from Castile, León and the military orders under the command of Diego Lopez de Haro. Pedro II of Aragon commanded the left wing, supported by knights of Santiago and Calatrava, while the right division was under the orders of Sancho VII of Navarre. Alfonso would have remained in the rearguard with the remainder of his knights, as a reserve division to deploy in case of emergency. Regrettably, the sources are not clear about the exact disposition of the men in their divisions, not only in terms of ratio but also in numbers between mounted and foot soldiers.

The battle was joined early on Monday morning, 16 July 1212, when the Crusaders opted for an all-out heavy cavalry attack all along the line, led by Diego Lopez. But this attack was repulsed after fierce hand-to-hand fighting between the knights and their Muslim enemies on foot. The sources confirm that the battle ebbed and flowed throughout the morning, with both sides attacking each other with their cavalry forces, hoping, no doubt, to break their enemy's resolve to continue the fighting: 'The battle was joined, but neither side was overcome, although at times they pushed back the enemy, and at other times they were driven back by the enemy.'[11]

What happened next turned the tide of the battle in favour of the Christians. The *Latin Chronicle of the Kings of Castile* mentions a number of Christian knights who were responsible for spreading panic amongst their comrades by crying out that the Christians were overcome. There are countless cases in medieval military history of Europe where panic was caused by fear of the enemy, or by a surprise attack, or a growing feeling of unrest and anxiety during the night after a disastrous battle. But Verbruggen has argued a long time ago that it is a mistake to explain these examples of panic in terms of lack of discipline.[12] History has shown many times that even the best troops may be subject to panic, but one of the best means of avoiding panic in battle is the use of two or three fighting lines in depth. The soldiers who are tempted to break ranks in a panic are usually then halted and rounded up not far from the front.

Therefore, at that crucial stage of the battle, Alfonso VIII took a momentous decision that would save the day for the crusaders:

> When the glorious and noble king of Castile, who was prepared rather to die than to be conquered, heard that cry of doom, he ordered the man who carried his standard before him, to spur his horse and hasten quickly up the hill where the force of the battle was; he did so at once. When the Christians came up, the Moors thought that new waves had come upon them and fell back, overcome by the power of our Lord Jesus Christ.[13]

The King of Castile's quick reaction to commit his reserve unit to battle at that crucial moment proved absolutely right. Alfonso ordered his reserves to join the two wings under Pedro II and Sancho VII, and this action shattered the Almohad line, with Sancho breaking through the enemy lines and reaching al-Nasir's tent. Sancho managed to take al-Nasir's pavilion despite the valiant efforts by the caliph's black African élite guard, who mounted a stiff resistance. Al-Nasir fled the field and escaped back to Jaen, while his army was annihilated as the Crusader divisions completely overwhelmed them in the early evening hours.

CONCLUSIONS

Perhaps it would be an anticlimax to the reader to begin this section by spelling out, first and foremost, the numerous misunderstandings that have emerged about the geo-political significance of Las Navas de Tolosa for European history. Undoubtedly, the high appraisal of the battle has its roots in the contemporary accounts – both Christian and Muslim – of its outcome, when often the crushing defeat of the Muslims is described in biblical terms, or a degree of significance is attributed to it, which surely exaggerated its actual impact on Iberian and European geo-politics.

Therefore, contrary to both medieval and modern perceptions that consider the Battle of Las Navas de Tolosa as the clash that was responsible (or served as a catalyst) for the eventual decline and fall of the Almohad regime in Spain, historians in recent years have been more cautious in making such sweeping remarks about the Christian triumph of 1212.

Las Navas de Tolosa may have been a terrible blow to the prestige of the Almohads in Andalucía, but it did *not* lead to the downfall of al-Andalus, thus ensuring that a continued Islamic presence in the Iberian peninsula was no longer sustainable. Despite the continuous pressure mounted by the kings of León and Portugal through-out the following decades, boosted by the constant influx of crusaders from outside the Iberian peninsula (Gascony, Germany and the Low Countries), the reasons for the Almohad decline were, rather, internal. These can be summarized as the political paralysis of the Almohad caliphate, which was brought about by a financial crisis in northern Africa, coupled with the dynastic problems that arose from the premature death of the Caliph al-Nasir in 1213, which left his ten-year-old son, Abū Yaqūb Yūsuf, as heir to the throne.

It was only after the death of Abū Yaqūb in 1224 that a power vacuum was created, which led to in-fighting between the Almohad sheikhs in Spain and Morocco, to the breakaway of Tunisia, and worst of all, to increasing tensions between the Berbers and their Almohad suzerains. It was this political instability that allowed for the Christian kingdoms of Iberia to resume military operations, as the success of the following military campaigns by Ferdinand III of Castile (reigned 1217–52) after 1224 indicates: Quesada, 1224; Baeza, 1226; Jaén, Granada and Murcia, 1228; Garcíes and Jódar, 1229.

Furthermore, Las Navas de Tolosa did *not* re-shape the balance of forces in Iberia between the Christians and the Muslims. In fact, the military establishment of the Almohads was fully functional and able to protect the borders of the Muslim kingdom for the next twelve years, with notable success. Between 1214 and 1224 the borders between the Christian kingdoms of the north and Al-Andalus hardly moved in any direction.

Nevertheless, the battle had important consequences that shaped the geo-political face of late medieval Spain. First and foremost, it was a significant blow to Muslim mili-tary prestige in Iberia. It also allowed for the Christian kings to reclaim the military initiative in the peninsula because, following their defeat at Las Navas de Tolosa, the Almohads would never again be able to mount any large-scale military expeditions in the region. Furthermore, the battle proved decisive in giving the Christian kings the opportunity to recover the disputed lands between the rivers Tagus and Guadalquivir, a highly important strategic territory of Spain that had been the focus of military operations since the Christian conquest of Toledo in 1085.

Finally, the conquest of numerous castles and fortified towns in the Sierra Morena region of central Andalucía would pave the way for the Christian advance into the valley of the Guadalquivir and, eventually, to the conquest of Andalucía at the close of the fifteenth century.

12 THE BATTLE OF BOUVINES

The End of the Angevin Empire

Date 27 July 1214

Location Bouvines, between the villages of Sainghin and Cysoing, 12km (7½ miles) south-east of Lille, Belgium

THE HISTORICAL BACKGROUND

THE BATTLE OF Bouvines is considered by modern historians to be the decisive engagement between two European coalitions, which changed the political face of Europe and signalled the emergence of the French King Philip II (known as 'Philip Augustus', 1180–1223) as the Continent's foremost monarch. It also threw Germany into a state of political chaos, and forced King John of England (1199–1216) to grant his barons the famous *Magna Carta* in 1215. However, to be able to fully understand the complex currents of international politics that reached their climax and their resolution in 1214 in the fields of Flanders, we need to go back a century to the formation of the Angevin Empire.

The term 'Angevin Empire' is a product of the nineteenth century that defines the lands of the House of Plantagenet in both the British Isles and the Continent between 1154 and 1214.[1] The empire was formed in 1154, following the death of King Stephen (1135–54): as the legitimate son of Adela – the sister of Henry I (1100–1135) – and Stephen, Count of Blois, King Stephen had been struggling for nineteen years with Matilda for control over the Anglo-Norman realm; Matilda was Henry I's only legitimate child, and the wife of Geoffrey Plantagenet, Duke of Normandy and Count of Anjou, since 1128. This was an era commonly known as 'Stephen's Anarchy', when England suffered vast economic devastation in the course of a civil conflict that saw baronial armies fighting each other and erecting unlicensed castles all over the realm.

By the middle of the twelfth century, an assessment of political power and prestige in western Europe would put the King of France on top of the list. Louis VII (1137–80) ruled not only the traditional Capetian royal principalities that stretched from Compiègne in the north to the neighbourhood of Bourges in the south, but through his marriage to Eleanor, the daughter of William X (1099–1137) of Aquitaine, he also became Duke of Aquitaine, lord of a territory covering roughly one third of the area of modern France.

But their marriage was annulled in March 1152 after no male heir was produced.

Immediately after the annulment of her marriage, Eleanor married Henry Plantagenet, son of Geoffrey and Duke of Normandy and Count of Anjou since the death of his father in 1151; on their marriage, Eleanor conveyed Aquitaine to Henry.

When Henry was crowned King of England in 1154, he became the most powerful ruler in Europe, having completely overshadowed his nominal overlord, the King of France. He would eventually rule a realm that would encompass, at its largest extent, the Kingdom of England, the Lordship of Ireland and, through various levels of vassalage to the King of France, the duchies of Normandy, Gascony and Aquitaine as well as the counties of Anjou, Poitou, Maine, Touraine, Saintonge, La Marche, Périgord, Limousin, Nantes and Quercy. Therefore it would be the growing influence of the House of Plantagenet on both sides of the English Channel that would bring it into conflict with the House of Capet.

The biggest challenge to Henry's reign was the Great Revolt of 1173–74. This was a rebellious act by three of his disaffected sons, which escalated quickly and decisively with the involvement of other European powers such as France, Scotland and Flanders. It witnessed baronial revolts breaking out in England, Brittany, Maine, Poitou and

The Angevin Empire – Henry II's possessions in France in 1154.

Angoulême, while Flemish, French and Breton armies repeatedly invaded Normandy and England. Later, in 1186, Philip II of France was threatening to invade Normandy, opening the issue of the English succession to the Vexin, a county between Paris and Rouen. Philip also invaded Berry, and Henry mobilized a large army, which confronted the French at Châteauroux. Further crisis was avoided because of papal intervention.

Relations between Philip and Richard broke down a few years later because of Richard's decision to break his betrothal with Philip's sister Alys, in 1191. The following year, and while Richard was away on crusade, Philip made contact with John, Richard's brother, whom he convinced to join the conspiracy to overthrow his brother. In 1193, while news of Richard's captivity on his way back from the Holy Land had reached Paris, Philip had John pay homage to him for his lands in France, and together with Count Baldwin of Flanders, invaded Normandy and the Vexin. War between Philip and the freshly arrived Richard went on until 1197, focusing on eastern Normandy and the counties of Vexin and Berry, but it started turning against the French king after many Norman lords reaffirmed their allegiance to Richard in 1198. By the autumn of that year, Richard had regained almost all that had been lost in 1193.

In May 1200, Philip formally signed a treaty with Richard's successor John, intending to bring peace to Normandy. The terms of John's vassalage included Anjou, Maine and Touraine, while the English king agreed to the abandonment of all the English possessions in Berry. Baronial rebellions were brewing in Aquitaine, secretly supported by Philip, thus allowing the latter to summon John in his Court as his feudal lord in France to answer the charges. In 1203, Philip took the offensive, and by the end of 1204, most of Normandy and the Angevin lands, including large chunks of Aquitaine, had fallen into Capetian hands. John reacted by launching an invasion of France in 1206: this ended in disaster, and eventually lost him his patrimonial lands in France.

The issue of the antagonism between the Plantagenets and the Capetians became even more complicated with the involvement of two more key players: the Pope and the German emperor. Pope Innocent III (1198–1216) was the most powerful and intelligent of all lawyer Popes that the western Church had even witnessed, and he so happened to begin his pontificate a year after the death of the German emperor, the Hohenstaufen Henry VI. The latter had died at a young age, but the major issue was that his heir, Frederick II, was only two years old. At stake was Henry's claim, which included Germany and the Norman kingdom of Sicily.

Animated by the theory of papal monarchy, and determined to prevent any encroachment of papal lands by the German emperors, Pope Innocent would do his utmost to impose his political will on the leading monarchs of Europe, playing one against the other. His main aim was to break up the political connection between Germany and Sicily, and he sought his chance after the untimely death of the German emperor Henry VI. The two main questions were, first, whether the kingdom of Sicily would remain in German hands; and second, which claimant would succeed the deceased Henry VI – because his son Frederick was an infant, his claim was taken by his uncle, Philip of Swabia. The latter, however, had a rival who was elected by the barons of Saxony,

Otto of Brunswick, acting as the representative of the Welfs, a rival family to the ruling Hohenstaufen. To complicate matters even further, the Welf claimant was a nephew of John I of England, whereas the Hohenstaufen enjoyed the support of Philip II of France.

Innocent insisted on being the arbiter in this election dispute by virtue of his papal privilege of crowning the German emperor. In 1201, the Pope announced that he recognized Otto as the only legitimate king. In return, Otto promised to support the Pope's interests in Italy, and loosen imperial control over the German Church. But after Philip of Swabia's death in 1208, Otto repudiated his promise, prompting Innocent to support the claims of the – now of age – Frederick Hohenstaufen. Otto immediately worked to restore imperial power in Italy, and in 1210 he marched on Rome in a blatant show of force, which resulted in his excommunication. A grim civil war seemed to be brewing, and Frederick Hohenstaufen sought the alliance of Philip of France, to counter the long-standing alliance between Otto of Brunswick and John of England.

Two years before, in March 1208, Innocent had also placed an *interdict* on the Kingdom of England, prohibiting clergy from conducting religious services. It was the climax of a three-year dispute over King John's refusal to accept the papal nomination for the Archbishop of Canterbury. John was, finally, excommunicated in November 1209, after he seized the lands of members of the Church who had fled England.

This played well into the hands of Philip, who saw his chance to launch an invasion of England with the Pope's approval. Nevertheless, John and Innocent struck a deal at the eleventh hour, according to which John would rule England as the Pope's vassal. After a treaty was ratified in May 1213, Innocent immediately turned against Philip, calling upon him to reject plans to invade England. The latter, however, had other ideas: because Ferdinand, the Count of Flanders and Hainaut and *infante* (Prince) of Portugal,[2] had denied Philip his right to declare war on England while John was excommunicated, Philip decided to invade Flanders to punish him.

John was also making plans for a final campaign to reclaim Normandy from Philip. By the end of May 1214 he had obtained the allegiance of the Limousin and most of the great baronial houses of Poitou, to the north and north-east of Aquitaine. John further assembled a coalition of European magnates, which included Emperor Otto IV of Germany, Ferdinand Count of Flanders and Hainaut, Duke Henry I of Brabant, Count William I of Holland, Duke Theobald I of Lorraine and Duke Henry III of Limburg. The English king's plan was to land in Poitou and threaten the French from the 'rear' to divert forces from the main operational theatre of Flanders, where Philip would be facing Otto.[3]

THE PRELUDE TO THE BATTLE

JOHN LEFT FOR Poitou in February 1214, landing at La Rochelle on the 15th of the month. Many barons, especially from the north of England, refused to follow him because they claimed they were not bound by 'feudal' bonds with their suzerain – King John – to provide him with host service at their own expense outside the frontiers of the realm.[4] John overcame this complication by hiring mercenaries to fill the gaps.

John felt confident enough to go over to the attack at the end of May. First he threatened Nantes, on the mouth of the River Loire, hoping to win over the new Duke of Brittany, King Philip's cousin, Peter of Dreux, an ambitious operation that ended up in failure. Moving up the Loire, John entered Angers on 17 June. But when Prince Louis of France brought an army from Chinon on 2 July, John was unable to persuade the Poitevins to fight, and beat a hasty retreat!

In Flanders, Otto reached Nivelles, some 30km (18 miles) south of Brussels, around 12 July, and then marched another 70km (43 miles) south-west to Valenciennes where his forces had been concentrating; he was still there on 23 July. Within the next three days, Otto's army made a number of raids in the forests to the north-east of Cambrai, before moving 20km (12 miles) north to Mortagne. Meanwhile, on 23 and 24 July, the French army under Philip had marched north-eastwards from Douai towards Tournai, the invasion gateway to Flanders and Hainault, reaching the town on the 26th. The distance between the two armies was less than 15km (9 miles), prompting Philip to call for a council of war.

According to William the Breton, chaplain to Philip at Bouvines (c. 1165–c. 1225), the French king was dissuaded by his advisers from launching an attack on Mortagne because the ground between the rivers Scarpe and Scheldt was narrow and marshy, and hence unsuitable for cavalry. Philip changed his plans, and on Sunday the 27th the army struck camp early and left for Lille, some 25km (15 miles) to the west of Tournai, to 'find a more level way into the county of Hainaut and destroy it completely'.[5]

While the French army was marching from Tournai towards Lille via an old Roman road that led through Bouvines, Philip dispatched a rearguard under Viscount Melun and the Duke of Burgundy to the direction of Mortagne to check on the movements of Otto's army. Meanwhile, the allies had learned that Philip had struck camp, giving them the impression the French were retreating, and in the council of war it was decided to pursue them in the hope of meeting part of the French army still on the right bank of the River Marque at Bouvines, mid-way between Tournai and Lille. Otto's vanguard of Flemish knights was spotted by the French rearguard, who immediately alerted Philip and his barons that 'their enemies were fast arriving in battle order.'

After much deliberation, a decision was made to follow the original plan and retreat west by way of the small bridge at Bouvines, between the villages of Sainghin and Cysoing, the only crossing point of the Marque valley. Philip only realized that there was going to be a battle when an urgent message disrupted his lunch while his army was fording the Marque at Bouvines; the Duke of Burgundy was already in contact with Otto's Flemish vanguard and had difficulty in holding them back while the French were crossing the river. Quickly, a cry 'To arms, barons! To arms!' was heard in the fields.

THE OPPOSING FORCES

It is very common for medieval chroniclers to disagree about the numbers of opposing armies, or not to give any details about troop numbers. Regrettably, the only eyewitness

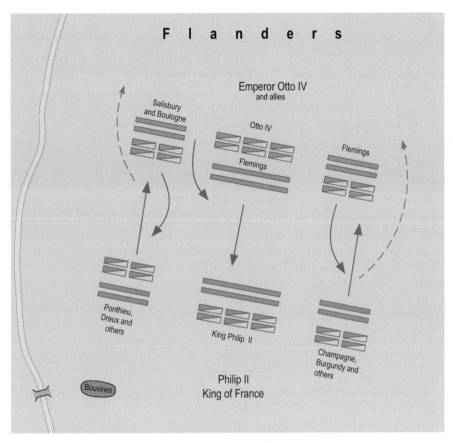

The Battle of Bouvines, 27 July 1214.

of the battle, William the Breton, gives no figures for his own side. Nevertheless, Verbruggen has painstakingly pieced together all the available information about the strength of the French army under Philip Augustus at Bouvines; he estimates between 1,300 and 1,400 knights, and between 5,000 and 6,000 foot soldiers. Otto's forces are also assessed to around the same numerical strength – some 1,400 knights and perhaps as many as 7,500 foot.[6]

Arms and Armament

Soldiers from both sides would have looked relatively indistinguishable in terms of arms and armament. Therefore, by the turn of the thirteenth century the couched lance had begun to dominate the battlefields of Europe as the weapon of choice for the mounted knights, all the way to the end of the Middle Ages. It was the principal offensive weapon of the Crusader knights, and it was Henry II's Assize of Arms of 1181 that specified the lance as the required weapon for knights on horseback.

A sword would have complemented the equipment of a knight of the period, with swords in general having changed little between the Carolingian period and the later thirteenth century; they consisted of a wide, double-edged blade with a rounded end, and were 65–95cm long.[7] Foot soldiers would also have carried a sword, if they could afford it, although the main weapons of a poor footslogger would have been the spear, which had not changed much since the Carolingian period, and the short-bow (in contrast to the long-bow of the thirteenth century) that was about 90cm (3ft) long and was drawn back to the chest.

Important changes in the design of armour were introduced at the turn of the thirteenth century. The established kite-shaped shield that features so prominently in the Bayeux Tapestry was gradually superseded by a smaller, lighter and more triangular shield, which, according to experts, reflects the adoption of leg-armour that made the older kite-shaped shield redundant.[8] The switch to the new shield seems to have come a bit later for the foot soldiers.

Side by side with the older conical helmet also depicted in the Tapestry came the slightly more rounded one, while the lighter *bacinet* with a visor would be used more widely after the middle of the century. This is also the period when the so-called 'great helm' was introduced to the ranks of the noble cavalry; in its simplest form, the great helm was a flat-topped cylinder of steel that completely covered the head and had only very small openings for the eyes and mouth. On the other hand, the so-called 'kettle hat' was a type of helmet made of steel in the shape of a brimmed hat; it was designed primarily as an infantry helmet, because the wide brim gave good protection against blows from above, such as from cavalry swords.

Finally, the hauberk was the kind of armour still favoured by the knights, and anyone else who could afford it, taking the form of the mail coat that was pulled on over the head. Foot soldiers would have had to do with any kind of padded garment for defence against enemy blows.

THE BATTLE

When Otto and his allies arrived in the vicinity of Bouvines, they found Philip's cavalry already arraying for battle. It was already mid-afternoon, and the sun shone on the shoulders of the French and in the eyes of the allies' coalition facing west. Philip used his cavalry as a screen for his slowly deploying infantry, knowing full well that the redeployment of an army after crossing a river is one of the most hazardous undertakings for any army in the field.

In fact the French king was in a tricky situation because not only did he have the bulk of his infantry force still on the other side of the Marque, but he also intended to fight with an almost completely reversed front, and with the small bridge of Bouvines behind him as the only route for retreat, for the Marque was reportedly impassable elsewhere. Hence Otto's reported astonishment upon his arrival when he saw the French army drawn up and ready for battle!

The French army was deployed into three main divisions (acies).[9] Philip ordered his knights from Champagne, Burgundy and Picardy into the right wing commanded by the Duke of Burgundy Eudes and his lieutenants: Gaucher de Châtillon Count of Saint-Pol, Count Wilhelm of Sancerre, Count of Beaumont, and Mathieu de Montmorency and the Viscount of Melun. The central division was commanded by Philip Augustus and his chief knights – William des Barres, Bartholomew of Roye, Girard Scophe, William of Garland, Enguerrand III de Coucy and Gautier de Nemours. The left wing, led by Robert of Dreux and Count William of Ponthieu, comprised troops from Brittany, Dreux, Perche, Ponthieu and Vimeux.

Otto also divided his army into three divisions: the right flank was put under the command of Renaud de Dammartin and William Longespée, the Earl of Salisbury, and it included Brabant infantry and English knights. William Breton reports of an innovative battle formation where Renaud launched a cavalry attack from a circular formation made up of spearmen; no doubt this was the kind of formation that would have offered protection to small units of cavalry that could launch their attack through the single entrance to the formation, and then withdraw inside to regroup or seek shelter in case their attack had been defeated.[10]

This is clear evidence of a combined arms tactics applied here, one which bears great similarities to the 'hollow infantry square' formation that was frequently employed by the Byzantines against the Arabs in eastern Anatolia since the first half of the tenth century.[11]

The centre was under the command of Otto and of Bernard von Horstmar, Otto von Tecklenburg, Conrad von Dortmund and Gerard von Randerath, along with knights from Saxony and Swabia, and infantry from Brabant.[12] The sources are not clear as to whether the knights or the infantry were put in the front ranks of the centre formation, but it is likely that because the German emperor had very few knights under his direct command (only 350),[13] he would have placed them behind the dense infantry phalanx in the front of the centre division – they could then exploit a gap in the enemy formation and attack at that exact spot. Otto stood in between, surrounded by fifty German knights. The left flank was left under the command of Ferdinand of Flanders and Hainaut with his knights, directed by Arnaud of Oudenaarde.

The battle opened with a cavalry charge by a unit from the French right, commanded by Bishop Guerin who seized the initiative and sent a contingent of 150 sergeants (non-noble heavy cavalry) forward to harass the Flemings on the left wing of the allied army. That did not work, however, since the Fleming knights despised the sergeants as their social inferiors and refused to come out against them. Furthermore, because the sergeants' horses had no armoured protection, they suffered heavy casualties from the enemy spearmen and archers, causing many of the men either to dismount and fight on foot, or to retreat to their starting point. Seeing an excellent opportunity to run them down, a number of the Flemish knights left their ranks – probably without orders – and charged against the confused and disorganized sergeants.

Following this initial setback, in the right wing the knights from Champagne quickly established French superiority in the field after attacking the Flemings and pushing them back to their lines with heavy casualties. Keeping with the momentum of the attack, the Viscount of Melun and his men succeeded in penetrating the enemy line to deliver many severe blows to the Flemish and Hainaulters. This was quickly followed by Gaucher de Châtillon and his men, who broke through the ranks of the Flemish knights, and then attacked them from the rear.

The disparity in discipline between the French and the allied forces was becoming apparent. Yet the Flemish and Hainaulters under Ferdinand would not give in after a three-hour fight with the French, despite their mounting losses – knightly honour kept them on the battlefield, where they defended themselves stoutly! The time was up for the men in the left wing of the allied army, only after two French knights cut their way through and took hostage the wounded Count of Flanders and Hainault, whose horse had been killed under him.

With the left wing of the allied army in disarray, the battle reached its climax with the clash between the two opposing centre divisions. Philip's infantry levies had arrived on the battlefield and had only just taken position in front of the formation of their king, when Otto and his centre division launched an attack against the opposite French units, where they could see the *Oriflamme* and Philip's standard of the fleur-de-lys. Otto's knights succeeded in breaking through the French infantry formation, cutting their way to the knights in charge of protecting the French king. Philip's position was threatened by Otto's foot soldiers, who managed to unhorse him, which shows that mounted men were scarce on both sides!

The final stage of the battle opened with a French counter attack against Otto's position. This attack pushed so deep into enemy lines that a French nobleman even tried to kill Otto with his dagger, but the blow glanced off the emperor's mail and struck his horse in the eye. Before Otto could get away and reach safety, he was grabbed by a knight called Guillaume des Barres, who put up a stubborn fight with Otto's bodyguard before Thomas St-Valéry and a contingent of fifty knights arrived to his aid. The German emperor managed to get off the battlefield, with the French soon after capturing the imperial waggon with the eagle and dragon.

Despite the collapse of the allied left and centre divisions, there was determined resistance put up by Renaud de Dammartin and his élite foot soldiers and small cavalry unit from Brabant, who applied their ingenious tactic of cavalry sorties from a solid round phalanx formation described above. They were fighting against the French units that had overwhelmed the allied left wing, and were now attacking the right-wing division from the flanks and the rear. But this combined arms arrangement worked well until the whole formation was overrun by fifty French knights and 2,000 of their supporting infantry. Renaud's horse was killed, and the count was taken prisoner and led away to the French king. Philip gave the order to pursue the fleeing enemy for only one mile as night was falling. It was all over!

CONCLUSIONS

The Military Perspective

From a military perspective, Bouvines offers a rare opportunity to study a variety of combined arms tactics used in high medieval warfare. In the first stage of the battle we see the clash between French sergeants and Ferdinand's undisciplined Flemish knights, who were later swept aside by the charge of the knights from Champagne, which began to penetrate the lines of the allied left wing in small-unit cavalry attack, slowly wearing down their enemies while probing for weaknesses. The next phase saw the general *mêlée*, with a French combined arms attack against the allied centre where Emperor Otto's banner could be seen, followed by an allied counter attack that posed a serious threat to the safety of the French king.

Finally, the last phase of the battle witnessed numerous failed cavalry attacks against a pike phalanx formation that was formed as a solid refuge for the small units of heavy allied cavalry. This battle tactic showcased the effectiveness that a disciplined and well-trained infantry formation can have over cavalry units that lacked the support of archers, but it also underscores the futility of the resistance of a phalanx unit in the face of relentless cavalry attacks when it, too, lacks the crucial support of archers and adequate cavalry to counter attack.

Detail of a miniature of a battle between Philip Augustus and John, King of England – Les Grandes chroniques de France (between 1332 and 1350).

© BRITISH LIBRARY, ROYAL 16 G VI f. 376v

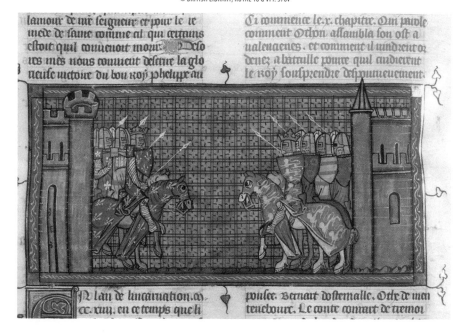

The Political Perspective

From a political perspective, the complex currents of European politics reached their climax and their dissolution in July 1214, dramatically changing the political face of Europe. Philip Augustus emerged as the strongest monarch in Europe, settling once and for all the dispute over the question of Normandy and Anjou, while the barons of Poitou reversed their allegiance to King John in favour of Philip Augustus.

Bouvines was also a turning point in the power balance between France and Germany in the High Middle Ages. The German magnates reluctantly acknowledged young Frederick as their emperor, and young Frederick, for his part, vowed to adhere to all the concessions originally granted by Otto to Innocent in 1208: recognition that Sicily was a papal fief and would forever remain separate from the empire, and securing the renunciation of all royal rights over the German Church.

At the peak of his political power in Europe, Innocent III then embarked on his greatest achievement of all: the summoning of the Fourth Lateran Council in 1215, what historians have dubbed 'the most imposing gathering of clerics since the Council of Nicaea in 325', to codify the reform of the Catholic Church.

For King John, the aftermath of Bouvines must have felt like the nadir of his political life; he had taken so much cash out of circulation to pay for the pursuit of his foreign policy objectives that burghers and barons alike complained that they were being forced to pay for the Crown's own folly. John's diminishing prestige and diplomatic failures paved the way for the uprising of the English barons that ended in the fields of Runnymede, in Surrey, in 1215 where they forced John to sign the *Magna Carta*, a revolutionary document that set forth principles of the rule of law that won recognition as fundamental law. This document eventually became part of the common stock of both British and American political thought, which has spread throughout the modern world.

13 THE BATTLE OF THE LAKE PEIPUS

Russian Halt to the Crusader Expansion

Date 5 April 1242
Location Lake Peipus, on the modern Estonian-Russian border

THE HISTORICAL BACKGROUND

> The Baltic crusades acted as one element in a cruel process of Christianization and Germanization, providing a religious gloss to ethnic cleansing and territorial aggrandizement more blatant and, in places, more successful than anywhere else.[1]

THIS IS HOW Christopher Tyerman, one of the greatest twentieth-century historians of the Crusades movement, recently defined the Baltic Crusades. It is fair to say that he pulls no punches when he describes the motives of the German Crusaders between 1000 and 1200.

The tenth-century East Frankish (German) rulers had inherited from their Carolingian predecessors a deep-rooted interest for converting the pagan Wends (west Slavs).[2] The campaigns of Henry the Fowler (919–36) and Otto the Great (936–73) led to the introduction of *burg*-wards (frontier towns) to protect German conquests in the lands of the Wends. This expansion was sustained by the obvious connection with 'pacifying' territory, driven by the Saxon nobility and the German clergy who insisted on the often brutal imposition of Christianity on the pagan Slavs. The monastery of Fulda was a powerful centre of missionary activity, while bishoprics were established at Meissen, Brandenburg and Havelberg to administer the 'pacified' territories.

By the middle of the twelfth century the process of German conquest accelerated, and many German colonies were established in Silesia and Pomerania, between the Elbe and the Oder (most notably, Lübeck in 1143). But the greed of the many local lords for land and plunder was often a real obstacle to conversion, as the German emperors were too busy to pursue a sustained expansionist policy in the region.[3]

In 1147, at the time when the Second Crusade was being prepared, a number of German (mainly Saxon) lords wished to campaign across the Elbe instead of Spain or the Holy Land: hence the papal letter, or *divina dispensatione*, which established the German crusade on the same lines as those in Spain or the Middle East. Throughout

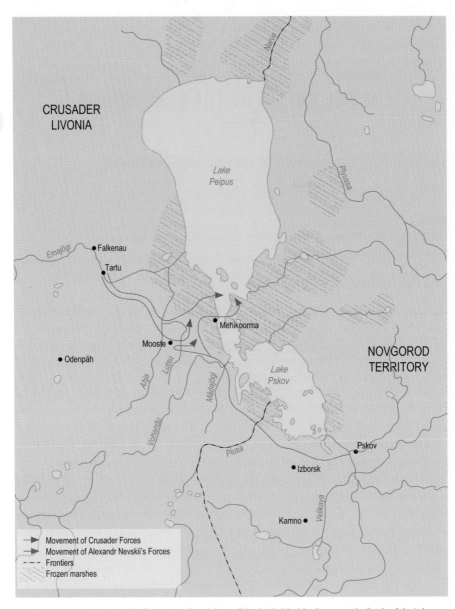

The movement of the Crusader forces (in red) and those of Nevskii (in blue) leading up to the Battle of the Lake Peipus.

the twelfth century the entire area between the Elbe and the Oder was drawn to the 'Catholic core', regardless of how superficial the conversion to Christianity might have been, by the quickening pace of economic development and trade of furs, wax and other profitable goods of the north, and by the interest of the local élites for land.

The main areas of German and Swedish expansion after 1200 comprised Prussia,

Livonia, Estonia and Finland. Although these wars directly served local political and ecclesiastical ambitions, great care was taken to justify them as defensive. When Pope Innocent III preached the Livonian Crusade in 1199, he made sure to emphasize the persecution of Christian missionaries and recent converts in Livonia, so that there would be explicit reference to the crusade conforming to the Christian criteria for war.

To simulate the Orders of the Temple and the Hospital in the Holy Land, Bishop Albert of Livonia (1199–1229) formed the 'Order of Sword-Brothers', committed to the expansion of Livonia and the conversion of its inhabitants. Their task was to lead the incoming crusaders, to establish and defend fortresses, to defend the missionaries, and to lead winter raids in enemy territory. These knights became notorious for their massacres of the local populations and for their land grab.

In 1237 the 'Sword-Brothers' were almost annihilated by the Samogitians of Lithuania. This disaster led to the transfer of a new force in the region, the Teutonic Order, which was founded during the siege of Acre in 1190 as a hospital order to care for the German sick in Jerusalem. Under its Grand Master Hermann von Salza (1210–39), the Order was transformed into a political and military force leading the Prussian crusades in East Prussia and Lithuania in the 1230s.

In 1237 they incorporated into their ranks the remnants of the 'Sword-Brothers', thus becoming known as the 'Livonian Order'. Their military skills and their great endowments in Germany, from which they could easily mobilize adequate funds for their eastward expeditions, earned them the leading role in the Christian expansion against the Baltic peoples, under the constant political and financial support of Pope Innocent III.

In the first half of the thirteenth century, the growing influence of Russian Orthodox Novgorod in the north Baltic Sea started to pose a serious threat, not just to the German policies in Livonia and Estonia, but also to the Swedish interests in Finland, an area where the Swedish kings had traditionally exercised great influence and were actively sending Catholic missionaries. Novgorod owed its rise to the gradual disintegration of the Kievan Rus that began in the eleventh century, following the death of Jaroslav the Wise (d. 1054), culminating in the largest civil disturbances that Kievan Russia had ever experienced, in 1068.

As Kiev declined, Novgorod emerged as a powerful polity with a huge hinterland that provided furs, wax and other items to supply and supplement its handicrafts industry, and it managed to establish an independent republic in 1136. The city of Pskov and its lands at the foot of Lake Peipus were part of Novgorod since the ninth century, but gained a *de facto* independence in the early thirteenth century after joining the Hanseatic League.

Prior to the expansion of the Crusaders in the Baltic countries, the government of Novgorod had shown little interest in the numerous different peoples of the region, as long as the trade routes with Scandinavia through the complex river systems remained open for trade. By 1200, Novgorod had imposed its suzerainty over the Karelians to the south of the Finnish peninsula, between Lake Ladoga and the Baltic Sea, partly to stop their raids in Novgorodian territory, but also to block the spread of Swedish Catholicism further east. Both Novgorod and Pskov tried to help the Estonians resist Swedish attacks in the 1210s, but it proved futile. Then in 1223, Novgorod had to face the combined threat of an outbreak of plague in the Baltic region, and a Mongol invasion that devastated southern Russia.

After their conquest of northern China and central Asia, the Mongols established their control over a vast area of Western Eurasia at the beginning of the thirteenth century. The first encounter with the Russians at the River Kalka in the south-east, in 1223, delivered an overwhelming victory to the Mongols.

The death of Genghis Khan in 1227 brought a lull to the Mongol expansion, but ten years later his grandson Batu Khan embarked on a more ambitious series of campaigns. He sacked Kiev in 1240, and then swept into central Europe like a 'whirlwind from Hell'. Seeing this as a great opportunity to deal with the growing threat of Novgorod, the Swedes and the Livonian knights made plans for an invasion of Novgorodian territories.

In the summer of 1240, a powerful mixed Swedish, Norwegian and Finnish force, led by the son-in-law of the King of Sweden, blocked Novgorod's access route to the Baltic Sea, the River Neva, although they were repulsed soon after by the forces of Aleksandr Nevskii, the *knez* (the medieval Slavic equivalent of 'prince') of Novgorod. This was a crisis period that called for heroic leaders to arise from among the Russian people.

THE PRELUDE TO THE BATTLE

The following spring (1241), a diverse army of Livonian knights and Estonian auxiliaries began encroaching into Novgorodian lands by taking the settlement of Kaporye, west of the River Neva and 15km (9 miles) south of the Baltic coast. They fortified the town with a stone castle, thus indicating their intention for permanent settlement.

Then in the early autumn of 1241, another mixed army of Livonian knights and Estonian vassals of the Danish king, led by Bishop Hermann of Livonia and Andreas von Felben of the knights, invaded Pskov territory to the south of Lake Peipus, taking the strategic town of Izborsk after a bloody battle with the citizens of Pskov on 16 September, before moving on the outskirts of Pskov to lay siege on the city itself.

The city soon agreed on a conditional surrender to the Crusaders. But the latter were contemplating their next strategic move, following the Mongol incursions into central Europe: the latter would prove a serious distraction for the Catholic armies that had been invading northern Russia. And while the Crusaders dithered, Aleksandr Nevskii struck again.

Nevskii's counter attack in the autumn of 1241 focused on the Gulf of Finland and the town of Kaporye, where resistance to his armies proved minimal and the Crusader stone castle soon fell. In the spring of the following year (1242), a combined Russian army of Nevskii's *družina* (stipendiary household troops), his brother's *družina* from

Suzdal, and militia from Novgorod and Pskov, headed south-west to push the Crusaders out of Novgorodian territory and to retake Pskov.

The city fell without a struggle on 5 March. Nevskii followed up his success by raiding Livonia, himself taking advantage of his enemies being on the back foot because of the Mongol invasion, which by now had alarmed the whole of Western Europe as it had reached Galich, in Poland, and was seriously threatening both Germany and Hungary.

Nevskii crossed the Velikaya river, to the west of Pskov, and marched north to the Estonian city of Tartu, bypassing Izborsk and its Crusader garrison while staying close to the western shores of Lake Peipus. However, the hurriedly raised defenders of Tartu scored a spectacular victory over the vanguard units of Nevskii's army just south of Tartu. While the survivors of the battle struggled to rejoin the main Russian army, Bishop Hermann advanced from Tartu with another force in an attempt to cut them off.

Nevskii would probably have learned that Hermann was joined by his vassals from Tartu and the rest of southern Estonia, which included the Danish king's vassals from Wierland (northern Estonia), along with a sizeable number of Livonian knights, thus amounting to a field force to be reckoned with. Nevskii's reaction was to beat a hasty retreat east to Novgorodian territory, over the still frozen Lake Peipus.

The campaigns of the Teutonic Knights in the Baltic region in the thirteenth century.

THE OPPOSING FORCES

Estimates as to the number of troops in the opposing armies vary widely among scholars, but historians agree that the Crusader army would not have exceeded 3,000 men, out of which some 1,000 would have been Estonian auxiliaries. On the other hand, the Russians would have fielded around 6,000 to 7,000 men, including 1,400 Finno-Ugrian tribesman and 600 Turco-Mongolian horse-archers.[4]

Arms and Armour

The Russian Army

A typical western Russian cavalryman of the middle of the thirteenth century would have been armed with a 'Lithuanian type' of spear and javelins. The spears would have been designed to penetrate plate armour, so would have had long triangular heads. The javelins are mentioned in the sources for the first time in this period, and would be carried by both infantry and cavalry troops against the Tatar archers. A Russian cavalryman would also have carried a straight-bladed sword imported from central Europe (Germany or Hungary), contrary to his south-eastern counterpart who would have preferred the 'Turco-Mongolian' curved sabre. Battle-axes and maces would only become widespread in the fifteenth century.

For protection, he would have carried either a conical or a dome-shaped metallic helmet, and a small rectangular wooden shield that curved down to a point at the bottom. Plate armour was adopted by western Russian knights around this period, in the middle of the thirteenth century; until then they would have worn a full-body mail coat, supplemented – perhaps – by additional lamellar protection for the torso.

Russian urban militiamen of the mid-thirteenth century would have worn quite similar equipment to their European counterparts. Depending on their financial standing, they would have carried a straight-bladed sword, a broad-bladed spear and a

The shore of Lake Peipus in spring.

'kite-shaped' wooden shield. Nevertheless, there are a number of distinctive features in their equipment: the conical iron helmet with a Mongolian-style padded undergarment, and the scale armour worn under a padded overcoat, which clearly reflects Mongol influence.

The light archer of the Russian armies in this period mirrors a native tradition with no outside influence. His sole protection would have been a thickly quilted coat. He would have carried a battle-axe, since this was a typical agricultural tool of a Russian farmer, together with a quiver and a semi-composite bow.

Finally, crossbowmen were a decisive element in the Russian armies of the period, with the crossbow being in widespread use all over Russia in the thirteenth century. The Russian crossbowman would also have carried a straight-bladed sword, and he would have been protected by a mail coat reaching down to his waist, worn over a padded undergarment, and a pointed, conical, narrow-brimmed iron helmet.

The Crusader Armies

The Crusader armies of the period largely consisted of German and Danish knights of the Teutonic Order – having incorporated the 'Sword-Brothers' in 1237 to become known as the 'Livonian Order'. Their arms would have included typically thirteenth-century arms and armour from Germany, imported to the Baltic regions from German manufacturing centres such as Iserlohn, in northern Rhine–Westphalia.

A Brother would have worn an iron helmet with a *visor* (face guard). The thirteenth century is a transitional period for the design of German helmets: when the Teutonic Knights arrived in Prussia in the early thirteenth century, they would have worn a variety of European-style helmets, from open-faced to conical or hemispherical and with just a nasal cover instead of a visor. A transitional form of flat-topped iron helm that did not cover the entire neck has been identified for the second quarter of the thirteenth century; this would eventually lead to the adoption of the *great helm*, which protected the whole head and would appear in Prussia at the close of the century.

Both the iron helm and the great helm were worn over a *coif*, a mail hood that provided additional protection to the neck and shoulders and was, itself, an integral part of the long-sleeved mail *hauberk*. The latter was a type of armour that proved very popular in the High Middle Ages, composed of interlinked rings of iron or steel that was formed into a mail shirt reaching down to the waist or, in the case of the Brothers, covering the entire body.

The *hauberk* was the dominant choice of armour for the knights in Prussia until the middle of the fourteenth century, when it was gradually superseded by plate armour. A small (around 50 × 70cm) triangular wooden shield with a leather holding strap would have complemented his equipment.

The most distinguished weapon of a knight in the Middle Ages was, beyond any doubt, his sword. Those carried by the Brothers in Livonia and Estonia would have been German in style and manufacture, straight-bladed and between 65 and 95cm long, although there is considerable variation in the types identified by archaeologists based on archaeological finds east of the Oder.[5] Before the turn of the fourteenth century, the sword blades were still wide and flat, with a narrow tip, which identifies the sword as a slashing weapon rather than a thrusting one.

Side-arms in use by the Brothers in the thirteenth century would have included a dagger with a two-edged symmetrical blade, and/or a battle-knife with an asymmetric one-edged blade. These were useful because they could kill an opponent by thrusting them between the mail rings, or in certain vulnerable parts of the enemy's armour such as the armpits or the neck.

THE BATTLE

The precise route of the two armies over the frozen lake is not known, but Nicolle has assumed that the most obvious course for the Russian troops back to friendly territory would have taken them through the Estonian fishing village of Mehikoorma, on the western shoreline of Lake Peipus.[6] Bishop Hermann may well have marched directly eastwards towards the same village, or perhaps a bit further to the north to cut the Crusaders off, if we accept that he would have had intelligence from his Estonian auxiliaries about the course followed by Nevskii.

Presumably Nevskii would also have had received intelligence from his scouts that the Crusaders were hot on his heels and would attempt to cut off his army from friendly territory: thus the *Chronicle of Novgorod* notes that the *knez* turned northwards after he reached the eastern (Russian) shoreline of the lake, in the direction of the place called 'Raven's Rock' – identified as the northern tip of the peninsula protruding towards Piirissaar Island in the middle of the lake.[7] That was the narrowest crossing point at Lake Peipus, and Nevskii would attempt to hold against the Crusaders at that spot.

The *Chronicle of Novgorod* comments that 'the Nemtsy and Chud men rode at them [the Russians], driving themselves like a wedge through their army', thus indicating that the Crusaders opened the battle by attacking in a wedge formation, a reasonable tactic for an army of heavily armed knights. The same source adds that Nevskii's army would have been deployed in battle array, ready to receive the enemy attack, although, as Nicolle emphasizes, the Russians would have been unlikely to have formed their ranks on the frozen surface of the lake, but rather on the icy banks, because in March the layer of ice covering Lake Peipus would have been between 20 and 50cm thick, which is dangerously thin to support heavily armoured men in close ranks.[8]

The *Livonian Rhymed Chronicle* refers to the first clash of the battle between the 'king's men' (probably the northern Estonian vassal knights of the Danish king) and the 'many archers' that were reported in the middle of the Russian formation. Hence we can assume that the Novgorodian militia and crossbowmen would have been deployed at the centre of the Russian formation, working as a 'screen' for Nevskii's *družina* immediately behind them.

It is likely that the Crusaders' plan was to break through the centre of the Russian line, where they could presumably see Nevskii's banner, whether to take him prisoner or kill him on the spot, and drive a wedge deep into the Russian infantry lines. If that was the case, then the Novgorodian militia performed well in 'shielding' the élite *družina* and causing the momentum of the Crusader attack to slow.

At that crucial stage of the battle it was Nevskii's turn to take the initiative by ordering his flanks to counter attack. These would probably have been the units of the Turco-Mongolian horse-archers who, according to their long military tradition forged in the steppes of Eurasia, would attack the enemy units in the flanks in an attempt to encircle them. Undoubtedly this would have come as a great surprise to the Crusader knights, and especially to their Estonian auxiliaries, who were certainly not accustomed to the battle tactics of the fast manoeuvring Turco-Mongolian horse-archers, with their showers of arrows and feigned retreats.

We also need to take into account the great difficulty of fighting on frozen ground for many hours – the Crusaders by that time would have been exhausted from the constant struggle of keeping their feet on the slippery surface of the frozen lake.

The statue of St Maurice in Magdeburg Cathedral (c. AD1240), with the saint wearing the long-sleeved mail hauberk and a coif. The sculpted features of Maurice's face and the colouring unambiguously identify him as a black man. In fact the name 'Maurice' is derived from Latin and means 'like a Moor'. Maurice was a legionary commander in the Thebaid region of lower Egypt, an early centre of Christianity. He was martyred after he disobeyed an order issued by the Roman emperor Maximian to suppress a Christian uprising in Gaul.

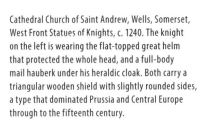

Cathedral Church of Saint Andrew, Wells, Somerset, West Front Statues of Knights, c. 1240. The knight on the left is wearing the flat-topped great helm that protected the whole head, and a full-body mail hauberk under his heraldic cloak. Both carry a triangular wooden shield with slightly rounded sides, a type that dominated Prussia and Central Europe through to the fifteenth century.

The attack of the horse-archers on the Crusader army's flanks was, probably, the tactical move that decided the outcome of the battle, as the Estonian auxiliaries soon broke off and fled towards their side of Lake Peipus. And it would have been at that stage of the battle that the Teutonic and Danish knights would have found themselves outnumbered and surrounded. Therefore the appearance of the fresh Novgorod cavalry made them retreat in panic. The *Chronicle of Novgorod* vividly describes the epilogue of the battle as follows:

> ... and there was a great slaughter of Nemtsy and Chud men. And God and St. Sophia and the Holy Martyrs Boris and Gleb, for whose sake the men of Novgorod shed their blood, by the great prayers of those Saints, God helped Knez Alexander. And the Nemtsy fell there and the Chud men gave shoulder, and pursuing them fought with them on the ice, seven versts [8km/5 miles] short of the Subol [Peipus] shore. And there fell of the Chud men a countless number; and of the Nemtsy 400, and fifty they took with their hands and brought to Novgorod.[9]

CONCLUSIONS

On purely ideological grounds, the Russian victory at Lake Peipus has been described as the battle that 'saved the Russian people from sharing the fate of the Baltic tribes and the Slavs of the Elbe who were enslaved by the Germans.'[10] This patriotic evaluation of the battle acquired a great significance in the twentieth century as a result of the two World Wars, and this Soviet appraisal of Nevskii's achievement would be shared by patriots of other persuasions throughout the Cold War. However, more recent studies have drawn a distinction between the great importance that the Battle of the Lake Peipus has undoubtedly had in the twentieth century, and its importance for contemporaries in the thirteenth century and beyond.[11]

For contemporary Russian sources such as the *Chronicle of Novgorod*, the outcome of the battle emphasized the help of 'God and St. Sophia and the Holy Martyrs Boris and Gleb' to Aleksandr Nevskii in winning back control of the strategic and rich city of Pskov. The traitors in Wierland (northern Estonia) and Pskov mentioned in the *Chronicle of Novgorod* had betrayed the prince, not Russia or orthodoxy, thus making it appear as a political issue rather than an ideological one, belonging exclusively in the context of local struggles for power.

Nevertheless, the legacy and decisiveness of the Battle of the Lake Peipus lies in the fact that it put a long-term halt on the eastward expansion of the Crusaders in the Baltic region. The peace negotiations that followed meant that the Crusaders handed back all the lands they had conquered, including the important castle of Izborsk, while the defeat opened a period of uprisings against Prussian and Danish rule in Courland (western Latvia) and Estonia that would last for the next seven years. Furthermore, it led to the re-evaluation of the Pope's foreign policy in the region, which would change from an aggressive military expansionism through military campaigns to a more conciliatory one that would make use of diplomacy.

The foreign policy of the Livonian Order would also change, focusing more on the Christianization of pagan Lithuania and Livonia rather than the encroachment into Russian territories; the Crusaders would not mount another serious challenge eastward.

The Battle of the Lake Peipus drew a distinctive geo-political line between the forces of Russia and those of Sweden, Denmark and Prussia, raising Nevskii as the 'God-sent' defender of Russian lands and allowing Novgorod to consolidate its power over the Arctic north and the Urals in the east. To add to that, the Bishop of Tallinn gained significant political autonomy from the Danish King, Eric IV (reigned 1241–50), eventually leading to the selling of Estonia to the Teutonic Knights in 1346.

Finally, with the benefit of hindsight and an aura of romanticism, many historians have been keen to emphasize that the battle also established a permanent border line through the Narva river and Lake Peipus, which divided Eastern orthodoxy from Western Catholicism.

14 THE BATTLE OF PELAGONIA

Ensuring the Byzantine Reconquest of Constantinople

Date July or September 1259
Location The plain of Pelagonia, south of Bitola

THE HISTORICAL BACKGROUND

FOLLOWING THE CAPTURE of Constantinople by the Latin armies of the Fourth Crusade in April 1204, and the dismemberment of its territory, the Byzantine Empire had effectively ceased to exist. According to the terms of the treaty between the Crusaders and Venetians, the emperor chosen for what can now be called the Latin empire was Baldwin of Flanders (reigned 1204–05), the primary military leader of the Crusade; he was crowned on 16 May 1204 in Hagia Sophia. The terms of the treaty specified that the new patriarch would be a Venetian, so Thomas Morosini (patriarchy, 1204–11) was elected as the first Latin patriarch of Constantinople.

With the Byzantine territories divided according to the infamous *Partitio Romaniae*, the Latin emperor received territories in both Asia Minor and Europe, but the greatest power was held by Boniface of Montferrat (1150–1207). He was the third son of William V of Montferrat and Judith of Babenberg, and the younger brother of William 'Longsword', Count of Jaffa and Ascalon, and of Conrad I of Jerusalem. He eventually refused to accept the territories assigned to him in Asia Minor, seizing instead Macedonia and Thessaly and installing himself as King of Thessalonica.

Boniface then turned his ambitions south into central Greece and the Peloponnesus. The Latin armies besieged all the major towns and cities of Peloponnesus, eventually managing to wrest control from the local lords within two years, 1210–12; only the potent fortress city of Monemvasia would defy the Latin invasion until 1248. The Latin *Chronicle of Morea* makes frequent mention of the devastating psychological effect the Latin siege machines (*perrières* and *mangonniaux*, the *trébuchet* and the *scrofa*) had on the native populations.[1] But it is surprising that the only pitched battle fought against the Latin invaders took place at the 'Olive Grove of Kountouras', in Messene in the south-west of the Peloponnesus in the summer of 1205, resulting in a victory of the Frankish knights and the collapse of local resistance.

Ultimately, Boniface installed Otto de la Roche as Lord of Attica and Voetia, while he lent his support to William of Champlitte and Geoffrey of Villehardouin to establish the Latin principality of the Morea (the Peloponnesus); the latter would become the most Westernized of the territories taken by the Crusaders in the Greek mainland.

In Thrace the situation was very different in terms of the balance of power between the multiple players in the region. In December 1204, the Latins of Constantinople defeated the ramshackle forces of the empire of Nicaea – one of the three main successor states – but their siege of Bursa proved a failure. The Bulgar tsar Kalojan (reigned 1197–1207) had emerged as a significant power broker in the southern Balkans, when he was involved in a local insurrection against the Latins that led to the siege and battle of Adrianople in April 1205. The defeat and capture of the Latin emperor, Baldwin, and the death of the Latin claimant to Nicaea, Louis I Count of Blois and grandson of Louis VII of France, radically changed the balance of power in Thrace and Asia Minor.

The outcome of the Battle of Adrianople left Theodore I Laskaris of Nicaea (reigned 1205–22) free to consolidate his gains in Asia Minor and, more importantly, to acclaim the title of emperor. The rapid rise of the Byzantine empire of Nicaea was confirmed in the ensuing victory of Theodore Laskaris over the Seljuk sultanate of Ikonion (Rum) at the Battle of Antioch-on-the-Meander, in 1211. The Turkish defeat and the death of the Sultan, who had previously concluded a treaty with the Latin empire of Constantinople, firmly established Nicaean hegemony of the Aegean coast of Asia Minor. In 1219, Theodore Laskaris married the daughter of the Latin empress Yolanda of Flanders. When he died in 1222, he was succeeded by his son-in-law, John III Ducas Vatatzes.

John III's victory at the Battle of Poimanenon over the brothers of Theodore Laskaris, who had sought the aid of the Latin empire to be installed on the throne in 1224, opened the way for the Byzantine emperor of Nicaea to greatly extend his territories in Asia Minor, in Thrace, and in the Aegean Sea. In 1235, John allied with Ivan Asen II of Bulgaria (reigned 1218–41), allowing him to extend his influence over Thessalonica and Epirus. Ivan Asen and John besieged Constantinople between 1235 and 1236, but the siege soon fell apart after Asen allied himself with the Latins.

Following the spreading threat of the Mongol invasion in the Balkans and the Near East in 1242, which left Nicaea surprisingly unscathed, John seemed determined to extend his empire's territories in the Balkans; a noteworthy catalyst in his victories in the Balkans was John's decision to recruit the élite steppe-mounted warriors of the Cumans that were being persecuted by the Tatars.[2] John's policy reached its climax in the seizure of Thessaloniki in 1246, and the capture of most of the Macedonian and Thracian territories that Asen had taken from the Byzantine despotate of Epiros in the previous decades. In 1245 John married Constance II of Hohenstaufen, daughter of Frederick II of Germany and Sicily.

John's death in 1254 seemed like the perfect opportunity for the Bulgar tsar Michael Asan (reigned 1246–57) to recover the lands lost between 1245 and 1246. What he did not contemplate, however, was Theodore II Laskaris' (reigned 1254–58) resolve to defend his father's conquests at all costs; the Nicaean-Bulgar war that broke out between 1254 and 1256, with the focal point of the operations being the areas of eastern Macedonia

(Serres) and Rhodope, confirmed Theodore as a skilled military commander. In 1256, Theodore concluded a favourable peace with Bulgaria, which helped to plunge the latter into a crisis of leadership. He then followed up his victory by expanding his control in western Macedonia and Epirus.

But the key to understanding the geo-political significance of the Battle of Pelagonia for the future of the Byzantine empire, and of the eastern Mediterranean in general, is to ascertain the complex network of political alliances that culminated in the powerful triple coalition of Michael II, the Byzantine despot of Epirus, and his Latin allies King Manfred of Sicily and Prince William II Villehardouin of Achaea (reigned 1246–78).

Following the fall of Constantinople to the Crusaders in 1204, and while the Nicaean rulers were stripping the Latin empire of most of its Anatolian and Balkan territories, the long-serving despot of Epirus, Michael II (reigned 1230–66/68), was expanding his own Balkan possessions in former European territories of the Byzantine empire (in modern-day western Greece and Albania). But it is interesting to see what brought the despot together in an 'unnatural' alliance with Manfred of Sicily, whose Norman ancestors had nurtured ambitions for the Byzantine crown, and with William of Achaea whose family had aspirations in conquering the rest of Greece. All three had a common enemy: the emperors of Nicaea!

As I mentioned earlier, a marriage alliance between John Vatatzes of Nicaea and Emperor Frederick II's daughter took place in 1245, which greatly alienated the papacy. But the situation changed with the death of Theodore II Laskaris in 1258, and the rise to the throne of a member of the powerful Palaeologus family, Michael VIII (co-ruler with the under-aged John IV Laskaris 1258–59; sole ruler 1259–82). This brief period of interregnum, during which it was unclear who held real power in Nicaea, seemed too good an opportunity to miss for Michael of Epirus to crush Palaeologus before the latter could consolidate his position.

Early in 1259, Michael of Epirus married his daughter Anna to William of Achaea, thus forming an alliance with the strong Latin principality of Peloponnesus. One year before, in early 1258, and while Michael was marching against Thessalonica with the hope of recovering the city from the Nicaeans, King Manfred of Sicily seized Dyrrhachium (in Nicaean hands since 1256) and its environs in the Albanian coast.[3] Michael came to terms with Manfred and sent him his daughter Helen as wife, ceding the lost towns and the island of Corfu as dowry.

It seems obvious that this 'triple entente' served each party in different ways.[4] Michael II's ultimate goal of conquering Constantinople had to be preceded by the capturing of Thessalonica, the metropolis of northern Greece, and for this he needed outside help and, particularly, the élite knightly cavalry of the principality of Achaea. Manfred also contemplated using the strategic Albanian ports of Dyrrhachium and Avlona, as his predecessors did in 1081 and 1107, as a springboard for further expansion in Macedonia, and perhaps even Constantinople. But for the moment, all he could do was to dispatch military assistance to his father-in-law.

Although more hypothetical than those of the rest of the participants, William's motives in joining the 'triple entente' could well have been the breaking of the Nicaean emperors' ambitions of restoring the Byzantine empire, which inevitably entailed the subjugation of the Latin states of central and southern Greece. William's aspirations to dominate Greece, or even take Thessalonica,[5] may have come second.

THE PRELUDE TO THE BATTLE

Michael VIII Palaeologus soon realized the seriousness of the situation, and tried to dissolve the triple alliance through diplomacy. He dispatched embassies to both Manfred and William, making lavish concessions and promises, but to no avail. Contemporary sources even talk about a Nicaean embassy to Rome, as Michael would have known very well that the Popes were mortal enemies of the Hohenstaufen, and that they also held immense political and moral power over the Latin states in Greece. In fact, Michael may even had contemplated a Union of Churches – already negotiated by John III Vatatzes before 1254 – in exchange for recognition of his claims to the Nicene throne. Surprisingly, the *Registers* of Alexander IV (papacy, 1254–61) contain no papal reply to Michael's embassy.

Michael Palaeologus was not disheartened by his diplomatic failure to resolve the crisis, and he prepared to go on the offensive by ordering his brother John to gather an army in Thrace and Macedonia and campaign against Michael II. Some scholars have argued that John's campaign took place in the winter of 1258/59, although Geanakoplos puts John's departure from the city firmly in September 1259.[6] John marched rapidly towards Lake Ohrid and Deavolis,[7] no doubt following the old Roman Via Egnatia that led from Dyrrachium to Constantinople, in an attempt to cut off the Epirot forces from friendly territory.

Palaeologus' aggressive strategy took Michael II by surprise, forcing the latter to withdraw his army from Kastoria, one of the biggest cities in western Macedonia and a strategic hub close to the Via Egnatia. Sources report that his withdrawal was so haphazard and chaotic that several of his troops were killed in the process.[8]

Michael retreated west towards the mountain ranges of Pindus, where he tried to conquer the town of Belegradion (modern Berat in central Albania, mid-way between Lake Ohrid and the port of Avlona) without success; he later withdrew to Avlona. Soon, towns such as Ohrid, Deavolis, Pelagonia and Belegradion fell to John – the spoils of a campaign that cut a deep swathe through Michael's territories in western Macedonia. But Michael had already called for reinforcements from his allies, and he soon received a picked force of German knights from Manfred, while William responded with a general levy of all available forces in his realm.

After his sweeping campaign in western Macedonia, John Palaeologus marched east over the Via Egnatia towards the town of Bitola/Monastir (ancient Heraclea), some 70km (45 miles) east of Lake Ohrid and situated at a major intersection of the Egnatia. He then moved against Prilep (ancient Stybera), a mighty fortress city 40km (25 miles) to the north-east that was in the hands of the Epirotes.

It was during the siege of Prilep that the Byzantine prince received the news that a large allied army led by Michael II was marching from southern Macedonia to relieve Prilep, probably following the valley corridor from Thessaly northwards via Servia and Kozani, to re-join the Via Egnatia on a north-westerly direction towards Bitola/Monastir via modern Amyntaio and Kleidi, and then north-eastwards towards Prilep. Alarmed, Palaeologus decided to move to the south of the Pelagonian plain in order to block the allied advance.

THE OPPOSING FORCES

The Nicaean Army

The Greek and French versions of the *Chronicle of Morea* provide a detailed account of the numbers and composition of the Nicaean army at Pelagonia: 300 'picked' German knights, 1,500 élite Hungarian mounted archers, 600 Serbian mounted archers, 500 Turkish mounted archers and 2,000 Cuman mounted archers. These accounts do not, however, include the Byzantine forces raised by John Palaeologus in Macedonia and Thrace, as the latter would have looked into recruiting every able-bodied man available. Nevertheless, modern historians have estimated their numbers to be between 2,000 and 3,000 men.[9]

The southern Balkan Peninsula around AD1260.

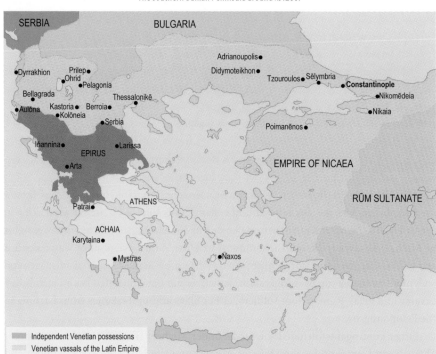

The plain of Pelagonia, south of Prilep.

The plain of Pelagonia, north of Bitola.

The Allied Armies

For the allied armies the information from the sources is sparse, to say the least, but we are still able to have an idea of the numbers and units that faced the Nicaean army in the valley of Pelagonia. King Manfred of Sicily had sent some 400 élite German knights to Michael II already before the conquest of Ohrid and Pelagonia by Palaeologus's army. The *Chronicle of Morea* notes that William of Achaea ordered for a general levy of all available forces in his realm, which would have included both Latin heavy cavalry and local 'Roman' foot soldiers, either Slavs and/or Tsakones from Laconia in the Peloponnesus.

Other contingents included the forces under Michael II's illegitimate son, John of Thessaly, and units under the Duke of Athens, and the Duke of Naxos, Euboea and

Salona – all vassals of Prince William. The Latin contingents may have numbered some
1,500 heavy cavalrymen, adding to that some 500–1,000 Thessalian cavalry, and perhaps
another 1,000 for the Epirot cavalry. The infantry numbers are much more difficult to
determine.

Arms and Armour

Byzantine Armament

A heavily armed Byzantine cavalryman of the post-1204 period would have been armed
and armoured with equipment that would have looked very similar to his Western counterparts, more so than in any other period in the Empire's history.[10] He would have been
protected by the old-fashioned but effective coat of mail, either full-bodied or reaching
down to his waist, although scale armour would also have been used. Padded or quilted
armour would have been preferred by the 'lower' (financially) soldiers, although the
padded overcoat (*pourpoint*) worn by the cavalrymen clearly came as an oriental influence. As would be the case in the rest of Europe, plate armour only became widespread
in Byzantium after the end of the thirteenth century, although Italian influences can be
detected in the iconography of the period.

A standard Byzantine helmet of the period was the *chapel de fer*, which would
usually have been onion-shaped with or without a wide brim, and it had mail aventails
attached to it, or it was worn over a mail *coif*. Simpler round helmets with reinforced
rims were also common. Armour would have been complemented by a triangular or
kite-shaped (rarely round) wooden shield, which would have been slightly curved and
between 1 and 1.5m tall.

The main weapon of a Byzantine cavalryman of the thirteenth century was his
sword, which would have been either long and straight, very similar to the Italian swords
of the period, or a curved sabre with undoubtedly oriental (mainly Turkish) influence.
The long lance or spear was also a principal weapon for both cavalry and infantry, comprising a long wooded shaft with an iron tip, usually between 1.5 and 3m long. Both the
club and the mace seem to have still been used by the cavalry, as we can discern from
the numerous depictions of military saints in the thirteenth and fourteenth centuries.

Allied Armament

A typical 'Latin' knight in Greece in the middle of the thirteenth century would have
worn similar equipment to that described for the German and southern French knights
at the Battle of Tagliacozzo: a full-body mail *hauberk* and a mail *coif* would have been
standard, complemented by a relatively small wooden shield (either triangular or oval).

Significant variations existed in terms of the metallic helmet worn by the warriors,
and that depended on the wealth of the knight, but also on the climate in which he
was operating; hence the German knight would probably have still worn the traditional
basinet (with or without a visor), though this would soon be replaced by the flat-topped
iron helm, while his Mediterranean counterparts would most likely have preferred the

chapel de fer (or 'kettle hat'). A knight's weapons would have included his straight-bladed sword, and possibly a dagger.

The Tsakones who served the Prince of Morea at Pelagonia were local Roman foot soldiers who inhabited the south-eastern Peloponnesian region of Laconia. Recently there has been an attempt to reconstruct their equipment, mostly relying on the great number of church frescoes in and around the regions of Laconia, Monemvasia, Geraki and so on.[11] They are described as being armed with a great array of weapons and armour, which varied according to the region, period and, of course, the source of the description: a full mail *hauberk* usually fitted with a *coif* and gauntlets; helmets similar to the Latin *chapel de fer* (in medieval Greek, *kranoi* or *kukla*); and padded surcoats, called *linothorakes*. They were armed with a great variety of weapons, including javelins, swords, battle-axes, crossbows and daggers.

THE BATTLE

Whether in July or in September 1259, it is most likely that the battle took place in the valley of Pelagonia: a flat basin about 15km (9 miles) wide and surrounded by high mountains, which forms the continuation of the valley that would have led Michael II's army from southern Macedonia to the area of Pelagonia. All Greek sources agree that, in deciding on his upcoming strategy, John was acting according to instructions conveyed to him by his elder brother Michael. Those were to avoid a pitched battle, but rather, to harass the enemy in a sort of a guerrilla warfare known to the Byzantines for many centuries.[12]

For that he was to take advantage of the light cavalry of the Cumans and the Turks, whose method of warfare included massive charges of mounted archers in hit-and-run tactics that aimed at frustrating the enemy, while the heavily armed Byzantine cavalry would withdraw in higher ground. In fact, the terrain in Pelagonia was ideal for this kind of warfare as contemplated by the Byzantines – although another important factor that would have prompted John to avoid a pitched battle with the allies would have been his army's numerical inferiority.[13]

John followed his brother's advice to the letter, as we read in Acropolites' *History*:

> A very large army was assembled and they set themselves in motion against the monarch's brother, the sebastokrator John. But he – for he had good advice from his brother the emperor – struck back at his adversaries strategically. With armoured forces that were equipped with breastplates, he held the strongest places, while the lighter foot-soldiers – for whom it was easy to move as they were nimbler – he ordered to join battle with the enemy in the plains … They engaged the enemy, striking them with arrows from a distance. They began to attack the enemy from a place whose name is *Borilla Longos*. They allowed them neither to march freely in the daytime nor to rest at night …[14]

It seems that the outcome of the battle was eventually decided not by the clash of arms in the battlefield, but by the use of stratagems. Pre-eminent among the allied army's weaknesses was the disunity resulting from the antagonism and great suspicion between the Greek and Latin contingents, and perhaps to a lesser degree, between the Germans of Manfred and the Franks from Achaea. Sadly, the Greek and Latin sources provide us with substantially different versions about what exactly unfolded between the leading figures in the allied army the night before the battle.

Interestingly, Gregoras' version describes an old stratagem that was used by John Palaeologus against Michael II: during the night, John secretly dispatched a false deserter to Michael, who would 'intentionally' be caught and would 'reveal' to the despot that his allies had made secret negotiations with him, and that the despot's only hope lay in flight.[15] Pachymeres' account may be more plausible, as the historian writes of the discord arising among the allies before the battle, and notes the secret negotiations between John and Michael II's stepson, John of Thessaly, to switch his allegiance and attack the Latins when battle was joined.

Whatever really happened that fateful night, we know for sure that Michael II of Epirus fled the allied camp, accompanied by one of his sons, Nicephorus, and a handful of trusted men; with his family, Michael eventually escaped to the Ionian islands of Leukas and Kephalonia. The following morning, after realizing with dread that they had been abandoned by their leader, the troops from Epirus deserted *en masse*. On top of that, John of Thessaly reportedly joined John Palaeologus in attacking William of Achaea's army.

Following Michael's desertion and John's switch of allegiance, John Palaeologus prepared his army to attack William. He put his picked German knights in the vanguard, flanked by the Cumans and Hungarian mounted archers to protect their wings, while attempting to disrupt any enemy attack. Behind the Germans, John deployed the Serbian and Bulgarian mounted archers, while he held the rearguard with the native Byzantine cavalry and infantry, supported by Turkish mounted archers. The *Chronicle of Morea* describes that William deployed his forces in a similar manner, in three successive divisions, with the vanguard led by the Lord of Karytaina and the middle division commanded by himself.

The Latin sources report that the battle was opened by the Lord of Karytaina's attack on the élite German vanguard of the Nicaean army, undoubtedly in a show of chivalrous bravado that was typical of Western knights in the late Middle Ages. The lord charged against the leader of the German mercenaries, even managing to unhorse him with his lance; the sources report that when his lance eventually broke, he grabbed his sword and began 'cutting down enemies like grass'. At that crucial stage of the battle, when the tactical situation seemed to be tipping in favour of the allies, John ordered his mounted archers to shoot down the enemy from a distance, aiming at their lightly armed horses rather than the knights – a tactic that had been applied against heavy cavalry armies long before Pelagonia.[16]

The involvement of the mounted archers proved to be the decisive tactical move that won the battle for John Palaeologus. The mounted Cuman and Hungarian units

| St Theodore Stratelates in his full armour except helmet – a miniature from the Fyodorovsky Gospel, c. 1330. | Fresco of St Demetrius by Manuel Panselinos in the Church of Protaton on Mount Athos, c. 1300. |

wrought havoc amongst the knights of the allied vanguard, even killing the Lord of Karytaina's horse, thus leaving him on foot. William saw the desperate situation of his vanguard, and rushed to send reinforcements – but his knights were also mown down by the skilled mounted archers of the Palaeologan army.

Having lost their mounts and effectively being put out of action, the Latin knights were reported to have surrendered; Gregoras writes that the 400 Germans sent by Manfred surrendered to only four Nicaeans (possibly high-ranking commanders), while the forces of William of Villehardouin scattered. Finally, the sources report that William himself, and more than thirty of his barons, were captured in battle; their captivity was to last for three years.

CONCLUSIONS

One of the greatest historians of the period, Deno Geanakoplos, has written about Pelagonia that '[it] was one of the most important battles of the thirteenth century, possibly of the entire later period of Byzantine history'. On the basis of the general strategy and battle tactics that were employed by both sides at Pelagonia, there is nothing extraordinary to report about the battle or, in fact, about the entire campaign. Surely, John Palaeologus was an acute and careful military commander who deployed several stratagems against his enemies, thus confirming the age-old military tradition of the Byzantines that:

> It is good if your enemies are harmed either by deception or raids, or by famine; harass them more and more, but do not challenge them in open war, because luck plays as major a role as valour in battle.[17]

But the underlying reason for the Nicaean victory was the defection of Michael II and John of Thessaly, a vivid illustration of Greco-Latin antipathy which caused the 'triple entente' to break down. To that end, we also have to add the manifested unwillingness of the local populations (especially in the cities) of the affected regions to take any side in this conflict, which they perceived as a civil war.

But the outcome of the Battle of Pelagonia had deep and decisive consequences for the geo-political future of the Balkans and Asia Minor. Following their victory over the Latins, John Palaeologus and John of Thessaly quickly moved south to the region of Thessaly to reinforce the local garrisons, while two other Nicaean generals took the city of Arta, the capital of the despotate of Epirus. However, John of Thessaly once again changed his allegiance and turned against the empire of Nicaea, marching back to Epirus and easily retaking Arta, while he relieved the siege of the strongly fortified city of Ioannina.

The following year also marked the return of Michael II who, with reinforcements from his son-in-law Manfred of Sicily, managed to defeat a Nicaean army in a pitched battle in western Epirus. But the tide had turned in favour of Michael VIII Palaeologus, as Pelagonia had irreversibly weakened Nicaea's main contender states in Greece, Epirus and Achaea, and had removed the menace of an attack from the west. Confident of victory, Michael VIII now was free to turn his attention to the recovery of Constantinople and the restoration of the Byzantine empire. After a prolonged but unsuccessful siege, the city would eventually fall to the Nicaeans by accident on 25 July 1261.

15 THE BATTLE OF TAGLIACOZZO

The End of Hohenstaufen Rule in Sicily

Date 23 August 1268
Location Between Tagliacozzo and Scurcola Marsicana, in the province of L'Aquila, in the Abruzzo region of central Italy

THE HISTORICAL BACKGROUND

THE BATTLE OUTSIDE the little town of Tagliacozzo, in the province of L'Aquila in the Abruzzo region of southern Italy, was the climax of a campaign of invasion led by Conradin Hohenstaufen, son of Conrad IV of Germany and Sicily (reigned 1250–54). Conradin was attempting to retake control of the Kingdom of Sicily from Charles of Anjou, the younger brother of King Louis IX of France, who had been offered the Sicilian crown by Pope Urban IV (papacy 1261–64); in fact he had already established himself in Sicily after defeating Conradin's uncle, Manfred, in the Battle of Benevento on 26 February 1266.

This would be a last-ditch attempt to secure the continuation of the German Hohenstaufen rule in southern Italy and Sicily, and to prevent the establishment of a new French dynasty, one with the closest of links to the French royal family of the Capetians, on the throne of the kingdom.

The enmity and antagonism between the papacy and the aristocratic Hohenstaufen family can be traced back to the reign of Frederick I 'Barbarossa' and his efforts, and those of his heirs down to the mid-thirteenth century, to consolidate their long-standing claims to northern Italy. Needless to say this was an ambition vehemently opposed by many northern Italian states and by the popes.

After Frederick, Duke of Swabia, was elected German emperor in 1152, he followed an aggressive policy to reassert German authority over the wealthy cities of Lombardy. This struggle reached its height during the pontificate of Alexander III (papacy, 1159–81), when the Pope backed the military alliance of the Lombard cities, known as the Lombard League, against Frederick.

The League's decisive victory at the Battle of Legnano, in 1176, forced Frederick to concede a *de facto* independence to the Lombard cities. After Legnano, the emperor shifted his ambitions to southern Italy and Sicily, arranging for his son and heir Henry VI (reigned 1190–97) to marry Constance (1154–98), the heiress of the Norman Kingdom of Sicily, in 1180. This spectacular political and diplomatic breakthrough, which would eventually see the political unification of southern Italy and Sicily with Germany under the Hohenstaufen, sounded alarm bells in Rome.

The premature death of Henry VI from malaria in 1197 left a power vacuum in his kingdom that led to a civil war in the German states and to the direct involvement of Pope Innocent III in the succession disputes between the great princes of the German realm and young Frederick Hohenstaufen. Eventually it was the Battle of Bouvines, fought in 1214, that reshaped the power balance in Europe and put young Frederick firmly on the throne of the Kingdom of Sicily, in 1215. Although in 1208 Frederick had conceded to Innocent III that Sicily would be ruled as a papal fief and would forever remain separate from the empire, after Innocent's death in 1216 he made it clear that he was not going to be bound by his promise.

Frederick II's policy of Italian unification under his command provoked fierce opposition by the popes, and the revival of the Lombard League. The power struggle with the papacy carried on, and resulted in Frederick's excommunication in 1227, as a punishment for failing to adhere to his promise to go on a crusade. He was excommunicated for a second time in 1239, this time as a result of his expansionist policies against the Lombard cities.

Frederick responded by expelling the Franciscans and the Dominicans from Lombardy, and electing his son Enzo as imperial vicar for northern Italy, while annexing the Romagna, and the Duchy of Spoleto, nominally part of the Papal States.

In 1245 Frederick was also condemned as a heretic by a church council at Lyon, and Pope Innocent IV (papacy, 1243–54) declared him deposed, calling for a crusade to rid the empire of its 'ungodly tyrant'. The latter action came as a direct result of the Pope's anti-Hohenstaufen policy, which led to Frederick's military show of arms in central Italy. But the imperial army's defeat at the Battle of Parma, on 18 February 1248, encouraged resistance in many Lombard cities that could no longer bear the fiscal burden of Frederick's regime: Romagna, Marche and Spoleto were, effectively, lost to the Hohenstaufen.

Frederick's death in 1250 was followed by his son Conrad IV's four-year reign, in which he successfully retook control of Italy from Frederick's vicar and bastard son, Manfred. But the Hohenstaufen rivalry with the papacy was left unresolved, and Conrad was not able to subdue the Pope's supporters. The period that followed Conrad's death in 1254 is known as the Great Interregnum, and is a period in which there were several elected rival kings, none of whom was able to achieve any position of authority. Conrad IV was succeeded as Duke of Swabia by his only son, two-year-old Conradin, in 1254. But Conradin had not been elected as heir to his father at an imperial diet, although he was recognized as King of the Germans, Sicily and Jerusalem by supporters of the Hohenstaufen.

Taking advantage of the Great Interregnum in Germany, including Conradin's young age and his status as the unelected only son of Conrad IV, was Manfred – the illegitimate son of the emperor Frederick II of Hohenstaufen. When his half-brother Conrad died in 1254, Manfred accepted the regency on behalf of Conradin, the infant son of Conrad, which caused the hostility of the Pope. He eventually defeated the papal army at Foggia on 2 December 1254, and soon established his authority over Sicily and the Sicilian possessions on the Italian mainland. He ruled as a vicar of the legitimate heir of the Hohenstaufen in Sicily, until he officially assumed the crown of the King of Sicily at Palermo, on 10 August 1258.

Pope Alexander IV (papacy, 1254–61) declared Manfred's coronation null and void, but the latter was determined to keep his prized possession. Undeterred, he sought to obtain power in central and northern Italy, where he named governors in Tuscany, Spoleto, Marche, Romagna and Lombardy. His political breakthrough was the marriage of his daughter Constance to Peter III of Aragon, in 1262. Terrified by these proceedings, the new Pope Urban IV (papacy, 1261–64) excommunicated Manfred, and in 1263 initiated discussions with Charles of Anjou, the younger brother of King Louis IX of France, who might, by force of arms, replace the Hohenstaufen south of the Alps.

Charles agreed that he would hold the Kingdom of Sicily as a vassal of the Pope, and he also promised that he would never claim the imperial title. He was crowned King of Sicily in Rome on 5 January 1266, and he immediately launched a campaign to consolidate his rule over his new kingdom. He led his troops across the Apennines towards Benevento, defeating Manfred's army at the Battle of Benevento on 26 February 1266. Refusing to flee, Manfred rushed into the midst of his enemies and was killed.

THE PRELUDE TO THE BATTLE

In November 1266, Manfred's staunchest supporters fled to Bavaria to persuade Conradin to assert his hereditary right to the kingdom. After Conradin accepted their proposal, Manfred's former vicar in Sicily, Conrad Capece, returned to the island and stirred up a revolt. Because Charles of Anjou had become detested by the majority of the magnates and people of the Kingdom of Sicily, it was easy to cause a revolt to flare up.

While the revolt was spreading from Sicily to the mainland and Charles was asserting his authority in Tuscany, Conradin left Bavaria for Italy in September 1267. Charles only grasped the seriousness of the situation in March 1268, when Pope Clement urged him to return to his kingdom. In late spring he began the siege of Lucera, a strategic town in north-western Apulia with a powerful fortress manned by Saracens; the town had followed the example of Sicily and rebelled against Charles' authority.

But with Charles occupied in Apulia, Conradin was free to invade northern Italy and push down towards Rome to join forces with his ally, Henry of Castile, who had occupied the city since the previous autumn (1267), and had defeated a small force dispatched by Charles to recover Rome sometime in the spring.

The distance between Rome and Lucera is, by modern standards, some 300km (190 miles) on a north-west to south-east axis. For Conradin's army based in Rome, there were two main routes that would have been suitable for the invasion of the Apulian province of the Kingdom of Sicily. First there was the old Roman Via Appia that connected Rome to Brindisi via Naples, which could take troops from Rome south to Capua and Benevento before turning east, either through Aquilonia and Venosa to Taranto and Brindisi, or following a course due east (Via Appia Traiana) through Troia and Canosa.

This would have been the course that Charles would have anticipated his enemies to choose; he knew this way very well, as he had defeated Manfred outside Benevento two and a half years earlier. But Conradin and Henry of Castile chose to invade Apulia from the Abruzzi to the north, following the Via Tiburtina by marching due east from Rome to Avezzano and Sulmona, before turning south to Lucera.

Conradin's army left Rome on 18 August, marching towards Vicovaro. They crossed the borders of the Kingdom of Sicily at Carseoli, then passed the small town of Tagliacozzo on their way to Avezzano. On the night of the 21 August, Conradin's army encamped at Scurcola, less than 8km (5 miles) to the east of Tagliacozzo, and on the following morning they came to realize that Charles' vanguard was blocking their way.

Charles had anticipated that his enemies would have taken the road via Cassino or Benevento, and he was swift to march his army to Ceprano, mid-way between Rome and Naples. From there, he could easily take advantage of the road network leading to the interior of the peninsula in order to intercept Conradin. According to Oman, Charles' spy network in Rome would have alerted him about the easterly route that his enemies were taking, hence his decision to march north, from Ceprano to Avezzano.

Eventually Charles succeeded in getting ahead of Conradin's line of march, though whether intentionally or by accident we will never know.[1] The two armies spent the night on opposite banks of the River Salto before battle was joined on 23 August 1268.

Battle of Tagliacozzo, MS from the workshop of Pacino de Bonaguida, c. 1340. In this illumination, Conradin is the figure in violet. In the first scene Charles of Anjou watches as the army led by his rival passes by, and pursues them in the second one.

SOURCE: *Il Villani illustrato. Firenze e l'Italia medievale nelle 253 immagini del ms. Chigiano LVIII.296 della Biblioteca Vaticana*, ed. CHIARA FRUGONI (FLORENCE: LE LETTERE, 2005), 155

THE OPPOSING FORCES

When Charles of Anjou was invited to invade the Kingdom of Sicily in 1266, he did so with an army of southern French and Provençal knights, and his household troops were always drawn from this pool of élite warriors. But he also welcomed many young French aristocrats who came to Italy to 'win their spurs'.[2]

At Tagliacozzo, Charles would have been in command of a cavalry force that numbered between 3,000 and 5,000 men. Conradin, together with Henry of Castile, would have brought to Apulia a mounted force of Germans and Castilians, between 5,000 and 6,000 in numbers, complemented by Italian mercenary knights.[3] In all accounts of the battle there appear nothing but horsemen, whether knights of aristocratic birth or sergeants of non-aristocratic origin. Hence, historians have presumed that the footmen would have played a marginal role in the whole campaign.

Arms and Equipment

The equipment of a German knight of the mid-thirteenth century would have been very similar to that of his contemporaries in France and England.[4] For defence, he would have worn a full-body mail *hauberk* under his heraldic cloak, and a *coif* for additional protection to the neck and shoulders. He would also have carried a small (around 50 × 70cm) triangular wooden shield with slightly rounded sides, a type that dominated Prussia and Central Europe through to the fifteenth century.[5]

Nevertheless, there would have been less uniformity when it came to the types of helmets seen in Italy at the time; for German knights, this was a transitional period from the traditional *basinet* (with or without a visor) to the flat-topped iron helm that did not cover the entire neck – the latter was the precursor to the *great helm* that protected the whole head and would appear at the closing decades of the century.

In hot climates, however, French and German knights were also known to have worn the kettle hat (*chapel de fer*), a steel helmet made in the shape of a hat. Although the southern Italian knights in the second half of the century seemed to have preferred the *basinet*, their northern contemporaries were among the first in Europe to adopt the 'flat-topped' *great helm*, probably as a response to an increased use of crossbow arrows.[6]

A knight's equipment in the mid-thirteenth century would also have included a sword that would have been either German or North Italian in style and manufacture, straight-bladed and between 65 and 95cm long, with a wide and flat blade with a narrow tip, which describes it as a slashing weapon rather than a thrusting one. Side-arms in use in the thirteenth century would have included a dagger, which had a two-edged symmetrical blade, and/or a battle-knife with an asymmetric one-edged blade.

THE BATTLE

The key topographical feature for the Battle of Tagliacozzo is the River Salto. Today, the Salto drains at the Lago del Salto, some 50km (30 miles) north-west of Tagliacozzo, a man-made reservoir built in 1940 when the Salto river was dammed in order to prevent the flooding of the Cicolano valley. Crossing a river while the enemy was deployed on the opposite bank has always been an undertaking fraught with danger, and in 1268 the Salto worked as a barrier between the two armies on the eve of the battle. Every medieval commander could condemn his army to destruction if he did not follow Vegetius' advice to take every precaution necessary to ensure the safe river crossing of his army before any armed clash took place:

> The enemy often launch rapid ambushes or raids at river crossings. Armed guards are stationed against this danger on both banks, lest the troops be beaten by the enemy because they are divided by the intervening river-bed. It is safer to build stockades along the bank on either side, and bear without loss any attack that is made.[7]

What Vegetius meant to say is that an army was at its most vulnerable while crossing a river, because the different units were disorganized and incapable of fighting any sort of battle until they were properly deployed for action. And it seems that Charles had heeded this warning, after Manfred's Sicilian knights' disastrous decision to cross the River Calore by a narrow bridge in the initial stage of the Battle of Benevento on 26 February 1266, which caused gaps in their formations and cost Manfred his Sicilian crown and his life. Therefore, the Count of Anjou was resolved to wait on the other side of the Salto and leave the initiative with his enemies.

Conradin drew up his troops on the north bank of the Salto, towards Tagliacozzo, deploying them in three divisions one behind the other: the vanguard was led by Henry of Castile, while the second and the third were under the command of Galvano Lancia and Conradin, respectively. The French were on the south bank of the Salto, also forming three divisions: the first two were deployed in column just before the bridge, commanded by Henry of Coutances and John de Clary, respectively. But Charles made an essential adjustment to his battlefield deployment, compared to how he had formed his troops at Benevento two and half years earlier: he concealed his reserve division of 800 to 1,000 handpicked men, under his command, in a lateral hollow of the hills behind his camp and out of sight of the enemy.

On the morning of the 23 August it was Henry of Castile who opened the battle by charging across the bridge, but they were checked by the French. Then Conradin ordered his second division, commanded by Galvano Lancia, to ford the Salto in rapid pace. They forded the river downstream and then wheeled eastwards, apparently wishing to attack the flanks of Charles' army while they were distracted fighting against Henry's forces around the bridge. And they seem to have been successful, as they caught their enemies totally by surprise and broke them.

Watching the confusion in the second division of the French, Henry ordered a renewed attack against the Provençal and Italian troops holding the bridge, and he succeeded in routing them. At that crucial point, Conradin also ordered his division to cross the Salto and join in the mêlée by attacking the French flank. With Charles' army faring badly, his troops being slaughtered and one of his commanders, Henry of

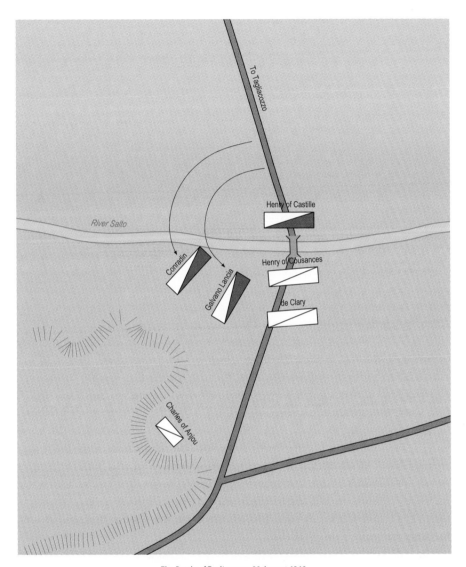

The Battle of Tagliacozzo, 23 August 1268.

Coutances, killed in action, it seemed that it was all over for Charles. But the Count had an ace up his sleeve!

While Henry of Castile's troops set themselves to pursue the routed enemy on the road leading south to Aquila, Charles was on the heights at some distance from the battlefield, and launched his attack when he saw his enemy scattered to loot. Making for Conradin's banners, his attack was initially misinterpreted by his enemies as Henry's units returning from the pursuit. But Conradin's knights could be deployed to receive the enemy attack at the last moment, thus engaging in a short but brutal onslaught with Charles' élite knights.

Meanwhile, Henry of Castile had apparently pursued many of the enemy, perhaps to the rising land near Magliano de Marsi to the north-east of Scurcola, when he realized what had happened – reversing his force he marched straight back to join the battle. The key move during this final stage of the battle was a feigned flight by a group of some forty knights, led by a certain Alard of Saint-Valéry – a veteran of the Crusades, who managed to lure some of Henry's forces out of their strong, packed formation. And as they broke ranks, they were attacked by both Charles' battle from the front and by Alard's unit from the flank. The exhausted troops under Henry's command were soon broken and fled the battlefield.

CONCLUSIONS

From a military perspective, the Battle of Tagliacozzo is a useful case study for historians to examine the strengths and weaknesses of a thirteenth-century mounted army. It demonstrates the rapid operational manoeuvres of the opposing forces, depending on the accurate flow of tactical intelligence by spies and field-scouting parties, with both armies covering huge distances in just a few days across relatively difficult country for cavalry to operate effectively.

Tagliacozzo also underlines the difficulties that a heavily armed mounted force had to overcome when operating in tight formations in a relatively broken, hilly or marshy terrain, which was also dominated by a river or an uphill castle: discipline, training and all the necessary precautions to avoid any ambushes or surprise enemy attacks were of paramount importance in order to avoid disaster.

Battle discipline was also central for a medieval commander, especially when leading diverse armies in the field; the Templars' Rule, for example, forbade a knight from undertaking individual attacks or to attack with a single unit before the order was given, with only one exception: it was permitted to go to the help of a Christian in danger. However, in the case of Tagliacozzo, battle discipline was not enforced in the case of Henry of Castile's troops during the second stage of the battle, when, after breaking through the two main divisions of Charles' army, and assuming their enemy had been defeated, they committed two serious tactical blunders: (a) they were involved in an uncontrolled pursuit of the enemy, and (b) they started looting the enemy camp.

Cavalry was also at its most vulnerable when regrouping after an unsuccessful charge. Order had to be restored forthwith, and the units had to be formed up again. But it took a significant amount of experience, training and discipline to be able to feign a retreat, in order to confuse the enemy and make him break ranks and follow you, before you reverse to make a fresh charge. This battlefield stratagem of the feigned flight had been known in Western Europe for centuries, but this does not negate the significance of its effective use at Tagliacozzo, where a small unit managed to lure away from the mêlée a much larger number of enemy troops, thus saving the day for Charles of Anjou.

The political ramifications of the Battle of Tagliacozzo were much more decisive for the history of Europe, and especially for Italy and Sicily. It finally broke the centuries-old political connection between Germany and the Kingdom of Sicily through the Hohenstaufen, ushering in a new French dynasty on the throne of the kingdom that had the closest of connections with the French royal family of the Capetians.

Nevertheless, the inhabitants of the realm, particularly those on the island of Sicily, resented Charles of Anjou and his army as occupiers. The so-called War of the Sicilian Vespers that followed the successful Sicilian rebellion against Charles' regime, in Easter 1282, was stirred up by Byzantine agents and by King Peter III of Aragon (reigned 1275–86), Manfred's son-in-law, who saw his wife Constance as rightful heir to the Sicilian throne. This prolonged conflict was fought in Sicily, Catalonia, and elsewhere in the western Mediterranean between, on one side, Charles of Anjou and his son Charles II, backed by the French monarchy and the papacy, and the kings of Aragon.

The war ended in 1302 with the Peace of Caltabellotta, which saw the division of the old Kingdom of Sicily: Charles of Anjou and Maine (future Charles II, King of Naples, d. 1309) was confirmed as king of the peninsular territories of Sicily (the Kingdom of Naples), while Frederick of Aragon (future Frederick II, King of Sicily, d. 1337) was confirmed as king of the island territories (the Kingdom of Sicily).

16 THE BATTLE OF SEMPACH

The Triumph of the Swiss Confederation

Date 9 July 1386
Location Close to the village of Hildisrieden, on the south-east side of the Sempach Lake, 15km (9 miles) north-west of Lucerne, Switzerland

THE HISTORICAL BACKGROUND

THE SERIES OF battles the Swiss cantons had to conduct in the fourteenth century came as a result of their will for self-determination coming under attack by the encroachments of the neighbouring Habsburgs of Austria and Burgundian lords, who wanted to impose their own power and socio-political structures on the Swiss communities. As a consequence, the Swiss warriors were forced to take up arms and develop a sort of militia-based armed forces to fight against some of the best trained and well equipped knightly armies of the late Middle Ages.

Three cantons played the greatest part in the formation of late medieval Switzerland: Schwyz, Uri and Unterwalden. They were the founding cantons that had agreed on the Federal Charter of 1291, an alliance against the encroaching interests of the Habsburgs. In the second quarter of the thirteenth century a *reichsfreiheit* was granted to Uri (1231) and Schwyz (1240): this was a privileged legal status in which they were placed under the direct rule of the Holy Roman Emperor. The reason for this was because the German emperors wanted to have the important pass of St Gotthard under their control: this was the main access point over the Alps, and although it was known since ancient times, it was not generally used until the 1220s. Its opening to traffic precipitated a reconfiguration in the balance of power in the region, hence the *reichsfreiheit* to Schwyz and Uri; Unterwalden had already enjoyed that status since 1173.

Despite their *reichsfreiheit*, the cantons came under threat from the expansionist policy of the Swiss family (from the canton of Aargau) of the Habsburgs, who, by the middle of the thirteenth century, had managed to bring much of the territory south of the Rhine under their control, extending their influence through Swabia (south-eastern Germany) to Austria. Things became even more complicated when the head of the family, Rudolph, was elected 'King of the Germans' in 1273, subsequently becoming the direct liege lord of these *reichsfreiheit* regions. Rudolph wanted to collect heavy tolls on the trade through the St Gotthard pass, and the pressure of taxes on the citizens of Uri, Schwyz and Unterwalden was becoming ever greater, thus inflaming the old urge of these cantons for independence. The signing of the Federal Charter of 1291 came as a reaction to Rudolph's death in the same year.

Habsburg rule over the alpine territories weakened until 1298, when Rudolph's son Albert prevailed over his adversaries for the German throne. He succeeded in bringing the three cantons under his rule from 1298 to 1308, but following his death, a protracted conflict erupted in which the Swiss cantons would eventually win their independence.

Tensions between the cantons and the Habsburgs reached boiling point in 1314, when the Habsburg Frederick the Handsome and Duke Louis IV of Bavaria (future Louis IV, Holy Roman Emperor) each claimed the imperial crown. It seemed obvious to the Swiss to side with Louis of Bavaria, for fear of Frederick attempting to annex their territories. This diplomatic manoeuvre prompted a swift reaction from the Habsburgs, with Frederick's brother Leopold assembling an army in Swabia to subdue the confederate Swiss cantons.

The host that Leopold of Austria assembled consisted of between 2,000 and 3,000 men altogether, including some 1,500 mounted knights and an equal number of crossbowmen and heavy infantry. He planned a surprise attack from the canton of Zug, directly south via Lake Ägerisee, on the borders between the cantons of Zug and Schwyz.

Leopold was unfortunately overconfident in his knights' ability to crush the Swiss militia, and the route he took ran through a narrow pass between steep mountains, presenting an excellent place for an ambush. The Schwyz commander Werner Stauffacher knew the area well enough to prepare a roadblock ambush at a point between Lake Ägerisee and Mortgarten Pass, where a small path led between a steep slope and a swamp. He deployed his army of between 2,000 and 4,000 footmen on a ridge above Lake Ägerisee, concealing them in a ravine atop the ridge; he then waited for the Austrian vanguard of heavy cavalry to appear.

As the marching columns were brought to a halt and piled up in the narrow mountain road, Leopold ordered the knights in the front to dismount and attack the Swiss. But with the defenders on the roadblock holding firm, the main body of the Swiss attacked from the ridgeline, throwing rocks and rolling down tree trunks, before following up with an all-out infantry attack. Shortly thereafter the Swiss halberdiers were inside the ranks of the enemy cavalry, wreaking havoc with their halberds, while a large number of knights drowned in the waters of the Lake Ägerisee below.

Leopold escaped, but around 1,500 of his Austrian troops suffered a horrific death at the hands of the Swiss militia, who, breaking with the chivalric code of conduct in battle, refused to ransom their social superiors – the knights. More importantly, the Swiss victory at Mortgarten consolidated the 1291 League between Schwyz, Uri and Unterwalden.

Capitalizing on their victory at Mortgarten, the three communities followed a policy of expansion. Uri entered a pact with the formerly Habsburg valley of Urseren in 1317,

Depiction of the Battle of Sempach in the 'Luzerner Schilling' (c. AD1515).

while in 1332, the city of Lucerne also joined the alliance. But when the city of Bern, the largest urban community south of the Rhine, threatened an alliance with the Swiss Confederation in 1339, the city's western enemies in Burgundy and in Freiburg laid siege to the city of Laupen, 16km (10 miles) south-west of Bern. The Burgundian contingent was joined by Freiburg lords, taking the total up to 12,000 infantry and 1,000 mounted knights. To raise the siege, Bern raised a force of 6,000, supported by troops from Uri, Schwyz and Unterwalden.

On the evening of 21 June 1339, the Swiss coalition army assumed a defensive position on a hill known as Bramberg, some 2 miles east of the besieged city of Laupen, rather than attempt a frontal attack on the Burgundian-Freiburger siege lines. The battle of Laupen opened in the afternoon when the Burgundian-Freiburger force, led by the cavalry and followed by the foot-soldiers, launched an assault up the Bramberg towards the Swiss all-round defensive formations, known euphemistically as 'hedgehogs'.

The Swiss pikemen and halberdiers stood their ground, but after some skirmishing, several ranks of the centre Bernese phalanx broke and ran for the woods. Undeterred, the Bernese commander Rudolf of Erlach ordered all his phalanxes to attack downhill, eventually shattering the Freiburger and coalition infantry. But the Burgundian heavy cavalry on the right re-formed and counter attacked the Swiss halberdiers, who reacted in turn by redeploying in a 'hedgehog', lowering their halberds and facing in all four directions to ward them off.

Seeing the halberdiers surrounded and being pounded by the élite cavalry, Erlach ordered his Bernese phalanxes to manoeuvre and strike the Burgundian cavalry, attacking the canton units. They caught the enemy horsemen in the flank by surprise, causing severe casualties and eventually a rout.

At Laupen, the Swiss pikemen and halberdiers showcased their unerring ability to choose a battleground that would favour their defensive formation against enemy cavalry attacks, an illustration of their tactical mobility and capacity that contrasted sharply with the Freiburger-Burgundian leadership's overconfidence in (chivalric) numbers, which saw no need for any other strategy except for a head-on attack on the Bernese infantry. The political outcome of the battle was equally significant for the Swiss cantons, as Bern was drawn closer to the Swiss Confederacy, eventually becoming one of the Eight Cantons in 1353.

All Eight Cantons pursued their own particular interests, most notably in the cases of the strong cities of Zürich and Bern, and it would be their aggressive expansionist policies in the following decades that would lead to further conflict with the Habsburgs of Austria. In the 1380s Lucerne – a Habsburg dominion between 1290 and 1332 – expanded its territory by claiming sovereignty over the valley of the Entlebuch and the formerly Habsburg city of Sempach – but in 1386 Leopold III of Austria reacted by assembling a powerful force to face the army of the Eight Cantons near Sempach.

THE PRELUDE TO THE BATTLE

As Lucerne expanded its sphere of influence over several smaller Habsburg towns and valleys, including Entlebuch, Sempach, Meienberg, Reichensee and Willisau, a small Austrian force defeated the garrison of Meienberg at the beginning of January 1386. A preliminary armistice between the Austrians and the Swiss Confederacy ended abruptly after just a few weeks, with the conflict escalating into a full-scale war.

At some time in the first week of July 1386, Duke Leopold III of Austria gathered his troops at Brugg, in the Swiss canton of Aargau, implying an impending attack on Zürich. But instead, the Duke moved south-west towards Lucerne, apparently with the intention of ravaging the Lucerne countryside, before concentrating his army against the town of Sempach, 15km (9 miles) north-west of Lucerne on the south side of the Sempach lake, on 7 July. After completely surrounding the city, he then placed advance guards along the road to intercept any relief forces marching west from Zürich and/or Lucerne.

Leopold would rightly have thought that it would be better to march against a smaller city of the Swiss Confederation, and let the stronger ones (Zürich or Lucerne) come to its rescue, rather than subject his army to a prolonged siege of one of the strongly fortified cities in the region. From a strategic point of view he would have the upper hand by choosing the battlefield and letting his enemies bring on the battle. And it seems that he was sensible enough not to repeat the tactical mistakes made by Leopold I at Mortgarten in 1316, by accepting battle next to a lake.

THE OPPOSING FORCES

The German Army

Leopold raised a powerful army of 4,000 men, which included some 2,500 foot-soldiers and 1,500 knights and mercenaries. Although mail was still favoured by many knights in the fourteenth century, the increasing effectiveness of archers (both longbow- and crossbowmen) led to the gradual adoption of plate at the end of the century. Hence, a German knight of the late fourteenth century would have been fully covered in plate armour, while also wearing a *basinet* – an open-faced military helmet that resembled an iron or steel skullcap, which extended downwards at the rear and sides to afford protection for the neck. This would have been complemented by a *visor* (face guard).

The German knight would have carried a sword with a blade, which, by the beginning of the fourteenth century, would have been narrower so that the sword could be used for thrusting rather than slashing, in response to changes in armour. He would also have carried a long lance and/or a dagger.

A German infantryman would have worn a mail coat under a surcoat, supplemented by gauntlets and metallic leg pieces, and he would have been carrying a circular wooden shield. His main weapon would have been the sword or the falchion – a short, single-edged weapon with a very broad and slightly curved blade, similar to a modern machete.

The Swiss Army

The strength of the Swiss army at Sempach was between 6,000 and 8,000, with the vanguard comprising between 1,500 to 2,000 levies. At the end of the fourteenth century, the Swiss had equipment well suited to fighting against armoured cavalry. Swiss armies had crossbowmen only as an auxiliary branch, because the strength of their armies lay in the heavily armed pikemen and the halberdiers.

By far the most notorious weapon in the hands of a Swiss was the halberd, wielded with both hands, which meant that the men could not carry a shield, but often wore short mail shirts and iron plates instead. They also had a *habergeon* under their helmet, which protected their head and neck. The halberd was a combination of a spear and an axe, consisting of a fairly broad blade with a spike projecting from the top secured to the end of a long pole, which was around 2 metres long. In the hands of an experienced warrior it could be used both as a thrusting weapon – a spear – and as a war-axe, reminiscent of the Viking axes in the north of Europe.

Because the halberd, unlike the long pike, was used for hand-to-hand fighting at close range, the halberdiers were placed behind the pikemen in the middle of the Swiss phalanx formation, where they could wreak havoc among the enemy horses and knights with their heavy weapons.

The tactical role of the pikemen was to work as an impenetrable wall of 'metal points' to frustrate the enemy cavalry charge, because their long weapons were practically useless for fighting at close quarters. The pike measured, on average, some 5m and weighed around 2.5kg. It consisted of a haft of ash and a metallic 'leaf-shaped' head.

THE BATTLE

The two sides approached each other on 9 July, with the Austrians setting off eastwards from Sempach, although they had no clear idea about the whereabouts of their opponents; it seems that Leopold may have had intelligence that his enemies were approaching from the direction of Lucerne. According to Delbrück, the Swiss presumably thought that they would catch the Austrians at Sempach itself, with their backs against the lake so they were denied the tactical mobility of their heavy cavalry.[1]

The two armies eventually met at a short distance to the east of Sempach, close to the village of Hildisrieden, where the terrain rises steeply from the lake, forming terraces that are cut by many ravines. In front of Hildisrieden there is a small plateau where the opponents would most likely have first spotted each other. The sources confirm that this was to the mutual surprise of both armies, as neither was in battle order.

After spotting the advance guard of the Austrians marching in three columns[2] towards them, the Swiss vanguard took their positions on the steepest spot just under the village of Hildisrieden, a place of wooded hilly ground, surrounded by small streams and cattle fences, which made it unsuitable for cavalry manoeuvres, but ideal for defensive action.

Aware of the ability of the Swiss phalanx to resist mountain attacks, whilst realizing the unsuitability of the terrain for any kind of cavalry attack, Leopold ordered his knights to dismount and attack uphill on foot, while his light crossbowmen would harass the Swiss and attempt to create gaps on their phalanx. The Duke proved reckless – or confident – enough not to wait for the full deployment of his forces from marching into a battle formation, perhaps because he believed that he had the entire Swiss army ahead of him.

The ferocity of the attack of the heavily armed knights under Leopold had the desired effect on the morale of the Swiss units that received them. Not long afterwards, Swiss losses began to mount, and the phalanx formation began to break apart. As the banner of the city of Lucerne fell into Austrian hands, Leopold prepared to order a general cavalry charge against the disintegrating Swiss phalanxes. But the Duke had misjudged the situation on the ground, and while he prepared to order an all-out attack, the main body of the Swiss army appeared over the rise near the village: they rushed to form for battle, and immediately attacked the dismounted knights from the flanks.

The flank attack by the Swiss troops overwhelmed the knights fighting on foot. Exhausted by the mid-summer heat and by hours of fighting in full armour, the latter were soon retreating in panic towards their rear, where their squires were holding their horses, while part of the Habsburg army was still advancing towards the battlefield. These advancing troops could have saved the day, and Leopold did order them to rush to the rescue of their retreating comrades, with himself leading them into the fray.

But in the swirling mêlée, Leopold and his knights were found dead, cut down by enemy halberdiers, while the rest of the army retreated down the hill. Coalition casualties numbered around 1,800 men, including the duke himself; Swiss losses were surprisingly low, about 120 men, mostly among the vanguard.

CONCLUSIONS

Coupled with the Battle of Näfels (9 April 1388), the last Swiss-Austrian battle of the fourteenth century, the Swiss victory over the Habsburg alliance east of Sempach has been perceived, already since the fourteenth century, as the turning point in the territorial expansion of the Swiss Confederacy. This point marked an evolution from a loose anti-Habsburg confederation of cities and cantons in the fourteenth century, to a powerful political and military federation and a key regional player at the turn of the fifteenth century.

Following the division of hereditary Habsburg lands after the Treaty of Neuberg, agreed between the Habsburg duke Albert III (reigned 1365–95) and his brother Leopold III (reigned 1365–86) on 25 September 1379, the outcome of the Battle of Sempach decisively tipped the balance of power west of the Rhine in favour of the Swiss Confederation. This allowed the cities, especially Lucerne and Bern, an unchecked expansion into the Habsburg lands, and eventually would lead to the establishment of the state of Switzerland.

From a military point of view, the Battle of Sempach offers an excellent case study of a military revolution that was unfolding in Europe in the fourteenth century with regard to the tactics of foot-soldiers. By the middle of the tenth century, wars were fought almost exclusively by men on horseback, and foot-soldiers were largely considered an expendable mob of armed peasants, who would mostly be used in siege operations or in defence of the lord's castle. Nevertheless, the tactical importance of foot-soldiers in medieval Europe varied greatly depending on the society from which they came.

In regions where the 'feudal system' prevailed, the peasants and burghers could not develop their full potential because the knights had the upper hand; a typical example were the many 'brotherhoods' of peasants in twelfth- and thirteenth-century France.[3] But where geography did not favour the rise of a land-based social élite, then armies of foot-soldiers emerged who were sometimes the only branch of the army, and were therefore, naturally, important. Regions such as the deep valleys of Wales, the Highlands of Scotland, the mountainous Swiss cantons, the marshland of Dithmarschen on the Elbe, or the urbanized regions of northern Italy and Flanders, were never dominated by a landed élite in the same way as their neighbouring regions, and would therefore develop some of the most effective infantry-based armies in Medieval Europe.

Up to the beginning of the fourteenth century, the foot-soldiers played a motionless defensive role and never mounted any attempt to attack enemy knightly formations. It was believed that a heavily armed infantry unit could withstand an attack by heavy cavalry if it kept its formation unbroken, and if it had adequate support from units of

The Battle of Sempach, woodcut by Niklaus Manuel (c. 1520).

cavalry and archers. However, its slow speed and limited ability for manoeuvre made any counter attack a very precarious undertaking, if not unthinkable, even for well-trained professional soldiers, because any counter attack leaves the unit with its flanks exposed to enemy attack and encirclement.[4]

At Dyrrachium (1081), the élite Varangian Guard fought dismounted in the centre front line of the whole formation but projected a few yards forward, and was encircled and annihilated by the Normans when the units of the main Byzantine army failed to keep up with the advancing Saxons in what, we suspect, would have been an imperial order to an all-out counter-attack.

At Civitate (1053), the Swabian infantry could stand their ground and deny the Normans their advantage in mobility and numbers, but as soon as their flanks became exposed because of the retreat of their Italian allies, their encirclement became inevitable.

At Bouvines (1214), Renaud de Dammartin and his élite foot-soldiers and small cavalry unit from Brabant, who applied their ingenious tactic of cavalry sorties from a solid round phalanx formation, worked well until the whole formation was overrun.

At Legnano (1176), the repeated attacks of the German knights were shattered on the thick hedge of long Milanese pikes, but the day was saved by the timely return of the Milanese knights, who charged against the German flanks. About fifty years later, in 1237, the Milanese foot-soldiers again successfully tackled another German army at Cortenuova, in Lombardy, resisting their repeated cavalry attacks while Frederick II issued an order for the attacks to halt, and to wait while archers thinned down their thick formations; this action allowed the Milanese to slip away during the evening lull.

At Falkirk (1298), the tightly packed Scottish *schiltrons* were left without cavalry reinforcements, and despite the fact that their flanks were covered by archers and their front by a marsh, they were left helpless when the English archers opened up gaps in their ranks through which the English cavalry could pour and cut them down.

It was only at the beginning of the fourteenth century that really important victories were won by foot-soldiers: by then not only had they become the chief or, in some cases, the only fighting arm, but they were winning the field by (counter) attacking their social superiors. The first victory of infantry over cavalry was at Courtrai in 1302, when the Flemish militiamen proved capable of defeating knights, first by thoughtfully choosing and preparing a battle terrain that enabled them to protect the flanks of their thick phalanxes, and by counter attacking at a key stage of the battle when the enemy knights had become bogged down and confused.

At Kephisos (1311), the large force of Latin knights from Athens were defeated by a much smaller, largely infantry army of the Catalan Company, who waited until the Latin army's mounted charge became disordered and was brought to a halt by the marshy conditions of the battlefield, thus enabling a mobile and lighter infantry counter attack to defeat them. Then in 1314 the Scottish foot-soldiers achieved a very similar, and equally brilliant, victory over the Anglo-Norman nobles at Bannockburn.

The following year at Mortgarten, as we have seen, the Swiss scored their first important victory over the knights of the duke of Austria, by ambushing the Austrians in a narrow mountain pass and denying them the chance to properly deploy for battle before falling upon them with extreme ferocity. At Laupen (1339), the Swiss halberdiers and pikemen resoundingly defeated the Burgundian mounted nobility by, again, choosing a battleground that denied their enemies their tactical mobility, while their experienced commander ordered his phalanxes to manoeuvre and strike at the flank of the Burgundian cavalry.

It seems that some lessons were learned by the French and the English about sending knights against a solid infantry line. At Mons-en-Pévèle (1304), the French avoided a frontal attack, and went instead for a push against the flanks of the Flemish militia; at Cassel (1328), the French chose to besiege the Flemish who were deployed in a foothill, forcing them to break their defensive formation and mount a failed attack on the French camp. At Dupplin Muir (1332) and Halidon Hill (1333) the English chose, 'contrary to the customs of their forefathers', to receive the enemy attack by fighting dismounted and flanked by longbowmen, thus wiping out two successive Scottish armies. This tactic was so successful that they 'exported' it to France, as at Crécy in 1346, Poitiers in 1356, and in Iberia – Najera in 1367, and Aljubarrota in 1385.

Therefore, the outcome of the Battle of Sempach in 1386 represents the climactic victory of a purely infantry army over its social superiors, the knights, which had dominated the European battlefields for almost a millennia. Dubbed as the 'infantry revolution'[5] of the fourteenth century, this period witnessed the gradual transformation of the tactical role of infantry forces in Europe from fighting motionless and in a purely defensive role as a 'screen' for the heavy cavalry units, to being the main (or only) arm of an army in the field of battle, and exploiting the exhaustion of the knights after the failure of their charges to go over to the attack.

This was made possible in regions where the landed élite was less strongly in force, and where infantry training and fighting had become institutionalized, either through regular community service – citizen militia fighting for their communities – or through professionalism – mercenaries.[6] Therefore, the independent and rich cities and states in northern Italy, Switzerland and Flanders were the only ones capable of putting large battle-worthy infantry armies in the field against the aristocratic knightly armies of the Middle Ages.

17 THE BATTLE OF NICOPOLIS

The Failure to Stem the Ottoman Expansion in Europe

Date 25 September 1396
Location South of Nikopol on the Danube

THE HISTORICAL BACKGROUND

The background to the Crusade and the subsequent Battle of Nicopolis in 1396 is to be looked for in the Ottoman expansion in the Balkans in the second half of the fourteenth century. Overcome by factionalism and religious and political infighting that frequently led to civil wars, the Byzantine Empire gradually began to lose its protagonist role in Thrace and western Anatolia after the death of Michael VIII in 1282, thus becoming an easy prey to the Ottoman Turks. Following the Ottoman conquest of Bursa, in north-western Anatolia (Bithynia), in 1326, political factions in Constantinople began to turn to the Ottomans for political and – more importantly – military assistance. Ottoman leaders now became supporters of competing Byzantine pretenders to the throne, regularly sending mercenary forces to Constantinople and Thrace, no doubt in an effort to prey on the weakness of Byzantium to defend its territories.

The Ottoman expansion in Anatolia and the Balkans was expertly organized and conducted by two adept rulers: Orhan 'Ghazi' (ruled 1324–59), and his son Murad (ruled 1360–89). Orhan's conquests of the Nicaean peninsula, following his rout of an imperial fleet at Pelekanon (modern Maltepe) in 1328, not only transformed the Ottoman state in one of the strongest Turkoman principalities in the area, it also reinforced the position of its ruler as the leader of the war against the infidel.

Then in 1346, Orhan led his nomads into Thrace in order to help John VI Kantakouzenus (reigned 1347–54) secure the Byzantine throne; in return John gave Orhan his daughter Theodora as a bride. Six years later, in 1352, Kantakouzenus handed over to Orhan the strategic fortress of Tzympe, in the European side of the Dardanelles, thus stimulating a new phase in Orhan's conquests in Thrace.

In reality, however, it was Orhan's second son, Murad, who was the real builder of the Ottoman Empire in Europe, using his father's base in the Dardanelles to conquer Thrace, Macedonia, Bulgaria and Serbia. Politics in the southern Balkans presented Murad with an ideal opportunity to expand, as Stefan Dušan, the great Serbian king who reigned from 1346 to 1355, died suddenly in 1355. Dušan had managed to take under his control most of Macedonia, Epirus and Thessaly, even holding Thessalonica for a brief period in 1349, and had become one of Byzantium's most serious enemies.

Dušan's successor, Stefan Uros (reigned 1355–71), proved unable to hold together his father's empire, but neither was Byzantium capable of reclaiming its protagonist role. On top of that, the Latin principalities in Greece and the Morea were weakened by internal divisions, while the Aegean islands were ruled by a mixture of Greek, Venetian and Genoese dynasties, who found it impossible to cooperate against the Ottomans.

Murad's expansionist strategy in the Balkans aptly demonstrates his acute strategic mind and knowledge of the region's geography and politics. He quickly signalled his intentions by conquering Adrianople (modern Edirne) in 1362, thus gaining a capital and a new powerbase in the Balkans from where to control the strategic region between the Rhodope mountains, the Maritsa river and Constantinople. The obvious targets after Adrianople were the cities of Philippopolis (modern Plovdiv), Serdica (modern Sofia) and Naissus (modern Niš), as Murad would have wanted control of the two main road networks giving access to the northern Balkans.

The first route ran northwards from Adrianople (Edirne) and along the valley of the Maritsa, to Philippopolis, then north through the so-called 'gates of Trajan'; it then proceeded to Serdica, over the mountains to Naissus, and then followed the valley of the Morava north to Viminacium and Singidunum (modern Belgrade). The alternative route travelled north from Thessaloniki, through the Rhodope range along the Axios (Vardar) valley, then via Stoboi (Stobi) up to Naissus, and north to Viminacium and Singidunum.

The Ottoman conquest of Adrianople prompted the first of many Christian efforts at united action against the Ottomans: the formation of an allied Serbo-Hungarian army, which in 1364 marched to the River Maritsa in the hope of inflicting a decisive defeat on the Ottomans before it was too late. But Murad ambushed their camp near Edirne in a battle known in Turkish history as the 'Rout of the Serbs'. Then, following a papal bull calling for a crusade issued in December 1366, a Byzantine ally, Count Amadeus VI of Savoy (reigned 1343–83), also decided to lead a Savoyard crusade, even managing to capture several Bulgarian maritime cities, though he failed to take the important port of Varna. By this time, however, the Ottomans were too well entrenched in the Balkans to be dislodged.

The next phase of Murad's expansion in the Balkans followed the strategy – well established since the time of Osman and the Seljuks – of dividing the frontier areas into three principalities, each commanded by an *üç bey*: the left, the right and the centre. The right flank aimed at conquering the Bulgarian Black Sea coast, thus cutting off Constantinople from the rest of Europe by land. However, the Bulgarians were unable to put together any resistance following the death of Tsar Ivan Alexander (reigned 1331–71) in 1371, because of disputes about succession among his sons.

The left flank targeted Macedonia and the ports in the Aegean Sea, and crucial for the Ottoman expansion in the Balkans was the Battle of Maritsa, near the village of Chernomen (modern Ormenio) on 26 September 1371. In this battle the Ottoman forces clashed with the armies gathered by the Serbian King Vukašin Mrnjavčević and his brother, despot Jovan Uglješa, ruler of the Aegean coast of Macedonia in Serres. Wishing to exact revenge for the defeat of 1364, the Serbs nevertheless suffered a devastating defeat, with Uglješa and Vukašin perishing in the carnage.

The outcome of the Battle of Maritsa resulted in Macedonia and parts of Greece falling under the Ottomans, while many of the local Serbian lords in Kosovo, Zeta (modern Montenegro) and Macedonia were forced to become their vassals (1371–75). Murad also invaded Bulgaria, taking Sofia and forcing the Tsar in Tarnovo, Ivan Shishman (reigned 1371–95), to become an Ottoman vassal in 1376.

The middle flank targeted the lands of Prince Lazar of Serbia, and the Ottomans initially suffered a setback, first at the Battle of Dubravnica (1380 or 1381) in central Serbia, where Lazar's forces emerged victorious, while a second Serbian victory over the Ottomans followed five years later at the Battle of Pločnik (1385 or 1386). But undeterred by these setbacks, Murad personally led a sizeable army into Prince Lazar's territory, capturing Niš in 1386 and forcing the Serbian prince to accept Ottoman suzerainty and pay tribute.

However, since the encounter at Pločnik in 1386, it was becoming more and more apparent to Prince Lazar that a decisive battle with the Ottomans was imminent. Hence he sought to make peace with Sigismund of Hungary, to secure his northern borders, while he also agreed on military support from Vuk Branković, the ruler of modern south-western Serbia, and the first King of Bosnia, Tvrtko (reigned 1377–91). But the outcome of the Battle of Kosovo on 15 June 1389 demolished the last organized resistance south of the Danube, thus opening Serbia to Ottoman conquest, and it left Hungary as the sole defender of Christian Europe against the Ottoman tide.

The appearance of Turkoman raiders at Hungary's southern borders was a crude awakening call to the King of Hungary and the elector of Luxemburg, Sigismund (reigned 1387–1437), concerning the grave danger that the Ottomans posed to his kingdom. He set out to form an anti-Ottoman coalition, and by early 1393 he was in secret negotiations with the ruler of the Tsardom of Vidin, a semi-independent Bulgarian principality between Niš and the Danube ruled by Ivan Sratsimir, a half-brother of the Tarnovo Tsar Ivan Shishman.

Sratsimir remained inactive while Bayezid's campaign of 1393 devastated Tarnovo Bulgaria and reduced the principality of his half-brother Shishman to Nicopolis and some small towns along the Danube; Bayezid claimed that this was a punitive expedition for Shishman's secret negotiations with Sigismund in 1393. Eventually, on 3 June 1395, Bayezid returned to Bulgaria to claim Nicopolis and execute Shishman.

Sigismund was also in negotiations with another powerful Christian lord of the region, Mircea I of Wallachia (ruled 1386–95). Following the Ottoman victory at Kosovo in 1389, Mircea was actively involved in supporting his Bulgarian neighbours, hoping to sustain them as buffer zones for his own principality on the north side of the Danube. But his actions attracted the hostility of Bayezid, who in 1394 crossed the Danube at the head of 40,000 men in an attempt to defeat Mircea in battle. The latter, however, withdrew his forces into the Wallachian mountains, and chose rather to use guerrilla warfare to fight the Ottomans.

The two armies finally clashed on 17 May 1395 in the Battle of Rovine, where Mircea won a prestigious victory. However, although this outcome saved Wallachia from Ottoman conquest, Mircea was nevertheless forced to accept Bayezid as an overlord to avoid further Ottoman intervention.

Before his Wallachian campaign, Bayezid was also conducting diplomatic manoeuvres in order to strengthen his position in the newly conquered territories in the southern Balkans. In 1394 he summoned a meeting of all his Balkan vassals in Serres, in eastern Macedonia, where he decided to place Prince Lazar's son Stephen Lazarevic as the vassal leader of the Serbs, with the latter faithfully maintaining his loyalty to Bayezid to the end of his days.

However, Bayezid's relations with the Byzantine Emperor Manuel II Palaeologus (reigned 1391–1425) were much more complicated, owing to the decades-old involvement of the Ottoman rulers in the empire's succession disputes. Manuel had been living in the Ottoman Court in Bursa as an honorary hostage, but after his father's death in 1391, he escaped back to Constantinople to impose his authority. In 1394, Bayezid established a blockade of Constantinople, which lasted until 1402, bringing much suffering and starvation to the people of the city.

Meanwhile in western Europe, Pope Boniface IX (papacy, 1389–1404) proclaimed a new crusade against the Ottomans in 1394. Then in March 1395, Richard II of England (reigned 1377–99) reached an agreement with Charles VI (reigned 1380–1422) to marry his daughter Isabella in the interests of peace between the two kingdoms, which were gripped by the evils of the Hundred Years' War.

The peace with the King of England allowed for the French aristocracy to respond enthusiastically to the call to defend Christianity from the infidels: Philip of Artois, Count of Eu, Jean Le Maingre, the Marshal of France, John of Gaunt and Louis of Orleans, all declared their intention to participate in the crusade. Finally, Philip II of Burgundy (ruled 1363–1404) sent his son and heir, John (to be known as 'the Fearless'), to take part in the crusade because of his eagerness to increase his and his house's prestige. The Venetian Senate also agreed to join the crusade by dispatching warships, while the Order of the Hospital of Saint John was also keen to join because of the Ottoman threat to their garrisons at Rhodes and Smyrna (modern Izmir) in the southern Aegean Sea.

At this point, however, I should pause and quote a key passage from one of the greatest crusades historians, concerning the evolution of the crusades movement in the Late Middle Ages:

> [...] the crusade leagues which became such a feature of the movement after 1332 should be treated as mutations, rather than as true crusades. In them, crusading was adapted to the needs of emerging states. They never claimed to represent the whole of Christendom, but were defensive alliances between certain front-line powers, the forces of which were granted crusade privileges.[1]

THE CAMPAIGN TO NICOPOLIS

We will never know with certainty the actual plans for the Crusade of Nicopolis in 1396, but historians have surmised that Edirne would have been the most likely target for the Crusader League in 1396. The Christian leaders would probably have envisaged an invasion of Bulgaria following the course of the Danube through Belgrade, since a campaign could have been easily sustained by naval convoys down the river – hence the need to take the strategic port town and crossing point of Nicopolis. Thereafter they would march the remaining 350km (220 miles) south to Edirne, possibly counting on the support of the local Christian Bulgarian lords.

The departure point for the crusade was fixed at the Burgundian city of Dijon, some 2,100km (1,305 miles) from Nicopolis, and the different contingents had planned to depart on 30 April 1396. Although it had been agreed that Philip II of Burgundy would be the official leader of the crusade, accompanied by John of Gaunt, 1st Duke of Lancaster (ruled 1340–99) and Louis I of Orléans (ruled 1392–1407), all three eventually withdrew from the Crusade. Most likely, their political ambitions for the throne of France, for which all three were rivals, necessitated their stay in France. However, Burgundy retained control of the enterprise under the young John, Count of Nevers, the Duke of Burgundy's eldest son, who summoned Enguerrand VII, Lord of Coucy, the most experienced warrior of the French realm, as chief military counsellor.

After setting forth from Dijon around 30 April, the Franco-Burgundian armies headed across Bavaria towards Strasburg, wishing to reach the upper Danube, from where they had plans to join Sigismund of Hungary in Buda. Other German contingents from Bavaria, Meissen, Thuringia, Alsace, Swabia, Luxemburg and Saxony also travelled south to Buda.[2] Most of the contingents had reached Vienna between 21 and 24 May. A fleet of seventy Venetian ships was also dispatched down the Danube from Vienna to Buda, followed by the main Crusader army, which finally arrived in Sigismund's capital in July.

Leaving Buda in the mid-summer of 1396, the Crusaders had no intelligence about Bayezid's whereabouts; allegedly, the Ottoman ruler had proclaimed that he would attack Hungary by May, yet he was nowhere to be found by the end of July. The Crusaders began to march down the left bank of the Danube, while part of the Hungarian army diverged north to gather the forces of Wallachia under Mircea, and to expel a pro-Ottoman rival of his, Vlad. They then crossed over to the right bank of the Danube at the Iron Gates gorge (modern Orşova), and carried on south towards Vidin, the capital of the former Bulgarian principality, a march accompanied by excessive pillaging and burning. At Vidin, the former Tsar Ivan Sratsimir, although an Ottoman vassal, threw open the gates of the city in September, resulting in the massacre of the Ottoman garrison.

The next target was Oryahovo (modern Rachowa), a strong fortress located 80km (50 miles) east from Vidin, on the borders between the former Bulgarian principalities of Vidin and Tarnovo. After extensive negotiations between the Bulgarian and Turkish inhabitants and the leaders of the Crusade, the former agreed to surrender their city if

Map of the Crusade of Nicopolis in the summer of 1396 – the march of the Crusaders from Budapest to Nicopolis.

their lives were spared. Sadly, the French contingents broke the agreement, and once the gates were thrown open in early September, they massacred the population and ransacked the city.

This event can be seen as the first sign of strain in the relations between the different Christian contingents that were marching across Europe against the Ottomans.[3] On 12 September, the Crusaders came within view of the fortress of Nicopolis and set up their plans to besiege the city.

Bayezid was besieging Constantinople at the time, but the Ottoman governor of Nicopolis, Doğan Bey, was certain that his master would come to the aid of the town, and was prepared to endure a long siege. Thus immediately after learning of the Crusader departure from Buda, Bayezid sent a unit of light cavalry under Evrenos Bey to scout on enemy movements through the Balkans. He also instructed his field forces in the region not to attack the Crusaders, but rather to concentrate between Edirne and Philippopolis.[4] Nevertheless, the Crusaders were determined that the siege of Nicopolis would be the prelude to a major thrust against Edirne – and possibly Constantinople? – and did not believe that Bayezid would offer them a battle.[5] They were in for a surprise!

THE PRELUDE TO THE BATTLE

The main Ottoman army headed from Edirne towards Tarnovo, while the Serbian vassals of Bayezid under Lazarevic set out from Philippopolis; both armies joined forces at Tarnovo on 22 September, when they were finally spotted by the Hungarian reconnaissance squadrons. On 24 September, Bayezid established his camp on one of the hills that surround the city of Nicopolis to the south of the city, in order to survey the scene and plan his course of action.

The Crusaders, on the other hand, were caught between a rock and a hard place, as they were trapped between an enemy army and an enemy garrison, with no well fortified camp or base to fall back to, and with the Danube blocking any retreat to friendly Wallachia. No doubt their desperate strategic situation affected their decision, in a war council on the 24th, to take the offensive against the Ottomans. Bayezid, on the other hand, would have been content to blockade the Christian camp until the Crusaders ran out of supplies.

THE OPPOSING FORCES

The number of combatants at the Battle of Nicopolis is widely contested by modern historians. Johann Schiltberger was a German follower of a Bavarian noble and was an eye-witness of the battle; he was captured for thirty years by the Ottomans, but when he returned home he wrote a narrative of the battle, in which he estimated the crusader strength at 17,000, although he overestimated the troops under Bayezid at around 200,000.[6] Şükrullah (1388–1488), a fifteenth-century Ottoman historian and diplomat who wrote a famous universal history in the 1460s titled *Behçetu't-Tevârih*, reported the

Crusader army as being some 130,000 strong, and the Ottomans at around 60,000 – though both numbers were absurdly high.[7]

According to moderate estimates, the Crusaders probably totalled some 16,000 men, bearing in mind that it took them just eight days to cross the Danube at the Iron Gates, while the Ottoman troops would have numbered around 10,000, supplemented by another 5,000 allied/vassal troops such as the Serbians.[8]

Arms and Armour

The Ottoman Army

The *Sipahis* were the Ottoman equivalent of the European knights, and their potency as warriors lay in their mobility and their fighting, not only with the mace and the sword, but also with the composite bow. The main components of *Sipahi* armour were the *char-aina*, the *zirh* and the *shishak*.

The *char-aina* was the typical body armour widely used between the fifteenth and eighteenth centuries in Anatolia, Persia, India and eastern Russia, although its origin is certainly earlier and probably Mongolian, going back at least until the thirteenth century.[9] Its name is Persian (*chahār-āyneh*), and it translates as 'four mirrors', which is a reflection of how these pieces would have looked. It consisted of a large round or rectangular plate that would have been worn over the chest and back, flanked by several rectangular or triangular pieces, with the whole set piece hanging from the shoulders on straps. But because these plates were not very big, they were worn over a coat of mail, itself worn over a quilted *kaftan*.

The *Sipahi's* protection would have been complemented by the *shishak*, a pointed conical helmet with cheekpieces, a mail aventail, and a fixed peak with an adjustable nasal guard secured by a staple and spring catch or wing. Another version was the 'turban' *shishak* without cheekpieces, aventail or nose guard, but with a turban wrapped around it. The *Sipahi* would also have carried a circular or convex shield of gilded copper or the pointed 'Hungarian'-type shield, strapped over his left shoulder.

For weapons, the *Sipahi* carried a short lance, a light curved sabre between 70 and 100cm long (the *kilij* or *sajf*), a composite bow with a quiver, and a mace, the latter being particularly liked by the Turks as the Christian sources frequently confirm.[10]

The Allied Army

The Franco-Burgundian, Hungarian and German knights who would have fought at Nicopolis would not have differed much from each other in terms of arms and armour. The second half of the fourteenth century was a transitional period for European armour design, from the coat of mail that was largely abandoned by the middle of the century, to the introduction of plate armour and the plate *cuirass*. The change started in the second half of the thirteenth century, when plate armour was made from large pieces of iron plate, both independent breast- and back-plate, and plates to cover the joints, held together by leather straps, and by the end of the fourteenth century it had evolved to cover most parts of the body as a solid plate *cuirass*.

A knight's armour would also have included a *basinet* with a full-face visor, or a *chapel de fer*, worn over a chain-mail aventail. The style of the shield would have varied somewhat, from the western European circular or convex-shaped shield, to the Hungarian style used both in Hungary and parts of Germany (but mainly after the 1450s), which was rectangular at the bottom, but the upper edge swept upwards forming a curve; the elongated upper edge was designed to protect the head and neck against sabre cuts.[11]

The main weapons of the knights and men-at-arms were the sword and the lance, though others, such as the mace, might have been used. Swords remained largely unchanged until the 1350s, after which they were designed to be shorter and used for thrusting rather than slashing, largely as a response to the introduction of plate armour. Other side-arms in use by the knights in this period would have included a dagger, which had a two-edged symmetrical blade, and/or a battle-knife with an asymmetric one-edged blade.

THE BATTLE

The Battle of Nicopolis was fought on 25 September, in an open field not far from the city. Although the precise location of the battlefield is fiercely debated, we will not be far from the truth if we imagine the opposing armies clashing in the area between Nicopolis (modern Nikopol) and the modern villages of Byala Voda (18km/11 miles south-east of Nikopol) and Debovo (15km/9 miles south of Nikopol). Beyazid's camp would have been on higher ground to the south-east of the city, and he would also have used the topography and natural features of the land to bolster his position, including the woods to his left and the broken ground on his right.[12]

Following a heated discussion during the war council on the previous evening (24 September), the Crusade leaders agreed on the disposition of the troops and the leadership of the diverse units of the Crusader army that would be deployed against the Ottomans the following morning. It was decided that the centre of the army would be arrayed in two divisions, one behind the other, with the Franco-Burgundians taking up their position at the front under Philip of Artois. Behind Philip's division, and along a broader front, would come the rest of the European knights – Hungarians, Germans, Hospitallers, Bohemians and Poles, under the command of Sigismund. The two flanks of the Crusader army would be protected by the Transylvanians on the right and the Wallachians on the left, while a rearguard under Nicholas II Garai, one of the most powerful Hungarian nobles, would guard the army's access to their camp; it would also offer protection from any attack from the garrison of Nicopolis.

The Ottoman army would have been deployed in their usual fashion, with the foot-archers placed in the front ranks, ahead of the heavy infantry of the Janissaries and the rest of the foot-soldiers.[13] They would have been followed by the heavy *sipahi* cavalry, which would – usually – follow up an initial attack by attacking in three main divisions;

the wings would be formed in smaller units and be projected slightly forward, which often gave the impression of a crescent formation. Because the battle was taking place on European soil, the Rumelia (European) cavalry was placed on the right – obviously to deliver the knock-out blow – while the Anatolian cavalry was on the left. In front of the whole formation Bayezid would have placed wooden stakes to guard against a frontal knightly attack, and he also deployed the irregular lightly armed *akıncı* horsemen in front of the stakes to harass the enemy and frustrate their attack.

Crucially, Bayezid placed his Serbian vassals under Lazarevic on the extreme left of the formation, while he and his household troops would have been deployed in between the main army and the camp, some distance to the rear. Nicolle felt confident in writing that Bayezid's household unit and the Serbs would have been obscured by the shape of the hill, on top of which the Ottoman ruler had placed his camp.[14]

The battle opened on the morning of the 25th, with the Franco-Burgundian knights, accompanied by their mounted archers, riding ahead to meet the Turks. The Hospitallers, Germans and other allies stayed with the Hungarian forces under Sigismund in the second division. Sigismund had ordered his allied leaders to avoid rushing against the

The Battle of Nicopolis, 25 September 1396.

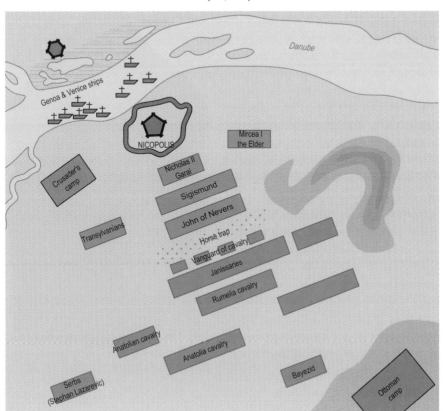

enemy, thus abandoning their defensive position on the field, but, in what has been a disputed sequence of events, Philip of Artois ignored the advice of his most senior and experienced councillors and attacked the *akıncı* horsemen in the vanguard of the Ottoman army. The Franco-Burgundian charge brushed aside the irregular horsemen in the Ottoman front line, who anyway would not have been either trained or equipped to offer much resistance to these heavy cavalry units.

Thereafter they advanced (whether on horseback or on foot is still debated) into the lines of the heavy Ottoman infantry, though the knights came under heavy fire from archers, and were hampered by the sharpened stakes designed to skewer the stomachs of their horses. But instead of rushing to support Artois' attack, the more experienced de Coucy insisted on waiting for the orderly advance of Sigismund's division.

At that crucial point of the battle it would have seemed more reasonable for the Franco-Burgundians to have halted their advance and to have waited for the main division of the Crusader army to catch up, because there was a serious risk of them being cut off and surrounded. But Artois and Jean II Le Maingre (called 'Boucicault', 1366–1421), both young and impetuous knights, pressed on with the attack, and within a short period of time, managed to break through the stakes and get amongst the infantry units of the Janissaries and the rest of the – relatively unarmoured – foot-soldiers. The Crusader attack was so fierce that even the heavy *sipahi* cavalry on the third line was involved in the fighting, probably plugging the gap that had opened on the infantry line ahead of them.

By now, the Franco-Burgundians had exhausted the impetus of their cavalry charge, while some of them were fighting on foot having lost their horses, and they were in real danger of being surrounded. It may seem reasonable to assume that Artois and Le Maingre would not have expected to find a third line of enemy units waiting behind the wooden stakes and the infantry immediately behind them; they would, rather, have looked forward to pillaging the Ottoman camp. Instead they were met by the sharp sword tips of the Ottoman *sipahis*, who very soon attacked them on their left and right flanks.

As the *sipahis* surged forwards sounding trumpets, banging kettle drums and yelling 'Allāhu akbar' ('God is great!'), the desperate situation of the Franco-Burgundians was

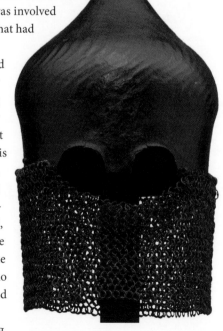

Ottoman turban helmet, fourteenth to fifteenth century, fitted with an aventail of riveted links suspended from a rod through seven iron vervelles.
SOTHEBYS

readily apparent, and some knights broke and fled back down the slope and towards their camp. The rest fought on and engaged the Ottomans in a desperate *mêlée* and with a ferocity that has been described by a contemporary chronicle as 'no frothing boar nor enraged wolf [fought] more fiercely'.[15] These remaining Latin knights held on, forcing the *sipahis* to withdraw back to the flanks.

Modern historians have been frustrated by the hazy sequence of events as described by both Latin and Ottoman contemporary and later sources; thus, at what stage of the battle did the Hungarians join the battle? Are we talking about two 'separate' battles, in which the Crusaders were defeated in a piece-meal fashion? Or did the battles overlap? The main division of the Crusader army under Sigismund seems to have moved forwards to support the reckless advance of the Franco-Burgundians, perhaps before the latter were attacked on the flanks by the *sipahis*.

At this stage of the battle, and while watching the stampede and massacre taking place between the Franco-Burgundians and the Ottomans, Tuchman has concluded that the Wallachians and Transylvanians thought that the day was lost and fled back to Nicopolis and the crossing point of the Danube.[16] They both must have felt that Bayezid was close to victory, hence they rushed to protect their territories from the threat of Ottoman retaliation and/or invasion.

Some accounts tell of the Hungarians and other nationalities in the main Latin division as being in confused combat on the plain, probably against the re-grouped Ottoman infantry, and of 'unspeakable massacre' on both sides. But the Hungarians pressed on, and then clashed with the Ottoman divisions of the *sipahi* cavalry, who would have moved forwards with their infantry down the hill slope. At this stage, Bayezid used his trump card of the Serbian cavalry under Lazarevic, which may have been concealed in a wooden area to the west of the battlefield, and he ordered them to attack Sigismund's division.

Lazarevic's intervention was decisive. The Serbian attack managed to bring down the Hungarian royal banner, and Sigismund's forces were quickly overwhelmed. While the Hungarian king and the Grand Master of the Hospitallers made their escape to a fisherman's boat on the Danube, and then boarded a Venetian ship anchored in the river, a deal was struck according to which the Crusader army surrendered, completing their defeat in detail.

CONCLUSIONS

> For thoughtful men life is not worth living after that thunderbolt, that deluge, which, although not engulfing the whole world, was worse than the first one [the biblical flood] in that it bore away men nobler than those of that time.

> *(Manuel II's letter to his teacher, Cydones, in 1396.)*

The disastrous outcome of the Crusade of Nicopolis in 1396 was a huge blow to the Byzantine Emperor Manuel's foreign policy against the Ottomans, as Bayezid soon

Left: Saint Theodore of Tiron, Mount Athos, Greece,
by Manuel Panselinos, c. 1300.

Above: Saint Theodore of Tiron's famous mirrored
clivanion (Κλιβάνιον) reconstructed by Dimitris
Katsikis, Greece.

resumed the siege of Constantinople, and Anadolu Hisari (the Anatolian fort) was built on the Bosporus to control Byzantine access to the Black Sea. But the siege was pushed only half-heartedly, probably because of the concerns of Bayezid's advisers not to provoke another European Crusade.

Then in 1397, an Ottoman army invaded southern Greece and the Peloponnesus, meeting with virtually no opposition and capturing Athens and Argos. Manuel sought aid and promises of money and armies in the royal Courts of western European rulers, but the only outcome of his European 'tour of charm' produced little results for the beleaguered empire: in 1399, Charles VI of France sent Jean Le Maingre with six ships carrying 1,200 men to Constantinople.

Finally, the miracle that the Byzantines had been anxiously waiting for came from the East rather than the West. Tamerlane (ruled 1370–1405), the Mongol chieftain whose armies had swept from Samarkand into Afghanistan and India, north into Russia, and west into Georgia, Armenia and Asia Minor, had crushed the independent Turcoman emirates not yet incorporated into Bayezid's empire, and then in 1400, they invaded Ottoman territory. Tamerlane's invasion of Anatolia culminated in the Battle of Ankara on 28 July 1402, which was a complete victory for the Mongols. Following Tamerlane's victory, civil warfare soon broke out among the sons of Bayezid, and this further aided the Byzantine recovery in Anatolia.

For the rest of the European participants in the Crusade of Nicopolis, the ramifications of the Christian defeat were wider and more complicated. For Mircea I of Wallachia, this was a period during which he had to defend his throne from Ottoman involvement; while Bayezid tried to install his rival, Vlad, into the Wallachian throne in 1397, Mircea prevailed with the help of a mixed Hungarian and Transylvanian army. But it would be in the aftermath of Ankara, in 1402, that Mircea would expand his authority in the strategic Dobruja region in the Danube Delta.

The disaster at Nicopolis is also considered by many modern historians as the end of the hopes for the revival of the Bulgarian Empire, as the last Tsar of Bulgaria, Ivan Sratsimir, was exiled in Bursa and strangled.

Political instability also rocked the kingdom of Hungary: Sigismund soon lost popularity among the Hungarian nobility, and a rival claimant to the crown was called in to replace him – Ladislaus of Anjou-Durazzo. Finally, for the Moravian Serbians and their leader, Stefan Lazarević, the opportunity to discard Ottoman suzerainty would come after Ankara in 1402, a period during which they would survive and slightly expand as the despotate of Serbia until 1459.

But perhaps the most crucial consequence of the disaster of Nicopolis was on the morale of European leaders and the public in general. For a long time following the Ottoman victory in 1396 there were to be few more 'saints in Paradise', to use the words by Jean Le Maingre's biographer. Bayezid's most important strategic achievement that early autumn day, was that it discouraged the formation of another European coalition (Crusader League) against them for another half a century, thus providing the Ottoman leadership with the time it needed to recover from the setback of the Mongol invasion.

The Battle of Nicopolis, as depicted by Turkish miniaturist Nakkaş Osman in the Hünername (1584–88).

18 THE FIRST BATTLE OF TANNENBERG

The Mortal Blow to the Teutonic Order

Also known as the Battle of Grunwald, and the Battle of Žalgiris.

Date 15 July 1410
Location Between the villages of Grunwald (Grünfelde) and Stębark (Tannenberg), Poland

THE HISTORICAL BACKGROUND

The Battle of Tannenberg involved the clash of three armies: those of the kingdom of Poland, the Grand Duchy of Lithuania, and the Prussian state of the Teutonic Order. Since the second quarter of the thirteenth century, the Teutonic Order had turned into one of the key political players in central and north-eastern Europe, harvesting great ambitions in a region where the expansion of Catholic Christendom had been blessed by the papacy a century before. By the middle of the thirteenth century, the Knights directly controlled a great stretch of the Baltic coast from the River Vistula to Königsberg, while Livonia became an autonomous province of the Order under the patronage of the Bishop of Riga.

The main characteristic of the Prussian Crusade (1217–74) was the brutal behaviour of the combatants, during which any native Prussian (whether noble or peasant) who resisted baptism was killed or exiled, thus paving the way for the gradual assimilation (or 'Germanization') of the Old Prussian population. This was a policy of colonization, rather than crusading for the love of God!

After Prussia, the Order's expansionist policies turned west, to the Polish corridor of Danzig (Gdansk), which would have allowed the Knights to unite their territories with Germany. The Order was then embroiled in a succession dispute between the Grand Duke of Poland Władysław I and the Margrave of neighbouring Brandenburg over the Duchy of Pomerelia. In 1308, the Margrave occupied the region, while the Grand Duke asked the Teutonic Knights for assistance. The Knights evicted the Brandenburgers and captured the prized city of Danzig – but instead of ceding the city and the region to the Poles, they annexed it!

Then in 1309, the Order moved its headquarters from Venice to the relative safety of

Marienburg (Malbork), a move seen as a reaction to the persecution and abolition of the Knights Templar in 1307. In the same year they also purchased Brandenburg's supposed claim to the duchy. War between the Order and the Poles only ended with the Treaty of Kalisz in 1343.

To gain reconciliation with Pope Clement V (1305–14) on the issue of the conflict with Poland, and allegedly 'waging war on such people against Christ, and with various cunning ruses', the Order's attention turned to the Lithuanians, flaring up into a 100-year war that was conducted with great ferocity on both sides. The Order's enemies were now, conveniently, committed pagans, turning the fighting into a bloody business that included massacres and excessive looting.

It was during the leadership of Grand Master Winrich von Kniprode (1351–82) that the Order reached the peak of its international prestige, hosting numerous international knights for seasonal campaigns in a form of 'crusader tourism', with many renowned warriors of the period such as King John of Bohemia and Marshal Boucicault of France going to fight alongside the Teutonic Knights in Lithuania. However, as the fortunes of the crusades movement against the Ottoman Turks dwindled, following the decisive defeat of the crusading army at the battle of Nicopolis in 1396, more and more Western knights would view the Baltic as an outlet for their religious enthusiasm.

The Influence of the Lithuanians

But who were the Lithuanians?[1] They belonged to the Balts, in the same language group as the Prussians and Letts. Their society mainly consisted of a peasant lower class, dominated by a mounted warrior class that owned the land ('boyars'); they inhabited a region in the densely forested basins of the rivers Niemen, Neris and Viliya, east of Prussia. Warfare in this region was led by the hereditary prince or kinglet of one of the nine main regions of ancient Lithuania, and groups of aristocratic retinues would go out raiding every spring, and return with cattle, slaves, silver and weapons, preparing for the anticipated retaliation the following spring.

Geographically, Lithuania was surrounded by the Teutonic Knights and Novgorod to the north, and the Catholic princes of Mazovia, Little Poland and Volhynia to the south. As was the case for the Novgorodians in the 1230s, this was a crisis period for Lithuania, which called for heroic leaders to arise from among its people.

The *Livonian Rhymed Chronicle* recorded that Mindaugas, the duke of southern Lithuania, had acquired supreme power in the whole of the country by the mid-1230s. Civil strife within his kingdom forced Mindaugas to be baptised in return for military assistance from the Teutonic Knights in 1251, although soon after he converted back to paganism.

The Grand Duchy of Lithuania became the largest state in Europe in the following century, reaching its height under Grand Duke Gediminas (reigned 1316–41), who intro-duced a strong centralized government and established an empire that spread from the Black Sea to the Baltic Sea. In 1321 Gediminas even captured Kiev, while throughout the fourteenth century, Novgorod became an occasional dependency of the Grand Duchy. In 1380, a combined Lithuanian and Russian force defeated the Mongols of the Golden Horde at the Battle of Kulikovo, after which the Mongol influence in the region declined.

Lithuania became a Christian state with the baptism of Jogaila, Grand Duke of Lithuania between 1377 and 1434 (later Władysław II Jagiełło, King of Poland between 1386 and 1434). This was a political decision with massively important ramifications for the geo-political future of eastern Europe and the Baltic region. It involved the union with another kingdom, Poland, in 1386, when Jogaila married Jadwiga, the under-age Hungarian-born heiress to the Polish crown. It might have seemed obvious that the Lithuanian conversion to Christianity and its union with another Catholic country would have forced the Teutonic Knights to cease their expansion (or 'crusade') into their territory, but Jogaila's baptism failed to that end, as the Teutonic Knights claimed that his conversion was a political trick.

The Brothers were actively involved in the Lithuanian civil strife between Jogaila and his cousin Vytautas, who had emerged as a contender to the Lithuanian throne, a war that lasted between 1389 and 1392. They took the side of Vytautas, even besieging Vilnius in the autumn of 1390. Jogaila and the Teutonic Knights signed the *Treaty of Salynas* on 12 October 1398, by which Samogitia (north-western Lithuania and the 'Baltic corridor' from Teutonic Prussia to Teutonic Livonia) was ceded to the Order, while the Knights agreed to assist Lithuania in a campaign to seize Novgorod.

But another war broke out soon after, in 1401, when another of Jogaila's brothers stirred up a revolt and declared himself Duke, though not without requesting the military assistance of the Order, in January 1402. The war was brought to an end in May 1404, when Jogaila reconfirmed the handover of Samogitia to the Teutonic Knights.

The issue of Samogitia was to prove so delicate that it would come back to haunt both parties in the years to come. An uprising by the Samogitians in May 1409 was 'highjacked' by Jogaila, who, perhaps wishing to draw the Order's attention away from Pomeralia, threatened the Knights that if they supressed the Samogitian rebellion he would intervene militarily to protect the native populations. The Order responded by declaring war on Poland on 6 August 1409. A series of indecisive campaigns led to the signing of an armistice on 8 October, which was due to last until St John's Day, 24 June 1410.

THE PRELUDE TO THE BATTLE

In the months of truce that followed, both parties prepared for the inevitable showdown that would reach its climax at the Battle of Tannenberg. The Order forged a network of alliances stretching from Livonia in the north to Hungary in the south. Lithuania, on the other hand, was backed by Novgorod and Pskov, with Moldavia also promising to send troops. By December 1409, Jogaila (Władysław II Jagiełło) and Vytautas, recognized as the Grand Prince of Lithuania following the reconciliation of 1401, agreed on a common strategy: both the Polish and Lithuanian armies would merge into a single force and march against the capital of the Teutonic Knights, Marienburg.

The two countries had different strategic objectives: the Lithuanians wished to recover Samogitia, while the Poles wanted the return of Pomeralia, which the Knights had annexed a hundred years earlier. They were both led, however, by their overwhelming desire to crush the Order. They would launch their invasion in June 1410.

Even in modern times, any military campaign involving multi-ethnic forces require high levels of planning, coordination and precision between the different units taking part – hence the first major challenge for the united Lithuanian-Polish army would have been the gathering point at a strategic location close to the Prussian border. This designated meeting point was set at Czerwinsk, about 80km (50 miles) south of the Prussian border, where the joint army would be able to cross the Vistula. All units managed to overcome this first major obstacle in a week, from 24 to 30 June 1410. The combined armies of Poland and Lithuania then began their advance northwards towards Marienburg on 3 July, crossing the ill-defined Prussian border and assaulting Lautenburg (Lidzbark) on 9 June.

The Grand Master Ulrich von Jungingen (served 1407–10) had concentrated his forces in Schwetz (Świecie), in the heartland of Prussia from where troops could respond to an invasion from any direction. When intelligence alerted him to the allied invasion plans and their perceived course of invasion, the Master left 3,000 men at Schwetz (Świecie) and rushed to organize a line of defence on the River Drewenz (Drwęca), near Kauernik (Kurzętnik).[2] That was the last natural line of defence, and it not only had a strong castle that commanded the heights above the river, but it was further reinforced with stockades.

On 11 July, after an allied council of war, it was decided that the Polish-Lithuanian army would simply bypass the Drewenz towards its headwaters further to the north-east; no major rivers would then stand between it and Marienburg. Having left Kurzetnik, the Polish-Lithuanian army marched east towards the small village of Wysoka, where the Grand Master had reinforced the garrison of the nearby castle of Soldau (Dzialdowo). Meanwhile the Teutonic army crossed the River Drewenz near Löbau (Lubawa), and then moved east in parallel with the Polish-Lithuanian army. The latter were marching in a north-easterly direction, and on 13 July ravaged the town of Gilgenburg and stormed its castle.

On 14 July the allied army spent the night near Dabrowno, while early in the morning of the following day (the 15th) they moved off through mist and fog towards the village of Faulen (Ulnowo). Scouts had reported that the Teutonic camp was pitched some 2 miles to their north, between the villages of Grunwald, Tannenberg (Stębark) and Ludwigsdorf (Łodwigowo).

THE OPPOSING FORCES

Calculations as to the total numbers of men who clashed at the Battle of Tannenberg vary greatly, but the commonly accepted figures are 27,000 men for the Teutonic Order against 39,000 who fought for Poland/Lithuania.[3] The styles of armour worn by the

Polish knights and the Teutonic Knights would not have looked markedly different from each other, as they both would have conformed to the style that dominated Central Europe at the beginning of the fifteenth century.

Armour Design

This is a period of transition for the evolution of armour design in Europe, and the armour of a knight in the fourteenth century would have differed dramatically from the armour that his counterpart would have worn a hundred years later, owing to the design and construction of new kinds of weapon. By the middle of the fourteenth century mail armour had been largely superseded by plate armour, which had come to dominate both the tournament and the battlefield, with the exception of those angular parts of the body that were difficult to protect with a solid plate. Coats of plate, usually worn over a mail *hauberk*, were used by the Teutonic Knights at Marienburg in the second half of the fourteenth century until the early 1400s.[4]

This style was the precursor to the full-body plate armour that developed from the practice of joining the plates into bigger and more solid parts, from a *cuirass* consisting of a breast- and back-plate, plate gauntlets for the arms, and greaves for the legs (c. 1330s–c. 1400s), to a 'plate suit' that appeared around the beginning of the fifteenth century. However, Nowakowski has argued that breast- and back-plates (including plate gauntlets and greaves) were more popular among the Teutonic Knights at the beginning of the fifteenth century than full-plate armour, based on the inventories of armours in several of the Order's castles.[5]

A mail *coif* would have covered the back and neck, while a smaller mail skirt – reinforced with metallic scales – would have provided additional protection to the lower torso and the groin.

Arms and Armament

The Polish and Teutonic Knights would have carried a small (around 50 × 70cm) triangular wooden shield with slightly rounded sides, a type that dominated Prussia and Central Europe throughout the fifteenth century.[6] Chivalrous shields known as *pavisses* are also reported for this period in the Prussian, Bohemian and Polish sources; these were larger (even 90cm high), almost rectangular, convex wooden shields covered in leather.

The helmet worn by these knights would not have been the great helm of the thirteenth century that covered the entire head and neck, as this style had proved a failure due to the great discomfort experienced by the knights in battle. Rather, the knights in Central Europe in the fourteenth and early fifteenth centuries preferred the following types of head protection: first was the *kettle hat*, a type of helmet made of steel in the shape of a hat, very similar to British helmets in World War I, and worn by both infantry and cavalry in Prussia and Poland through the fifteenth century. Then there was the so-called 'pig-faced *basinet*', which was also popular in this period, because it featured a removable visor, thus offering superior flexibility, and it had better defensive qualities than the great helm.

The armour of the Lithuanian knights seems to have been very different in appearance. The predominance of mail and lamellar armour over plate shows that the influence was undoubtedly Eastern. The light mail and scale cuirass, combined with a mail *coif* and a Mongolian-style padded overcoat with a heavy fur-lined cloak, displays Russian influence, although the plate gauntlets and greaves would have been imported from Germany or northern Italy. Another Eastern tradition that would remain a Lithuanian/Russian characteristic is their preference for tall and pointed helmets.

In general, the arms that would have been carried by the knights on both sides would have looked more alike compared to the types of armour just examined. German-style swords would have been favoured by the knights on both sides: these would have been straight-bladed and between 65 and 95cm long, with the blades made narrower and with a tapered point to be used as a thrusting rather than a slashing weapon.

Other side-arms in use by the knights in this period would have included a dagger, which had a two-edged symmetrical blade, and/or a battle-knife with an asymmetric one-edged blade. There are also miniatures illustrating the use of lances by the Teutonic Brothers at Tannenberg, but Nowakowski has argued that the drawings are idealized rather than realistic, as heavy lances would have been incompatible with the kind of war that was practised in the Baltic region, and only a small number of them would have been stored in some Teutonic castles.[7]

THE BATTLE

The battlefield in which the armies were deployed covered around 4sq km (1.5sq miles), in a north-east to south-west axis along a depression that ran along the road from Tannenberg to Ludwigsdorf. This was a wet, boggy and heavily forested area, with numerous small ponds and marshes that have long since dried up, undoubtedly making it an inconvenient – to say the least – battlefield for heavy cavalry manoeuvres.

The allied army was positioned in front and to the east of Ludwigsdorf. Although it is impossible to determine the exact way the units were deployed, historians presume that the Polish heavy cavalry would have formed the left flank of the allied army, with the Lithuanian light cavalry being assigned the right flank, while various (primarily Bohemian) mercenary groups linked up the two armies in the centre. Their men would have been arrayed in three lines of wedge-shaped formations, probably about twenty men deep each.

Opposite the allied army were the Teutonic forces, having arranged their units in the same axis along the road, and with their left flank anchored at Tannenberg village. They massed their élite cavalry on the left flank against the Lithuanians, commanded by the Grand Master Ulrich von Jungingen, while other mounted troops in the centre and right screened the Teutonic gunpowder artillery, archers and dismounted light riders behind them. One chronicle reported that the Brothers had dug pits to hamper an enemy mounted attack.[8] Furthermore, the wet conditions would certainly have affected the use of cannons that had been brought from Marienburg, as only two cannon shots were fired during the battle.

The battle was opened by Vytautas, the commander of the Lithuanian cavalry on the right flank of the allied army: observing the movement of units in the Teutonic left flank directly opposite his position, which suggested to him that the Brothers were regrouping for a major attack, he decided to take the initiative and charge. It may also have been a reaction to the firing of gunshots from the Teutonic cannons, which were cleared a field of fire by the mounted knights who had been screening them since the early hours of the morning.

Supported by a few Polish units from the centre, Vytautas launched his attack on the left flank of the Teutonic forces, where they encountered fierce resistance and a hail of crossbow bolts coming from the Brothers. After almost two hours of relentless fighting,

The campaign of Tannenberg in July 1410.

the Lithuanian cavalry began a full retreat back to the relative safety of their lines, thus prompting the Knights to break ranks and pursue them, assuming that victory was theirs and wishing to gather much loot before returning to the battlefield to face the Polish troops.

This event has been interpreted as everything from a panicked Lithuanian rout to a perfectly executed feigned retreat in the finest Mongol/Tartar tradition.[9] Whatever the case, the retreat spread to the mercenary Bohemian units in the centre of the allied army, who also began to fall back, until Vice-Chancellor Mikolaj Traba of Wislicz halted them.

The Lithuanian retreat that prompted the Teutonic counter attack may have worked in favour of the allies, as it was the turn of the Polish cavalry to get involved in the battle against the Prussians – and what better opportunity than to attack them while they had broken ranks and were pursuing their Lithuanian comrades in search of loot. Heavy fighting broke out between the Polish and Teutonic forces, but it seems that six units (banners) of the Teutonic left flank, commanded by Kuno von Lichtenstein, concentrated on the right flank of the Polish army instead of pursuing the retreating Lithuanians. The sources report fierce fighting around the banner of Krakow, and it seems that the standard may have fallen for a while until another standard bearer held it aloft again.

During that crucial stage of the battle, both commanders-in-chief reacted promptly and tried to gain the momentum for their side. From his position on a small hill behind the left wing of his army, Jagiełło ordered the deployment of his reserves – the second line of his army – to support the right flank fighting the Prussians. Ulrich von Jungingen then personally led sixteen units (banners), almost a third of his force, to the right Polish flank and into the ongoing mêlée.

According to Turnbull, the direction of Jungingen's advance is interesting in that he did not launch a frontal assault, but swung to the left past Tannenberg, and then turned south to hit the Poles in their right flank. One explanation is that he may have wanted to collect survivors from the pursuit of the Lithuanian cavalry during the first stage of the battle.[10] Then, Jagiełło's swift reaction was to commit his last reserves, the third line of his army.

By now it was becoming obvious to the Poles that Jungingen's attack was directed against King Jagiełło, as a unit of the attacking Knights forced its way through to the royal banner, and even managed to seriously threaten the king's life. Eventually it would be the return of the reorganized and regrouped Lithuanian cavalry under Grand Duke Vytautas that would save the day for the allied army at Tannenberg. The Grand Duke ordered an attack on Jungingen's rear to relieve the mounting pressure on the Poles.

There is no doubt that the Teutonic Knights would have been outnumbered, and by now were becoming increasingly desperate in fighting both the Polish and the Lithuanian cavalry. We also need to bear in mind that Vytautas' forces would have had time to regroup and catch their breath after hours of fighting at the peak of a midsummer's day, whereas by this time the Prussians would have been exhausted.

At this crucial stage of the battle, Ulrich von Jungingen met his death with a lance thrust through his neck. Surrounded and leaderless, the Teutonic Knights fled towards their camp. This move backfired when the camp followers turned against their masters. The Knights attempted to build a *laager* (an improvised wagon fort), but their desperate attempts proved futile and they were soon overrun. Jagiełło ordered his units to pursue the Knights retreating towards the swampy ground between Tannenberg and Grunwald, but he then withdrew his order once the sun began to set; it was around eight in the evening and the battle had been raging for over ten hours.

Hundreds of Teutonic troops lay dead, and 14,000 prisoners were taken. According to the *Soldbuch*, the payroll book of the Order, only 1,427 men straggled back to Marienburg to claim their pay.[11] Of 1,200 men sent from Danzig, only 300 returned.[12]

Probably because of the losses suffered that day, Jagiełło was in no position to follow up his victory, while Heinrich von Plauen, commanding the Order's forces left in West Prussia, defended shrewdly. The siege of Marienburg began only eleven days later, on 26 July, and was eventually lifted on 19 September, as the allied army was ill prepared for a prolonged siege of such a powerful fortified city. The Knights also appealed to their allies for help, and Sigismund of Hungary, Wenceslaus, King of Bohemia and Germany, and the Livonian Order promised financial aid and reinforcements. But Jagiełło managed to raise a fresh army and dealt another crushing defeat to the Knights in the Battle of Koronowo on 10 October.

The *Peace of Thorn* was signed in February 1411. Under its terms, the Teutonic Order was forced to cede the Dobrzyń land to Poland, and to renounce their claims to Samogitia during the lifetimes of Władysław II Jagiełło and Vytautas. In addition to that, the treaty imposed a heavy financial burden on the Knights from which they would never recover. They had to pay an indemnity in silver, estimated at ten times the annual income of the King of England, to raise, which their recourse was to borrow, confiscate from churches and increase taxes.[13] Two major Prussian cities, Danzig (Gdańsk) and Thorn (Toruń), would soon revolt against these tax rises.

CONCLUSIONS

The outcome of the Battle of Tannenberg would irreversibly reshape the face of Eastern Europe within half a century after the battle, as the victory of the allied Lithuanian-Polish armies dealt a mortal blow to the future of the Teutonic Order. Because of the high number of casualties suffered during the battle, the Order was never again able to take the offensive against any of its neighbours. Combined with the swift Christianization of Samogitia, which, along with Poland and Lithuania, was now firmly within the 'Catholic core' of Europe, it deprived the Order of the crusading appeal it had held until the turn of the fifteenth century, thus making it exceedingly difficult to recruit new volunteers.

As the Order finally lost its *raison d'être*, it came to rely all the more on expensive mercenaries. The costs of these troops, and the indemnities imposed on the Brothers by the Peace of Thorn, bore heavily upon the cities, merchants and knightly settlers in Prussia, with the result that there was mounting resistance against the despotic rule of the Order and its Grand Master.

The Battle of Tannenberg set the seal on the changing balance of power in Eastern Europe in favour of the rising star of Poland-Lithuania. By Jagiełło's death in 1434, both realms were firmly ruled by members of his dynasty, only to be ruled again by a single monarch in 1447, Casimir IV Jagiełło. With the influence of the Jagiełłonian dynasty in Europe growing rapidly during the fifteenth century, in 1471 Casimir's son Władysław became King of Bohemia, and in 1490 also of Hungary.

At the same time, the future of the Teutonic Order dwindled, with citizens from the towns of Danzig, Thorn and Elbing establishing the Prussian Union in 1440 as an alternative government to the Teutonic Order. By the spring of 1454, every Prussian fortress of the Order except Marienburg and Stuhm (Sztum) was in Union hands. And although the leader of the Union had offered Prussia to King Casimir IV in 1454, Prussia was only formally incorporated into the Polish kingdom following the Second Peace of Thorn, signed in 1466, which ended the Thirteen Years' War (1454–66) between the Kingdom of Poland, allied with the Prussian Union, and the Teutonic Order.

As Royal Prussia now became the exclusive property of the Polish Crown, eastern Prussia remained with the Teutonic Order as a Polish fief until 1525, with the Grand Master's seat of power now being transferred to Königsberg.

Engraving of the Battle of Tannenberg by Marcin Bielski, Kronika wszytkiego świata, 1554.

19 THE SIEGE OF ORLÉANS

The Watershed of the Hundred Years' War

Date 12 October 1428–8 May 1429
Location Orléans, the River Loire, north-central France

THE HISTORICAL BACKGROUND

THE FATES OF England and France had been intertwined for centuries because of the tenurial relationship of their rulers, until their ultimate clash in 1337 that severed their bonds in the fourteenth and fifteenth centuries. Enmities between the two crowns reached a climax between 1154 and 1204 when the landholdings of the Angevin kings in France were at their greatest extent, encompassing an astonishing range of territories such as Normandy, Maine, Anjou, Touraine, Poitou and Aquitaine. By the first quarter of the thirteenth century, the rapid expansion of the Capetian realm came largely at the expense of the English, and almost all their territories overseas were lost to the resurgent French. But luck changed when Edward III inherited the throne in 1327, ushering in an era of English expansionism in the Continent.

The Treaty of Paris that was signed between Henry III of England (reigned 1216–72) and Louis IX of France (reigned 1226–70) in October 1259, confirmed the English tenure of Bordeaux, Bayonne and their hinterland known as Gascony, and the promised reversion of the old duchy of Aquitaine. A further complication was introduced when the county of Ponthieu, in the mouth of the Somme, came to the English king in 1279. But the most important aspect of the Treaty was the confirmation of the English kings as vassals of the French Crown, obliging them to pay homage to the French king for their continental lands. This served to increase Anglo-French hostilities, because one sovereign ruler to be the vassal of another flew in the face of political realities.

When the issue of the succession of the French Crown erupted in 1328 after the death of Charles IV (reigned 1322–28) earlier that year, the diplomatic relations between the two countries reached a tipping point. An assembly of aristocrats and lawyers had already decided that no woman was eligible to inherit the throne of France, thus excluding Charles' daughter from posthumously succeeding her father; instead, the assembly designated Philip of Valois as the rightful heir, the deceased king's cousin. But there was a third party, which sent a delegation to Paris to argue against the assembly's decision:

the *Grandes Chroniques de France* tells us that an English delegation did come to Paris to argue that Edward III was the closest relative of Charles, basing their arguments on the fact that Edward's father had married Charles' sister, Isabelle.

Nevertheless, it is difficult to know how seriously Edward III took the matter of the claim to the French throne. In fact, it was not until 1340 at Ghent that the English king openly asserted his claim to the Crown of France, some three years after the outbreak of hostilities. Curry believes that Edward was merely trying to use his hereditary rights to the French throne as a bargaining counter, and 'the promoting of the claim as an apparent war aim arose as a *result* of the outbreak of the Hundred Years' War, not as its *cause*'.[1]

War had already broken out in 1337 in Gascony, as it had several times in the previous century (especially 1294–98), because of struggles to dominate the wine trade that passed through this rich and fertile region of the south of France. It was the revenues from the wine trade that helped balance the losses incurred from the Anglo-Flemish tensions in the Low Countries over the wool trade. Therefore it was royal status, and the status and financial exploitation of dependent territories such as Gascony, that lay at the heart of the struggle that erupted in 1337.

The most fascinating thing about the Hundred Years' War, though, was not its causes but the way in which it was fought. In a nutshell, the English strategy was to harass the French with bands of soldiers some few thousand strong, led by nobles who were relying increasingly on common infantry armed with pikes, spears and the famous longbow. The English performed what is known in Western medieval history as *chevauchée*, using the French term: limited warfare verging on brigandage, which emphasized raiding and looting, usually of livestock.

Whether this strategy intended to avoid battle or not is still open for debate; nevertheless, the fact remains that surprisingly few large-scale pitched battles took place – yet whenever they did, the English usually won.[2] The first major battle took place in 1346 at Crécy, when the French halted the English 'retreat' (or 'searching for the enemy', depending on your point of view) through Flanders. The English archers triumphed!

After Crécy the English forces, led chiefly by the heir to the throne – Edward, known as the Black Prince – returned to their successful strategy of *chevauchée*; in 1355, the so-called *grande chevauchée* cut a ruinous swathe through the richest parts of the French south, from Bordeaux, on the Atlantic coast, to Narbonne on the Mediterranean. In 1356 another large battle took place at Poitiers, with even greater results for the English, who not only defeated the French but captured their king for ransom, thus creating a governmental vacuum in France.

The Treaty of Brétigny, agreed in May 1360, ended the first period of hostilities between the two Crowns, providing Edward with a huge ransom for King John, major territorial concessions, and the renunciation of Valois sovereignty over English lands in France. In return Edward offered to abandon his claim to the French throne.

The war reopened in 1369 after Charles V (reigned 1364–80) summoned Prince Edward to Paris to answer certain charges brought by a coalition of Aquitanian nobles. The Black Prince's illness and Edward III's declining years left the command of

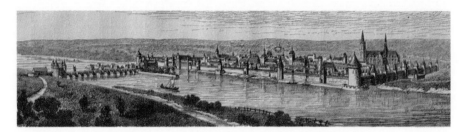

View of fifteenth-century Orléans, by Anatole France, Project Gutenberg.

E-TEXT 19488

English forces in incapable hands. Furthermore the French realized that their strategy of confronting the English in pitched battle had brought nothing but disasters; under the talented Marshal Du Guesclin they now refused to be brought to battle, and the *chevauchées* launched by commanders such as Sir Robert Knolles and John of Gaunt, Duke of Lancaster (1340–99), achieved little. Minority regimes on both sides of the Channel after 1380, and the Peasants Revolt of 1381, dragged the war to a stalemate. A short truce agreed on 18 June 1389 led in time to a twenty-six-year truce in March 1396.

When Henry V (reigned 1413–22) invaded northern France in August 1415, he was taking advantage of two political factors in French politics that worked in his favour: Charles VI's insanity, and the competing factions of the Burgundians and the Armagnacs. Already in 1411, and again the following year, two large expeditions had been sent from England to aid the Burgundians in their struggle against the royalist Armagnacs. The politics in France, coupled with Henry's hard-line foreign policy, led to the campaign of 1415 that culminated at Agincourt – a victory that effectively wiped out the Armagnac leadership and produced the modern myth of the dominance of the humble longbow in the field of battle over the knight in shining armour.

Henry's astonishing success plunged France into one of its darkest periods. After Agincourt, the English went on to conquer a large part of northern and central France, with the Valois Dauphin Charles being too young and inexperienced to mount any form of resistance. Following the assassination of John the Fearless, the Duke of Burgundy, by the Dauphin's followers in 1419, the Duke's son and successor Philip was forced into an alliance with the English. In 1420 they forced the mad king Charles VI to sign the Treaty of Troyes, by which Henry would marry Charles' daughter Catherine of Valois, and Henry and his heirs would inherit the throne of France, while the Dauphin was declared illegitimate. Everything seemed to be lost for Charles VII, as Henry formally entered Paris later that year.

Following Henry's death in 1422, the diplomatic priority for the English was to maintain the Anglo-Burgundian alliance against Valois France and to convince the French people to accept Henry's son – Henry VI (reigned 1422–61) – as their legitimate king. For the Dauphin it also seemed paramount to break the aforementioned alliance and crown himself king at Rheims Cathedral, where Clovis was baptized by Saint Remi in 496, which lay in territory controlled by the Anglo-Burgundians. Throughout the

1420s, the Anglo-Burgundians worked to stabilize the frontier with Valois France, roughly along the River Loire. Valois attempts to break through to Rheims were beaten back twice in 1423 and 1424 at a huge cost to the French.

In the following five years English power was at its peak, reaching from the Channel to the Loire, excluding only Orléans and Angers, and from Brittany in the west to Burgundy in the east.

THE PRELUDE TO THE BATTLE

It is crucial to stress the political and strategic significance of the city of Orléans for the military operations of 1428–29. The dukes of Orléans were at the head of a political faction of the Armagnacs, who were staunch supporters of the disinherited Dauphin Charles. The Duke of Orléans, also in line to the throne, was one of the combatants from Agincourt who remained a prisoner of the English fourteen years after the battle.

Finally, the Dauphin and his officers were acutely aware that if they left Orléans to fall to the English, they would lose control of the entire Loire valley. The French had to keep under their control the areas that lay just north of the Loire, and those that projected well into English territory in Maine, to interrupt the communications between the English-held areas in the north-west, and the English and Burgundian areas of operations in the east. The English knew that, and they were keenly aware of the strategic importance of the city of Orléans as a bridgehead to the south of the Loire and the cities of Chinon and Bourges – important Valois strongholds at Anjou and Berry.

In 1427, Valois forces relieved the siege of Montargis, some 80km (50 miles) east of Orléans, in what was the first effective French action in years. This success seems to have emboldened sporadic uprisings in the thinly garrisoned English-occupied region north of the Loire. However, the French failed to capitalize on the aftermath of Montargis, in large part because for the first half of 1428 the French court was embroiled in a power struggle between different factions surrounding the Dauphin.

Hence the initiative was left with the English and the regent John, Duke of Bedford, who availed himself of French paralysis to bring reinforcements from England in early 1428, under Thomas Montacute (Earl of Salisbury). Yet the target for the English in the summer of 1428 seems to have been the region of Maine and Anjou, to the west of Orléans, so as to preclude any relief of the city via the River Loire.

THE OPPOSING FORCES

The French Army

The French army after Agincourt was nothing but a shadow of its former self; because of the catastrophic loss of life in the field of battle, coupled with the years of anarchy and financial decline that followed, the entire recruiting system of the French Crown had been thrown into chaos. Hence, for the relief of Orléans the Valois regime had to rely on a mixture of local volunteers, urban militias and foreign mercenaries who were often left unpaid and had to live off the land.

Contemporary accounts regarding troop numbers under the Valois command are conflicting and confusing. Modern estimates put their numbers between 1,600 to 2,400 for the professional soldiers, and around 3,000 for the urban militia.[3] These numbers would have been reached after gradual reinforcement of the city and the occasional withdrawal of troops throughout the winter of 1428 and the spring of 1429, until the arrival of the armies of Joan of Arc. In fact, it was not until July 1429 that the French achieved numerical superiority over the English.

The English Army

English expeditionary armies rarely operated in a vacuum but were intended to be supplemented by, and coordinated with, the military structures established within the conquered territories – in this case, Salisbury's forces were complemented by levies from Normandy, Paris, Burgundy, Picardie and Champagne. England, unlike France, raised troops through the well-established system of indenture (a contract of fixed term, fixed conditions), one that was also agreed between Henry VI and the Earl of Salisbury on 24 March 1428.

The latter included the service of 600 men-at-arms and 1,800 archers raised in England, while an additional 200 men-at-arms and 600 archers were raised while the army was in Paris, probably drawn from garrisons in Normandy. Bedford would also have benefited from the service of 1,500 Burgundians and several hundred men from areas that recognized Henry VI as king, although their precise number is difficult to estimate.[4] Nevertheless, the English numbers would have fluctuated constantly for the duration of the siege of Orléans.

Arms and Armaments

In terms of armaments, there was little to differentiate the English from the French. The knights and men-at-arms would have worn plate armour, both independent breast- and back-plate, which gradually developed in the fifteenth century into a fully articulated suit of plate armour. For battle, the lighter *basinet* with a visor covering the face opening was preferred over the cumbersome great helm, while the already small metallic shield would disappear over the course of the war.

The main weapons of the knights and men-at-arms were the sword and the lance, though others such as the mace might have been used. Swords remained largely unchanged until the 1350s, after which they were designed to be shorter and used for thrusting rather than slashing, largely as a response to the introduction of plate armour.

Infantry relied more on brigandines – cloth or leather armour reinforced with metal strips that covered the entire torso, while their armour was often complemented by chain-mail hauberks, mail and plate gauntlets, plate arm and leg guards, and chain-mail *coifs*. The basinet was also used by infantry soldiers, although without a visor; they also rejected the old triangular wooden shield in favour of the smaller, round one.

By the beginning of the fifteenth century, the infantry spear had grown longer, into a pike. Yet evidence shows that the typical weapon for the infantry was the bow. Both the English and the French did use the longbow, but the latter largely preferred the crossbow because it had an intrinsically longer range. The longbow was cheaper and it had the advantage of being capable of releasing ten shots for the crossbow's two.

Finally, by the beginning of the fifteenth century another technological reality became apparent: gunpowder artillery. This had an enduring impact on siege warfare, with huge guns projecting massive cannonballs against stone city walls; already in 1377, Philip the Bold of Burgundy used canons that discharged 91kg cannonballs and obliterated the fortifications of Odruik Castle. At Orléans, each side had between fifty and seventy canons, although historians believe that the English canons were somewhat smaller.

THE CAMPAIGN

The Earl of Salisbury and his army from England landed at Calais on 1 July 1428, and he immediately headed for Paris for consultation with Bedford about their strategy for the coming summer. Initial plans for the invasion of Maine and Anjou were reluctantly revised to the more daring attack against Orléans, as both English leaders were well aware of the political turmoil in the Dauphin's Court at the time.

In the weeks preceding the beginning of the siege, Salisbury took considerable pains to capture Beaugency and Meung to the west, and Jargeau and Châteauneuf to the east of Orléans and on the south bank of the Loire, so as to have his flanks covered. All four castles had surrendered by early October, and on the 7th the English force recrossed the Loire to position themselves opposite the southern bridges of Orléans. However, despite the city appearing to be surrounded, the blockade was never complete.

Contemporary sources make it clear that the citizens of Orléans were anticipating a siege, and they had improved the defences under the command of the governor De Goncourt.[5] These included the five gates and the many towers and curtain wall that surrounded the city. Orléans' famous bridge had been built in the twelfth century, and it had twenty arches with several shops on top. On the southern end of the bridge there was the famous fortification of 'Les Tourelles', a twelfth-century fort with two towers that guarded the southern approaches to the city, and was reinforced by an eastern barbican or outwork.

The English began the bombardment of the city on 17 October, from the *bastille* they had built on the ruins of an Augustinian monastery that faced the Tourelles. Within a week from the beginning of operations, the heavy bombardment and the undermining of the fortifications by the English forced the defenders of the Tourelles to withdraw into the city, on the night of 23/24 October. Critical for operations was the fatal injury incurred by the Earl of Salisbury from a chance shot fired by a young boy who had

mounted the city's fortifications while the guards were having their lunch! Command
now passed to the more cautious Earl of Suffolk.

Orléans was reinforced by the arrival of fresh troops under Count Jean de Dunois,
who entered the city on the 25th. Nicolle has suggested that the forests to the east of the
city would have been much denser in the fifteenth century, and would have provided sufficient cover for reinforcements and supply convoys to get in and out of Orléans.[6] After
5 November, Suffolk commanded his troops to withdraw to specially prepared winter
quarters on the western and northern suburbs of the city, leaving a token force of a few
hundred to maintain the siege in the Tourelles.

France and England in 1429.

Legend:
- English holdings
- French holdings
- Burgundian lands allied with England to 1435
- ✗ Major battle

There were several sorties throughout November to harass the English, but to little avail, until the English reopened their attacks on the southern bridge of the city on 7 December. They were rejuvenated by the arrival two days earlier of John, Lord Talbot, a fiery warrior who would share command with the cautious Suffolk. Talbot immediately ordered a tentative attack against the French fortifications on the other side of the now broken Orléans bridge. Meanwhile, numerous forts were being erected by the English on the northern and eastern sides of the city to tighten the blockade – although supplies were still able to get through into the city.

On 12 February 1429 a French relief force under the Compte de Clermont was approaching the city from the south – the region of Blois – when it ran into an English convoy of 300 wagons that was transferring salted herring to the besiegers for consumption during Lent. It is likely that the French had accurate intelligence about the date and course of this supply convoy, and decided to intercept it. The battle that followed is widely known as 'The Battle of the Herrings'.

Despite the numerical superiority of the French force, which numbered between 3,000 to 4,000 mounted troops, they failed to break the defensive formation of the English, who, under Sir John Fastolf, received the French attack in a *laager* – an encampment or an entrenched position formed by a circle of wagons. A mounted English counter attack eventually routed the French forces, who in the meanwhile had dismounted, contrary to orders. Needless to say, this disaster had a shattering effect on

Siege of Orléans in 1428–29 (Vigiles de Charles VII, fifteenth century).

SOURCE: GALLICA DIGITAL LIBRARY, ID: btv1b105380390/f117

French morale, with several French leaders such as the Compte de Clermont and La Hire abandoning the city to its fate.

Joan of Arc

It would be Joan, a teenage peasant girl from Domrémy, in north-east France, who would save the city of Orléans, and who would ultimately change the course of the Hundred Years' War. Convinced that the voices in her head were coming directly from the Archangel Michael, Saint Catherine and Saint Margaret, Joan was granted an escort on 6 March to visit the Dauphin in his base at Chinon, to convince him of her divine mission to save France.

Joan's arrival on the scene effectively turned the longstanding Anglo-French conflict into a religious war, a risky course of action as many of Charles' enemies could easily have accused Joan of heresy unless her orthodox credentials were established beyond any doubt. Eventually, a commission of inquiry declared her to be of 'irreproachable life' in early April 1429.

Joan arrived at the besieged city of Orléans on 29 April 1429 at the head of a Valois army that had been gathering at Blois for weeks – in all, some 500 men under the command of officers such as Dunois and La Hire, who were escorting a convoy of supplies to the beleaguered city. Meanwhile, the English had almost completed the construction of the forts that would block the northern (so-called 'Bastille St-Pouair'), western (so-called 'Bastille St-Laurent') and eastern (so-called 'Bastille St-Loup') approaches to the city; however, their operational strategy was frustrated by the sudden departure of the Burgundian mercenaries.

The arrival of Joan at Orléans forced a change in the pattern of the siege. Until then, the defenders had attempted only one major offensive assault, which had ended in disaster. But on 4 May, Joan and the Armagnacs, at the head of some 4,000 troops, captured the outlying 'Bastille St-Loup', followed on 5 May by a march to a second fort in the southern approaches called 'Bastille St-Jean-le-Blanc', which was found deserted. The French remained on the south bank of the Loire for the final attack, on 7 May, against the main English stronghold of the Tourelles. Contemporary accounts confirm Joan as the heroine of the battle, because she was wounded by an arrow between the neck and shoulder while holding her banner in the trenches under the Tourelles. 'The witch is dead!' exclaimed the English – but she was not.

The final stage of the siege of Orléans had now been reached. The first day of the siege of the Tourelles (6 May) was spent in a largely fruitless bombardment, and attempts to undermine its foundations by mining and burning barges. On the following day (7 May), however, Joan concentrated the French attack on the Boulevard-les-Tourelles, the outlying fortifications protecting the approaches to the Tourelles on the south bank of the Loire – at which point she was seriously wounded.

Rumours of her death bolstered the confidence of the English defenders, but according to eyewitnesses, she returned later that evening and told the soldiers that a final assault would carry the fortress. Heartened by the news, the French troops rallied beside the Maid and mounted repeated attacks, aiming to dislodge the English from the Boulevard and throw them back into the Tourelles. But then the drawbridge connecting them gave way, and William Glasdale, the English commander of the Tourelles, fell into the river and drowned. The surviving English garrison surrendered soon after without a fight.

With the Tourelles complex taken, the English had lost the south bank of the Loire and so there was little point in continuing the siege, as Orléans could now be easily and indefinitely resupplied. Hence on 8 May the English prepared to withdraw their forces by forming up into two large bodies between the siege lines and the city's fortifications – though whether to provoke a pitched battle, or perhaps in a gesture of defiance, is not known. After a stand-off with the French units under Dunois that marched out to face them, and which lasted for about an hour, the English marched off to join other garrison units in Meung, Beaugency and Jargeau.

Despite their retreat from Orléans, the English retained control over the surrounding perimeter of the Orléanais region – Beaugency, Meung, Janville and Jargeau. However, the Loire quickly fell back into French hands after a series of brief sieges and battles at Jargeau (12 June), Meung (15 June) and Beaugency (17 June). English reinforcements under John Talbot had been gathering since the beginning of June, but these were of rather secondary quality, largely drawn from different garrisons in Normandy, and it also included French troops of dubious loyalty. They were eventually defeated at the Battle of Patay on 18 June. That was the first significant field victory for French arms in years, which included the capture of the English commanders, the Earl of Suffolk and Lord Talbot.

CONCLUSIONS

It was believed by contemporaries that the ultimate fate of the city of Orléans would reveal that of France itself, hence its survival through the appearance on the scene of Joan not only led to her becoming *la Pucelle d'Orléans* (the 'Maid of Orléans'), but allowed the Dauphin Charles to be consecrated as King Charles VII of France at Rheims on 17 July 1429. Hence, historians can say with confidence that the successful defence of the city of Orléans was the turning point in the hundred-year-old struggle between the English and the French Crowns, which eventually cut the umbilical cord that had kept the two countries together for four centuries.

The victories at Orléans and Patay showed the French how to fight, and, more importantly, how to win against an enemy that had prevailed in three hugely important battles, one of which – Agincourt (1415) – had been fought within living memory, with the carnage on the French side being so immense that it had devastating consequences on French morale. Orléans and Patay proved that the English were not invincible in the field of battle, and it provided a desperately needed boost to French fighting spirit. More importantly, Charles' control of the strategic Loire valley was confirmed, while he

conducted a medieval *blitzkrieg*, capturing many places on the way to Reims, where he
was crowned on 17 July as Charles VII.

Even though Joan's influence in the course of the conflict has been exaggerated,
especially by French specialists on the period, her capture and execution in 1431 was not
enough to change the tide of the war, which had, by then, irreversibly turned in favour
of the French and the Valois. A tell-tale sign of the changing political climate was the
decision of Duke Philip III of Burgundy to break his alliance with the English and throw
his support behind Charles VII by signing the Treaty of Arras (20/21 September 1435).

After that year, French pressure in Normandy began to tell, and Charles' war of
attrition gained him the strategic Norman ports of Dieppe and Harfleur. It had become
clear that the English were by now on the defensive, and were just looking to minimize
their losses. Nevertheless, the fact that the war carried on for another two decades is a
testimony to the massive military effort exerted by the English government, sending
around 10,000 troops to the defence of Calais and to Normandy.[7]

Although primarily a dynastic conflict, the Hundred Years' War gave impetus to
ideas of French and English nationalism,[8] and accelerated the process of transforming
each country to a centralized state. Both England and France eventually emerged as self-
contained national entities; in France, Charles VII and Louis XI reasserted the power
of the French Crown and expanded the frontiers of the country, while in England, the
dissatisfaction of English nobles became a factor leading to the civil wars known as the
Wars of the Roses (1455–1487).

20 THE BATTLE OF VARNA

Sealing the Fate of the Balkans and the Byzantine Empire

Date 10 November 1444
Location North of the city of Varna, on the Black Sea coast of Bulgaria

THE HISTORICAL BACKGROUND

TAMERLANE'S INVASION OF Ottoman territories in Anatolia and his defeat of Bayezid's army, coupled with the capture of the Ottoman ruler at the Battle of Ankara on 27 July 1402, had broader ramifications for the *status quo* in Anatolia. This was because the Ottoman Empire built during the fourteenth century contained important seeds of instability: first, the vassal system of Christian princes left them in a position to assert their independence whenever the central authority was troubled or weak; and second, the Ottoman army was moving away from the ghazi tradition of fighting and expanding the realm of Islam against the infidels. This process was accompanied by extensive pillaging of newly conquered regions and the acquisition of estates for his loyal troops, especially since the Eastern conquests offered nowhere near the degree of lure of the Balkan campaigns. Problems such as these had to be resolved by Bayezid's heirs after the battle at Ankara, if the empire was to be restored.[1]

Following Bayezid's death in captivity in 1403, his eldest son Suleyman was recognized as Ottoman ruler in Europe, based in Edirne, while Bayezid's other sons – Musa Çelebi ruling at Bursa, and Mehmet Çelebi at Amasya – both acknowledged the suzerainty of Tamerlane. So although the Ottomans may have retained control of all their existing territories, their prestige had declined enormously. This period would have presented a good opportunity for Christian Europe to push back the Ottomans from Europe. But the situation was not that simple!

At the turn of the fifteenth century, the leading European powers were in no position to take the initiative against the Ottomans. The English and French had temporarily halted their Hundred Years' War conflicts to join the Crusade of Nicopolis in 1395–96, but following the disastrous outcome of the campaign outside Nicopolis in September 1396, and although technically at peace, they again plunged into a period of hostilities. That period of 'cold war' lasted until Henry V's invasion of Normandy, which culminated at Agincourt in 1415.

Hungary was also in a state of political instability following the disaster at Nicopolis, and between 1401 and 1412 Sigismund was nowhere near its undisputed ruler. Led by the archbishop of Esztergom, in 1401 the Hungarian barons even imprisoned Sigismund for six months while they administered the realm in the name of the Holy Crown. Then in 1412, another group of barons offered the Hungarian Crown to Ladislaus of Naples.

At the same time, the office of the Pope was plagued by what has been known as the Papal Schism of 1378, a split within the Catholic Church that lasted between 1378 and 1417. During this time, two, and after 1410 even three, ecclesiastics simultaneously claimed to be the truly elected Pope.

After the Battle of Ankara, the Ottomans had managed to retain control of all the territories conquered by Bayezid in the Balkans, while the Ottoman army was far from being in disarray: in fact, the army in Europe and the newly formed slave military units (*kapikullari*) had remained almost intact and under the firm leadership of Suleyman. Therefore the most pressing concern for the Ottoman rulers after 1402 was not the rebuilding of defences against a possible European counter attack, but rather to restore united leadership, and to reassert Ottoman rule throughout Anatolia.

From the Ottoman capital in Edirne, Suleyman seized his chance and proclaimed himself ruler, but his brothers refused to recognize him. He then concluded alliances with Manuel II Palaeologus, to whom he conceded Thessaloniki in 1403. Suleyman was eventually defeated in battle and killed by his brother Musa in 1411, who had received the help of Palaeologus, Stefan Lazarevic of Moravian Serbia, and Mircea of Wallachia.

But Musa was himself soon defeated in battle by Mehmet, after the latter landed with his Anatolian troops on the Black Sea coast north of Constantinople, with Palaeologus' consent, in the summer of 1413. In the end, Mehmet prevailed over his brother because he managed to win the support not only of Byzantium, but also of the more important ghazi frontier leaders and Turkoman notables.

Mehmet moved fast to resume the ghazi tradition of expansion, which implied a return to the policy of avoiding conflicts with the Anatolian principalities, and instead, turning the state's attention to Europe. He faced a tricky political situation in the Balkans, where his Bulgarian, Serbian, Wallachian and Byzantine vassals had become virtually independent. On top of that, the Albanian tribal leaders had united and had massacred several Ottoman garrisons in the country, while Bosnia and Moldavia had officially declared their independence from Ottoman rule. At the end of the interregnum, Ottoman control of the Balkans had become precarious.

Mehmet's show of force quickly restored Ottoman rule in Albania and Morea (Peloponnesus), while intensive raids into Mircea's territory brought Wallachia back under Ottoman suzerainty. He also undertook a series of raids into Transylvania and Hungary, whose king, Sigismund, also nurtured ambitions in the area, and completed the conquest of the Dobruja. Finally, ghazi raids into Bosnia caused many of the region's feudal nobles to fall under Ottoman influence, leading King Tvrtko II (1420–43) to accept Ottoman suzerainty.

Mehmet's successor, Murat II (ruled 1421–51), would emerge as the founder of Ottoman power in Europe. He initially launched the sixth Ottoman siege of Constantinople, to punish the emperor Manuel II for his support of one of his rivals (summer 1422). Later he undertook the siege of Thessaloniki against the city's new defenders, the Venetians.

While the siege of Thessaloniki was under way, Murat campaigned against a Venetian anti-Ottoman coalition, which also included Hungary, Serbia, Bosnia and Wallachia – Hungary was the only real adversary of the Ottomans in the Balkans, as a result of raiding expeditions in Bosnia through Serbian lands (1426), the death of the Serbian despot Stefan Lazarević (19 July 1427), which plunged Serbia into a half-century of dynastic quarrels, and succession disputes in Wallachia after the death of Mircea (1418).

Murat's newly built fleet allowed him to launch a final assault on Thessaloniki, forcing the city to surrender on 1 March 1430, thus completing his control of the major ports in the Aegean Sea. Venice was forced to accept the Peace of Lapseki (July 1430), recognizing Ottoman control of Macedonia. Also in this period, Murat set in motion factors that would eventually lead to the introduction of the Cannon Corps (*Topçu Ocağı*), troops that were trained specifically to use this important new weapon that was about to revolutionize modern warfare.

In the 1430s, however, things were beginning to show that another anti-Ottoman coalition was taking shape. Although Murat had reclaimed direct control of the strategic coastal cities of Albania, including Epirus and its metropolis of Ioannina in 1431, he was only accepting tribute and military assistance from the rulers of Serbia, Bosnia, Wallachia, Ragusa, Venice and Bulgaria. But Sigismund's diplomatic involvement in Balkan politics would upset the fragile political situation in the region: he masterminded the replacement of the Ottoman vassal Voivode of Wallachia, Dan II (d. 1432), initially by Mircea's son Alexander, but when the latter died in 1436, then Vlad II 'Dracul' (ruled 1436–42) became prince in his place.

In 1434, Wallachia joined an anti-Ottoman coalition with the Bosnian king Tvrtko II, and also with the new Serbian despot Đurađ Branković (reigned 1427–56), who had restored Serbian independence and had allied himself with Hungary in the mid-1430s. Their timing was perfect, because in 1434–35 Murat was busy with foreign invasions of his Anatolian territories.

Sigismund's death on 9 July 1437 handed the initiative back to Murat, who was becoming increasingly concerned about the possibility of a new European Crusade effort, especially after the aspiration of John VIII Palaeologus (reigned 1425–48) to unite the Catholic and Orthodox Churches – a union that was ratified at the Council of Florence on 6 July 1439.

In the same year (1439), Murat invaded Serbia and captured Branković's newly established capital of Semendria, while another Ottoman army – supported by Vlad II Dracul, Prince of Wallachia – made an incursion into Transylvania. In Bosnia, the Ottoman leadership supported, both financially and militarily, a rival to Tvrtko II's right to the Bosnian Crown, a move that soon led to the splitting of its southern territories (to form modern Herzegovina).

But what gave the Balkan and European leaders enough encouragement to make a stand against the Ottoman aggressive expansion were the successes of the newly appointed Voivode of Transylvania, John Hunyadi (ruled 1440–56). He was put in office by the new King of Hungary and Poland, Ladislas (reigned 1440–57), and in 1441 pushed the Ottomans out of Semendria and then routed them several times in Transylvania. The following year, Hunyadi annihilated an Ottoman force of some 17,000 men (22 March 1442), a victory coupled by another triumph in September when he crushed a huge invading army (allegedly 70,000 strong) led by the governor of Rumelia.[2]

Ultimately, Hunyadi's victories in 1441 and 1442 turned him into the most prominent enemy of the Ottomans.[3] He would be renowned throughout Christendom, not only for his courage, but also for his military aptitude: he refrained from applying the usual tactics of attacking the enemy main body with mounted knights, but instead, attacked with his dismounted men-at-arms while his horsemen encircled the enemy and attacked their flanks.[4]

THE CRUSADE OF VARNA

Sparked by Pope Eugene IV (papacy, 1435–47), who published a crusading bull on 1 January 1443, there seems to have been very little initial response to the call for the upcoming Crusade from the military leaders of Europe. Nevertheless, there were considerable numbers of French and German knights who would attend in a personal capacity, while in April 1443 King Ladislas and his barons decided to take part in this major campaign against the Ottomans, after agreeing on a truce with Frederick III of Germany. Joined by forces raised by John Hunyadi and Đurađ Branković, the campaign was launched under a plan that looked uncomfortably like the disastrous Crusade of 1396. And it was to have the same disastrous outcome!

With the Crusade against the Ottomans officially proclaimed at the Diet of Buda on Palm Sunday 1443, an army of around 40,000 men, mostly Magyars, led by Ladislas and organized to the slightest detail by Hunyadi, the Crusade crossed the Danube and then marched down the Morava to take Niš and Sofia in November 1443. Both leaders were confident that the Ottomans would offer little resistance due to Murat's absence in Anatolia. The Hungarians then crossed the Balkan mountains in winter and defeated a Turkish army at the Battle of Zlatitsa (12 December 1443), moving closer to their target of Philippopolis (Plovdiv). But Hunyadi saw that supplies were running low, so he sensibly withdrew to Buda in February 1444.

A new Crusade plan was hatched in Buda that spring, which involved a march along the Danube to the Black Sea port of Varna, while Venetian ships would prevent the Ottomans from crossing the Bosporus straits. At the same time, the Byzantine despot of Morea would make diversionary attacks in the Peloponnese and Athens, and a revolt would break out in Albania.

But John VIII Palaeologus eventually concluded that his relationship with the Ottomans was too important to break; the same applied to Đurađ Branković, whose daughter was married to Murat. Nevertheless, now that the European chivalry scented the possibility of victory, thousands more Crusaders flooded into Hungary, and a great new Crusade army was mobilized at Buda under Ladislas. The Crusaders departed on 1 September 1444, and they were joined at Orsova on the Danube by Hunyadi and his host of Transylvanian knights, before proceeding towards Varna.

Meanwhile, after securing the borders in the east against the Karamanids of Anatolia, and having negotiated peace treaties with several notables in Serbia, Wallachia and Bulgaria, Murat abdicated his throne in favour of his son, Mehmet, and went into retirement in Bursa, in August 1444. But when the army commanders in Rumelia realized the gravity of the threat that was descending upon them, they quickly dispatched messengers pleading with Murat to come to their aid. Murat accepted the offer, and with the help of the Genoese fleet, transferred his Anatolian armies into Europe in early October.

The Crusader advance was rapid, as Ottoman garrisons were bypassed, while Bulgarians from Vidin, Oryahovo and Nicopolis joined the Crusaders marching along the Danube. On 10 October, some 7,000 Wallachian heavy cavalrymen under Mircea II also joined Ladislas near Nicopolis, before the Crusader army continued its march east towards Varna via Tarnovo and Shumen.[5] The two opposing forces were about to meet in battle near Varna, on the Black Sea coast, in early November 1444.

THE PRELUDE TO THE BATTLE

On 9 November, the Crusaders found out that a great Ottoman army was approaching Varna from the west, thus threatening to trap the Christians between the Black Sea (to their east), Lake Varna (to their south-west), the city of Varna (to their south) and the steep wooded slopes of the Franga plateau (some 3km/2 miles north of Varna). At a supreme military council called by Hunyadi during the night of 9/10 November, most

The two Crusades of Varna, in 1443 and 1444.

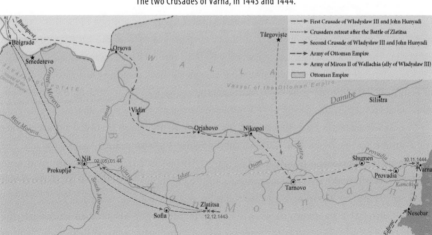

A Janissary, drawing by Gentile Bellini, c. 1470.

John Hunyadi on a hand-coloured woodcut, in Johannes de Thurocz's *Chronica Hungarorum* (Brno, c. 1490).

of the Crusader leaders were contemplating a withdrawal via Varna Bay with the help of the Christian fleet; Cardinal Cesarini argued that they should make a defensive enclosure with their wagons, known as *vozová hradba* in Czech or *Wagenburg* in German, until the ships arrived.

But Ladislas and Hunyadi dismissed this option, and instead, handed out orders for the troops to prepare for battle. Probably their hand was forced by news that the Ottomans were less than '4,000 paces' away from their camp, and were advancing rapidly.[6]

THE OPPOSING FORCES

The multi-ethnic Crusader army would have been composed of Hungarian, Polish, Bohemian, Wallachian, Czech, German, Teutonic, Bosnian, Croatian, Bulgarian, Lithuanian and Ruthenian knights. Historians estimate that their numbers would have varied between 16,000 and 20,000, but what is more important to highlight here is the disproportionate (even asymmetric) size of the two armies at Varna.[7]

Inalcik has suggested that the Ottomans would have mobilized between 30,000 to 40,000 troops from Anatolia, who were later joined by a further 7,000 Rumelian troops. Then, if we include the 'self-mobilizing' *akıncı* cavalry, it would be no surprise for the Ottoman army of Murad to have arrived at Varna totalling nearly 60,000.[8]

As Murphy points out, this disparity in army size between the Ottoman and European forces, already apparent in the 1440s, would remain characteristic of Balkan confrontations until the early decades of the eighteenth century.[9]

Arms and Armament

Already by the early fifteenth century, European knights would have ridden into battle wearing a full suit of plate armour, and as the century progressed, two styles of manufacture predominated in Europe: the 'Italian' (mostly Milanese) and the 'German'. Their armour would have included either a kettle hat, or a so-called 'pig-faced basinet', which was also popular in this period because it featured a removable visor.

Shields would have varied between the small triangular wooden shield with slightly rounded sides; the larger, almost rectangular, convex wooden *pavisses* that were reported for this period mainly in the Prussian, Bohemian and Polish sources; and the characteristically Hungarian shield, but used both in Hungary and parts of Germany (but mainly after the 1450s), which was rectangular at the bottom, but with the upper edge swept upwards forming a curve.

Besides the lance and the mace, variations in sword styles would mainly exist between the Hungarian, Moravian and Slavonian knights and the rest of the Europeans. By the beginning of the fifteenth century, the former would have made increasing use of the single-edge *kesek* small sword, which would have certainly set them apart from the Italian, German and French heavy cavalry of the period.[10]

The arms and armour of the élite Sipahi cavalry has been examined in detail in Chapter 17 on the Battle of Nicopolis, so we do not need to discuss this topic any further. The Janissary regiments of the early Ottoman armies would have been armed by a centrally controlled system of supplies, and in the first 200 years their weapons would have included bows, slings, crossbows and javelins, as their primary role in battle was that of élite infantry archers. They began adopting firearms as soon as such became available during the 1440s, and the sources report them being used in the wars against the Hungarians and the Transylvanians between 1440 and 1443.[11]

For the first two centuries of their growth out of the *kapikullari* corps, the Janissaries would have worn little or no armour. While in peacetime they would carry only clubs or daggers, in combat at close quarters they used axes, and the famous *yatagans* that were smaller and lighter than ordinary swords (*kılıç* or *sajf*) so as not to hinder them when carried at the waist on the march.

The *yatagan* has several characteristics that distinguish it from other types of early modern sword:[12] the pommel of the hilt, which would be made of bone, horn, ivory or silver, spreads out in two wings to either side, a feature that prevents the sword slipping out of the hand in battle. A broad, thick metal band covered the join between the hilt and blade. *Yatagan* blades varied between 60 and 80cm in length, and were slightly curved towards the sharp edge. While the back of the blade was made of iron, the sharp edge was made of steel to add strength.

THE BATTLE

The two armies clashed early in the morning of 10 November 1444, with both commanders-in-chief deploying their troops in a similar fashion – in three main divisions (left, right and centre), forming an arc between Lake Varna and the Franga plateau.

Deployment of the Ottoman Army

The sources agree[13] that Murat placed his Anatolian troops on the left wing, under Karaca Bey, consisting mainly of Sipahis and 'other forces on horseback' (probably irregular *akıncı*) that were around 30,000 strong. He then placed his Rumelian troops on the right under Şahin Paşa, who commanded 'the people of Greece, Turks as well as Christians', meaning the *kapikullari* and Sipahi foot and mounted men.

Murat led the centre, which was placed between the right and left flanks, but deployed slightly behind them behind ditches and barricades (exactly as at Nicopolis), and it included the Janissaries and levies from Rumelia. Janissary archers and *akıncı* light cavalry were also deployed on the Franga plateau.

Deployment of the Christian Army

Antonio Bonfini (1434–1503)[14] describes the deployment of the Christian army in detail, writing that the line was some 1,000 paces long and shaped as it was so that the right of the line was facing both to the front and towards the Franga plateau. Opposite the Ottoman right flank, thus on the Christian left, Hunyadi placed his brother-in-law, Michael Szilágyi, with a substantial force of Transylvanian cavalry, probably also accompanied by German and – perhaps – also Bulgarian heavy cavalry, a total of 5,000 men. The centre of the Crusader army was commanded by Hunyadi and held by Polish, Hungarian, German and Transylvanian heavy cavalry, both mercenaries and knights numbering some 3,500 men, while Ladislas held a few Wallachian and Hungarian units in reserve.

The rest of the army would have been deployed on the right flank, and on a much wider and deeper arc to prevent possible encirclement, numbering some 6,500 men. In overall command of the right wing was Bishop Jan Dominek of Varadin with his personal banner, while Cardinal Cesarini was in command of two units of German mercenaries, the Bishop of Erlau/Eger in the north of Hungary commanded his own unit, and the military governor of Slavonia, Talotsi, commanded one unit. It is probably in the right wing – or perhaps between the right wing and the Crusader camp by the sea – that Mircea II and his 4,000 cavalry would have been deployed.

The Opening Stages of the Battle

Sadly, the Muslim and Christian sources differ as to what exactly happened in the opening stages of the battle. The anonymous author of the *The Holy Wars of Sultan Murad* reports of a Christian attack that took place first from the right wing, led by Mircea and the Wallachians, who attacked the Sipahi from Edirne that were positioned on the flanks of the left wing under Karaca Bey.

Mircea's attack was swiftly answered by an Ottoman counter attack against Talosi's Croats, while at the same time the Ottoman right wing under Şahin Paşa was also manoeuvring for an attack, which was to be met by Hunyadi's units from the centre.

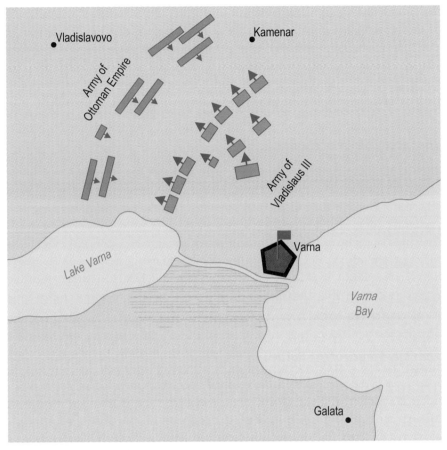

The Battle of Varna, 10 November 1444.

Then the author goes on to describe the course of the battle in the two wings of the battlefield: he reports that Karaca Bey's attack was thwarted by the Crusaders 'because the Anatolian troops were not loyal to Karaca Bey', who, betrayed by his own soldiers, fought a desperate battle like a 'male lion' and 'taking no account of their [Crusaders] numbers'. The same author later puts him in a suicidal attack against the entire division of Talotsi's Croats, which resulted in him being martyred.

According to Bonfinius and Jehan de Wavrin, the battle opened with the Ottoman left flank, probably the irregular akıncı as five decades before at Nicopolis, attacking Talotsi's Croats on the Christian right. Almost as soon as he saw the Ottoman charge coming down against his flank, Hunyadi rushed with his troops from the centre to support them: '...he charged them and, with a great lance that he was carrying, hurled Caraiabay [Karaca Bey] to the ground together with all the men who came up first.'[15]

Although the source certainly exaggerated the martial vigour of Hunyadi, the result of the Christian counter attack resulted in the death of the commander of the Ottoman left flank, thus throwing his troops into disarray. Hunyadi then ordered his cavalrymen to pursue the fleeing enemies uphill. Jehan de Wavrin reports that 'those in the rear [of the Ottoman attacking unit] were coming at such a speed that they drove them [those who were fleeing] back against the Hungarians, who killed them with their great knives and long swords.' What followed was Hunyadi's dispatch of more troops to the mêlée on the left flank, a move that eventually turned that fight in favour of the Crusaders.

The Second Stage of the Battle

The accounts of the sources become even more confusing for the second stage of the battle, although modern historians have reached some common ground on the basic sequence of events. Hence, we get some sense that Hunyadi led a fierce counter attack against the advancing right flank of the Ottomans under Şahin, probably with troops from his own centre division and from the Crusader left, which caused the Ottomans to retreat 'towards the mountains' – referring to the Franga plateau – with Hunyadi's forces in hot pursuit. But Şahin reportedly managed to rally his retreating troops and organize a counter attack, which clashed into the pursuing Crusader units, creating havoc amongst their ranks.

The Final Stages of the Battle

A key event in the course of the battle was the death of the commander of the Anatolian troops, Karaca Bey, which dragged his division into panic and disarray. The anonymous Muslim source paints an image of a heroic charge against Talotsi's Croats, which eventually forced the latter to retreat from the battlefield, although Karaca suffered a martyr's death fighting against the infidel. But there is no such mention in the Christian sources, so we are left with the 'bottom line' from both accounts: the death of the commander of the Anatolian troops.

At that point, all the sources describe how, what could have been one of Hunyadi's greatest victories, was turned rapidly into a crushing defeat. Perhaps believing that victory was at hand, or succumbing to peer pressure from his household knights, the young and inexperienced King Ladislas prepared to join the battle in person. This was something that Hunyadi had tried to persuade him not to do, because, unlike the king, the experienced and keen-eyed Hunyadi was not fooled into thinking that the Ottomans were beaten. But undeterred and 'untamed', Ladislas sought to 'win his spurs' by leading his household guard of 500 Polish and Hungarian knights directly against Murat's Janissary regiment that was positioned in the rearguard of the Ottoman army.

Despite initial success, Ladislas' charge was beaten back, and he was killed after a Janissary brought down his horse with a fatal blow of his spear. The Hungarian army very soon broke up into small groups and retreated. The Ottoman troops did not pursue them for at least a day, as apparently the losses were sufficient for Murad to state: 'May Allah never grant me another such victory.'

CONCLUSIONS

Hunyadi was able to escape the carnage but only with great difficulty, while thousands of European knights were slaughtered in the aftermath of the battle. Murad was pressured by the Ottoman notables and the officers of the Janissaries to keep his throne, on the grounds that his son Mehmet lacked the authority and strength needed to defend the state at this crucial time. Indeed, the sources report that Murat spent his remaining years (until 1451) in a series of campaigns to stabilize Ottoman rule in the Balkans by suppressing the vassals who had revolted during the previous campaign, especially those in Bulgaria and mountainous Albania, and by enforcing his direct rule in Greece and the Peloponnesus. But troubles would be stirred up again from the north, as Murad was desperate to secure his authority in Rumelia.

Hunyadi had been working to create a new Crusade army ever since his return to Buda in 1444, and four years later, the Transylvanian notable, who had been appointed as the regent of Ladislas' infant son, saw the right moment to lead a campaign against the Ottoman Empire. Once again he managed to collect an army of European chivalry, allegedly some 50,000 men, with whom he crossed into northern Serbia in September 1448, despite Brankovic's refusal to participate.

His strategy was based on an anticipated revolt of Balkan leaders (especially Skanderbeg in Albania), who would then merge with them into an anti-Ottoman coalition army that would head towards Edirne to crush the Ottomans in a single decisive battle – exactly what Varna and Nicopolis were aspired to be. But Murad's swift reaction to intercept the Crusaders proved fateful, and he routed the Crusader army at the Second Battle of Kosovo, on 20 October 1448.

The repercussions of the Ottoman victories at Varna and Kosovo for the future of Europe were two-fold, as the fate of both the Balkans and the Byzantine Empire were sealed. Having succeeded in removing a significant opposition to their expansion into central and eastern Europe, Murad now was left unopposed to impose his direct rule over the different nations and populations in the Balkans. He encouraged large numbers of Turkish tribesmen to settle in various 'sensitive' regions in the north and east of the Balkan peninsula, so that, in less than a century, they formed a majority of the population, while a large number of the Christian populations of the Balkans were left with no option but to become Ottoman subjects. He also boosted the expansion of the *timar* system in the Balkans, with members of the old Bulgarian and Serbian landed nobility being gradually absorbed by the Ottomans.

Ottoman prestige throughout the Muslim world was immensely enhanced after 1448, but that of Hunyadi was significantly weakened. The latter resigned from the office of Voivode of Transylvania in 1449, although he was confirmed as the guardian of the under-aged Ladislas V of Hungary for another eight years. After Varna and Kosovo, there would be no other Christian leader able to command the prestige that Hunyadi did in the 1430s and 1440s and put together a crusade against the Ottoman invasion into Europe.

With the rise of Mehmet II, called 'the Conqueror' (Fatih), into power in 1451, the Ottomans would inaugurate a new era of conquest that would soon extend the empire's borders across the Danube and into central Europe. The new Sultan and his advisers quickly concluded that their next target would be Constantinople, not only because the conquest of the city would give an immense boost to Mehmet's prestige as a Muslim leader, but also because it was an obvious strategic target at the confluence of two continents.

Furthermore, they needed a spectacular victory to fortify their political position against the Turkish nobility, and as long as Constantinople held out, there would always be the possibility of new crusade efforts to rescue it. Therefore, the fate of the Byzantine Empire had been sealed long before Mehmet's deployment of his canons outside the Theodosian walls in February 1453.

CONCLUSION

PERIODIZATION IN MILITARY HISTORY

IN AN EFFORT to study the history of medieval Europe in a more effective way, historians have divided the twelve centuries we have come to know as the 'Middle Ages', from the middle of the fourth to the middle of the fifteenth, into periods of study. Periodization, therefore, has become an inescapable part of the study of history at all levels. Military historians have not escaped this process of slicing up the past into pieces of varying sizes, and then allocating them special names, or 'labels', to help them demarcate each slice as something unique.

We have come up with a description for the period between AD400 and AD1100 as 'The Age of Migration and Invasion'. Undoubtedly, the impact of the migration of nomadic and semi-nomadic nations into the European landmass shaped the continent in a profound way. For over 2,500 years, the steppes of Eurasia have given rise to a series of pastoral peoples who have lived on and wandered through that great landmass, but have always remained on the fringes of great sedentary civilizations (China, India, Persia, Rome).

The relationship between the nomads and their settled neighbours was characterized by raiding and warfare, interspersed with periods of trading and alliances. The key to the nomads' great success in the battlefield was their strategic and tactical mobility, which came directly from their extraordinary relationship with two key components of war: the horse and the bow, and they mastered the use of both to perfection.

Nomadic people, such as the Huns, were loosely organized in a tribal manner, and fortunately for their neighbours, tended not to cooperate very often, unless a skilful leader emerged – such as Attila. Instead, they found it easier to conquer than to rule, extorting tribute money from their richer neighbouring leaders, who, most of the time, were happy to oblige. Hence before the middle of the fifth century, the nomads were rarely viewed as a serious challenge to Roman authority south of the Rhine and the Danube. However, when in 450 the fragile balance of power between the two halves of the Roman Empire and the Huns was interrupted, the experienced and intelligent Attila picked his target wisely: he moved against the West, clashing with the alliance led by the general of the western Roman Empire, Flavius Aetius, at the **Battle of the Catalaunian Fields**, in 451.

The early Germanic peoples who infiltrated Roman territories in the fourth and fifth centuries also had a notably fluid social structure, based in principle on the clan, or extended family, and their populations tended to group around military chieftains. These 'semi nomads' moved and fought largely on foot, and were known as ferocious warriors. But while there were innumerable confrontations along the Rhine-Danube *limes* over the centuries, Roman contact with the Germanic peoples for the most part benefited both societies. Roman imports were crucial signs of status and wealth within 'barbarian' society; these were procured through gifts, trade and, of course, raiding, and all three were fundamental to the construction of early 'barbarian' rulership.

On the other hand, the Empire employed the 'barbarians', either individually (*dediticii, laeti*) or en masse (*foederati*), to manage her frontiers and to help reduce the military threat by engaging one group to attack another. By the second half of the fourth century, their numbers were high enough to form separate divisions under their own leaders within Roman expeditionary armies. This was the case at the **Battle of the Frigidus**, in AD394, when the armies of the western Roman Empire, which to a great extent consisted of Gothic *foederati*, were annihilated by the Eastern armies of emperor Theodosius I.

Following the collapse of the western Roman Empire in the second half of the fifth century, the military forces of the Germanic 'successor' kingdoms reflected the fusion of Roman and barbarian elements that characterized the whole society. In the late fifth and sixth centuries, western European 'barbarian' identity rapidly became closely associated with warfare and military service, and perhaps the greatest transformation in this period was the creation of a new 'social élite', in which to be a 'barbarian' and a 'warrior' conferred social status.

Thus a new 'militarized' society was taking shape in western Europe, one which would come to forget the institution of a regular paid army, and would, instead, rely on an ethnically based army in which military service would depend on ownership of land and military obligation. Essentially, armed forces, like politics, would become increasingly privatized in the hands of powerful magnates. These 'new' armies would clash at the decisive **Battle of Vouillé**, in AD507, when the emerging power of the Salian Franks under King Clovis crushed the Visigoths of France and Spain, and settled once and for all the future of continental Gaul.

Further invasions of Europe in the ninth and tenth centuries came from three directions – the north, the east and the south – and their impact was considerable. Muslim pirates who plagued the southern coasts of Europe were but a distant echo of the disciplined Umayyad armies that had poured out of the Arabian peninsula in the seventh century. These early Arabian tribesmen constituted a unique sub-class of nomadic horse people, because although they used horses and camels for strategic and tactical mobility, their battle traditions differed greatly from those of the steppe tribes, having little emphasis on archery.

At the **Battle of Guadalete** in July 711, the Visigothic kingdom was eclipsed by the armies of the Arabs from Morocco, an event that radically changed the course of the history of Spain and Europe for the next five centuries, giving rise to the ideas of Christian Holy War. It would take the strategic brilliance of Charles Martel to defeat the ever-expanding emirate of Al-Andalus at the **Battle of Tours** in 732, a victory that secured Charles' position as the most powerful man in France.

Prior to that decisive victory in central France, the Umayyad army and navy was also decisively defeated in the outskirts of the Byzantine capital, following the unsuccessful **Second Siege of Constantinople** between the summers of 717 and 718. The Byzantine capital's survival preserved the empire as a bulwark against Islamic expansion into Europe well into the fifteenth century and the coming of the Ottoman Turks.

Emerging in the footsteps of Attila the Hun, the Magyars began to trouble the eastern borders of Europe in the middle of the ninth century. During the first few decades of their appearance in Europe they served as élite mercenaries, as the Magyar light horse-men were capable of rapid overland marches that could bypass or outrun local defences; they were a huge and able man-force that could be tapped by the political powers of Europe at the time. They took full advantage of the political instability in central Europe at the end of the ninth century, establishing themselves in the south-eastern marches of the German kingdom around AD896.

The Magyars' massive raids cut deep swathes of destruction through central and southern Europe for more than thirty years (900–930), defeating no fewer than three large German armies between 907 and 910. Therefore, the significance of the **German victory on the banks of the River Lech**, in 955, was crucial for the future and stability of the Holy Roman Empire, a victory that put a check on the Magyar raids, whilst also opening the way to their eventual Christianization.

Finally, from the north came the 'heathen' Vikings, who initially, at the beginning of the ninth century, were launching raids against lucrative targets in England, Ireland and France. Then in northern France during the eleventh century, the people who came to be known as the 'Normans' – the 'people of the north' – gained a strong reputation for their performance on the battlefield throughout the Mediterranean (Byzantium, Spain and Italy). While they were distinguished for their craftiness and cunning spirit, they were also known for their cruelty and bloodthirstiness, and their policy of destruction. Furthermore, two hugely important and decisive Norman victories in two completely different operational theatres of war helped to promote even further their reputation for martial prowess and invincibility in the battlefield.

The Norman establishment in Italy is particularly interesting, because by the middle of the eleventh century they had become the undisputed masters of the entire southern Italian provinces of Apulia and Calabria, owing to their decisive victory at the **Battle of Civitate** in 1053, where they solidified their political and military dominance in the South. And thirteen years later, in 1066, William, Duke of Normandy, made his bid for the English throne in the most remarkable and well planned of all enterprises conducted by a Norman leader in history, the climax of which was William's triumph at the **Battle of Hastings** in October.

Although the Battle of Hastings has left an indelible mark in collective memory as the epoch-making moment in the rise of the knight, it is the Mediterranean that provides an arena in which a historian can truly explore how, why and what made the knight such a popular and effective military system. While the processes that created the knight began in the tenth century, it was in the eleventh that the knight became part of a fully matured military system.

In Italy and Sicily, the Normans expanded their dominions through negotiation, tolerance, fear and diplomacy, and in an aggressive castle-building policy. They won their battles against a multitude of enemies from different 'military cultures' – Arabs, Byzantines, Lombards, Germans – relying on the effective use of the charge of their heavy cavalry units and the shock impact this would have on their enemies, especially if the latter's army consisted of infantry levies. This was coupled with the application of feigned retreat tactics and a clever exploitation of the topography of the battlefield in their favour.

The period between AD1100 and AD1500 has been described as the 'Age of Traditions in Conflict'. This is an age of political instability and expansion in the lands at the periphery of Europe – the Middle East, Livonia, Spain, Italy and Sicily – but it is also an age of social renewal in Western Europe, which in the century between 950 and 1050 gave rise to a new aristocratic social order and a new socio-military system that we have come to know as 'feudalism'. Although this term has been rendered obsolete for a number of reasons, it nevertheless describes a socio-political system of lord–vassal relations that was built around three major elements: the private castle, noble warriors on horseback (knights) and non-knightly soldiers.

The emergence of 'feudalism' in Europe after the middle of the eleventh century thrust into the spotlight the heavily armed knight as the élite warrior of his time, and as the main offensive strike force in a theatre of war. The knight used the horse for strategic and tactical mobility, although he could be deployed and could fight equally well on foot as on a horse. It was the social and economic superiority of the medieval knight that allowed him to be armed and armoured with the highest quality metalwork, and to be a warrior on a full-time basis and as a lifestyle.

The humble foot-soldiers, on the other hand, were poorly armed and led, and their tactical role in the battle was simply to boost the numbers of the 'feudal' armies of the period; they were much more effectively used in a siege operation than in actual fighting.

In the eleventh, twelfth and thirteenth centuries, while the Holy Roman Empire and the papacy were engaged in prolonged conflict from which neither would emerge fully victorious, England and France evolved into centralized states. The transformation from a 'sacred' into a bureaucratic monarchy was one of the most fundamental historical developments of the Late Middle Ages, and had a profound impact in the way that war was waged between AD1200 and AD1400. As the Capetian kings of France developed a state policy of expanding the royal demesne and tightening the royal lordship over the major dukes and counts of France in the twelfth century, it would bring them into direct conflict with the over-extended Angevin empire.

Philip Augustus's greatest achievement was the destruction of the Angevin empire, the crushing blow eventually coming at the **Battle of Bouvines**, in 1214. The outcome of the battle dramatically changed the political face of Europe, turning Philip into the strongest monarch in Europe, while plunging England into a political and financial crisis that would force King John to sign the *Magna Carta* in 1215.

In an age of expansion into Europe's periphery, the idea of Holy War brought Christian knights into conflict in theatres of war far removed from the Middle East and the Holy Land. The expulsion of the Muslims from Iberia – the so-called *Reconquista* – would last for over four centuries, and it certainly looked like a wild dream after the humiliating defeat of King Alfonso VIII of Castile at the Battle of Alarcos (19 July 1195). Nevertheless, the **Battle of Las Navas de Tolosa** in 1212 allowed for the Christian kings of Spain to reclaim the military initiative, and gave them the opportunity to recover the disputed lands between the rivers Tagus and Guadalquivir.

While Crusader expansion seemed to pick up pace in Iberia, it was dealt a crushing blow in the Baltic region. There, the political and territorial ambitions of the Teutonic Knights and of the Swedish and Danish kings clashed with the growing influence of Russian Orthodox Novgorod. The outcome of the **Battle of the Lake Peipus** in 1242 put a long-term halt on the eastward expansion of the Crusaders in the Baltic region, and drew a distinctive geo-political line between the forces of Russia and those of Sweden, Denmark and Prussia. The decisive blow to the very existence of the Order would be delivered about a century and a half later, when the victory of the allied Lithuanian-Polish armies at the **Battle of Tannenberg**, in 1410, would irreversibly reshape the face of eastern Europe within half a century after the battle.

The Crusader movement was dealt another massive blow in a different corner of Europe, in the southern Balkans. Following the divergence of the Fourth Crusade to Constantinople and the humiliating conquest of the Byzantine capital by the 'Christian' armies of Latin Europe in 1204, the Byzantine Empire had effectively ceased to exist. Nevertheless, there emerged two competing Greek-speaking empires that aspired to be the 'successor state' of Byzantium. Eventually it would be the empire of Nicaea, in western Asia Minor, that would defeat the combined armies of the despotate of Epirus, Sicily and the principality of Achaea at the **Battle of Pelagonia** in 1259. It was a decisive event in the history of the eastern Mediterranean that ensured the Byzantine reconquest of Constantinople and the end of the Latin Empire in 1261, marking the beginning of the Byzantine recovery of Greece.

The **Battle of Tagliacozzo**, in 1268, is interesting for military historians from both a political and a military perspective. On the one hand, the outcome of the battle underlines the difficulties that a heavily armed, mounted force had to overcome when operating in tight formations in a relatively broken, hilly or marshy terrain that was dominated by a river or an uphill castle. Order and discipline were paramount for a cavalry force, especially when it was re-grouping after an unsuccessful charge, hence the great tactical significance of the feigned flight manoeuvre that saved the day for the Sicilian king, Charles of Anjou. But Tagliacozzo should also be remembered for its political ramifications for the future of Italy and Sicily, as it irreversibly broke the centuries-old political connection between Germany and the Kingdom of Sicily through the Hohenstaufen.

For a military historian, the Middle Ages as an 'Age of Cavalry' received its most influential expression in the closing years of the nineteenth century, when Sir Charles Oman wrote his monumental *Art of War in the Middle Ages*. And although we have come to dismiss his romantic view of the 'Age of Cavalry' that began – with Victorian precision – at Adrianople in AD378, there is little doubt that European chivalry was dealt its mortal blow in the fields of Western Europe in the fourteenth century. This has been dubbed the 'Infantry Revolution' of the Late Middle Ages, which witnessed the transformation of the tactical role of infantry forces in Europe, from fighting motionless and in a purely defensive role, to being the main (or only) arm of an army in the field of battle, while (counter) attacking against their social superiors.

Therefore not only should the **Battle of Sempach** in 1386 be viewed for decisively tipping the balance of power west of the Rhine in favour of the Swiss Confederation, an outcome that would eventually lead to the establishment of the state of Switzerland. Sempach should also be appreciated as the climactic victory in a period when independent and rich cities and states in northern Italy, Switzerland and Flanders were capable of putting large, battleworthy infantry armies in the field against the aristocratic knightly armies of the Middle Ages, and crushing them!

The Late Middle Ages (AD1100–1500) was an age of global contact between different 'military cultures' through war and trade, and it was dominated by the Mongol explosion of the thirteenth century at the eastern end of the Mediterranean. The Crusades also brought Western Europe, Byzantium and the Muslim world, with its connections to Central Asia's nomads, into an extended period of competition and exchange. The Crusades, therefore, represent the culmination of this trans-cultural contact, connecting war and religion in a mixture that would be responsible for some of the worst massacres in history. The eventual fall of Byzantium at the hands of the Ottoman Turks would signal the end of an era, and would demonstrate that such transcultural contact could lead to a 'fight to the death'.

As the Ottomans emerged to be one of the local powers in western Asia Minor, following the political vacuum in the region around AD1300, they began to create an independent polity for themselves at the beginning of the fourteenth century; by the second half of the century they had grown to such an extent that they came to be viewed as the key geo-political players in the southern Balkans and Anatolia.

Christian Europe's reaction to Ottoman expansion on the south-eastern fringes of Europe came in the form of the *Christian League* – defensive alliances between front-line powers where the message of crusading was 'adapted' to the geo-political needs of the time. However, the defeat of the **Crusade of Nicopolis** on the outskirts of the Danube city in 1396 had a devastating effect on European morale, allowing the Ottomans crucial time to consolidate and expand their territories in the Balkans, while they were allowed to recover from the setback of the Mongol invasion in AD1402.

When the time was ripe again for another Crusade to stem the Muslim tide into European lands, a multi-national army from many corners of central and western Europe answered the crusading bull of Pope Eugene IV (papacy, 1431–47) on 1 January

1443. Nevertheless, the repercussions from the Christian defeats at **Varna**, in 1444, followed by the rout of the Crusader army at the Second Battle of Kosovo on 20 October 1448, were ground-breaking for the future of Europe. They sealed the fate of both the Balkans and the Byzantine Empire, while giving a great boost to Ottoman prestige in the Muslim world as conquerors and fighters for the Jihad. Their ultimate spoil would be Constantinople, five years later!

BIBLIOGRAPHY

CHAPTER 1

A Companion to the Roman Army, ed. by Paul Erdkamp, Wiley-Blackwell, Oxford, 2007.

Cameron, A., *The Last Pagans of Rome*, Oxford University Press, Oxford, 2011.

Claudian, Latin texts with English translation by Maurice Platnauer, Heinemann, London, 1922 (The texts are in the public domain: http://penelope.uchicago.edu/Thayer/E/Roman/Texts/Claudian/home.html).

Coulston, J. C. N., 'Late Roman Military Equipment Culture' in A. Sarantis and N. Christie (eds) *War and Warfare in Late Antiquity*, Brill, Leiden, 2013, pp.463–92.

Halsall, G., *Barbarian Migrations and the Roman West*, 376–568, Cambridge University Press, Cambridge, 2007.

Mitchell, S., *A History of the Later Roman Empire, AD284–641* (2nd edn.), Oxford University Press, Oxford, 2015.

Rufinus of Aquileia, *The Church History of Rufinus of Aquileia: Books 10 and 11*, trans. by Philip R. Amidon, Oxford University Press, Oxford, 1997.

Southern, P. and Dixon, K. R., *The Late Roman Army*, Routledge, London, 1996.

The Cambridge Ancient History (vol. XIII, The Late Empire, AD337–425) ed. by A. Cameron and P. Garnsey, Cambridge University Press, Cambridge, 1998.

The Ecclesiastical History of Sozomen, trans. by Edward Walford, Henry G. Bohn, London, 1846.

Vegetius, *Epitome of Military Science*, trans. by N. P. Milner, Liverpool University Press, Liverpool, 1993.

CHAPTER 2

Ammianus Marcellinus, trans. by J. C. Rofle, Heinemann, London, 1939.

Bishop Gregory of Tours, History of the Franks, trans. by E. Brehaut, Columbia University Press, New York, 1916.

Bury, J. B., *History of the Later Roman Empire from the Death of Theodosius I to the Death of Justinian*, McMillan, New York, 1958.

Hughes, Ian, *Aetius: Attila's Nemesis*, Pen & Sword, Barnsley, 2012.

Kim, Hyun Jin, *The Huns, Rome, and the Birth of Europe*, Cambridge University Press, Cambridge, 2013.

Lindner, Rudi, 'Nomadism, Horses, and Huns', *Past & Present* 92 (1981), pp.2–19.

MacDowall, S., *Catalaunian Fields AD451, Rome's Last Great Battle*, Osprey, Oxford, 2015.

Maenchen-Helfen, Otto J., *The World of the Huns, Studies in the History and Culture*, University of California Press, London, 1973.

Priscus, *The Fragmentary Classicizing Historians of the Later Roman Empire*, ed. and trans. R. C. Blockley, F. Cairns, Liverpool, 1981, vol. 2, pp.221–400.

Prosper of Aquitaine, 'Epitoma Chronicon' in *From Roman to Merovingian Gaul: A Reader*, trans. by A. C. Murray, Peterborough, Ontario, 2000, pp.62–76.

Sidonius Apollinaris, *Poems and Letters*, trans. by W. B. Anderson, Heinemann, London, 1936.

The Chronicle of Hydatius and the Consularia Constantinopolitana. Two Contemporary Accounts of the Final Years of the Roman Empire, ed. and trans. by R. W. Burgess, Oxford University Press, Oxford, 1993, pp.1–172.

The Gothic History of Jordanes, trans. by C. C. Mierow, Heinemann, London, 1915.

Thompson, E. A., *A History of Attila and the Huns*, Oxford University Press, Oxford, 1948.

Vita Aniani ep. Aurelianensis, ed. Bruno Krusch, *MGH* (SRM. 3), 1896, pp.104–17.

CHAPTER 3

Bachrach, Bernard S., 'Vouillé and the Decisive Battle Phenomenon in Late Antique Gaul' in *The Battle of Vouillé, 507 CE: Where France Began*, ed. Ralph W. Mathisen and Danuta Shanzer, De Gruyter, Gottingen, 2012, pp.11–41.

Bachrach, Bernard S., *Early Carolingian Warfare: Prelude to Empire*, University of Pennsylvania Press, Philadelphia, 2011.

Gregory Bishop of Tours, *History of the Franks*, trans. by Ernest Brehaut, Columbia University Press, New York, 1916.

Halsall, G., *Warfare and Society in the Barbarian West*, 450–900, Routledge, London, 2003.

Lecointre, C. 'La Bataille de 507 entre Clovis et Alaric', *Bulletin de la Société des Antiquaires de l'Ouest* 3rd ser. 4 (1916–18), pp.423–56.

Rouche, M., *L'Aquitaine des Wisigoths aux Arabes, 418–781: Naissance d'une region, éditions de l'EHESS*, Paris, 1979.
Wood, I. N., *The Merovingian Kingdoms, 450–751*, Taylor & Francis, London/New York, 1994.

CHAPTER 4

Browning, Robert, *Byzantium and Bulgaria, a Comparative Study Across the Early Medieval Frontier*, Temple Smith, London, 1975.
Hupchick, Dennis P., *The Bulgarian-Byzantine Wars for Early Medieval Balkan Hegemony*, Palgrave, Basingstoke, 2017.
Maurice's Strategikon: Handbook of Byzantine Military Strategy, trans. G. T. Dennis (2nd edn.), University of Pennsylvania Press, Philadelphia, 1984.
Nicephorus, Patriarch of Constantinople, *Short History*, trans. by Cyril Mango, Dumbarton Oaks, Washington DC, 1990.
Pavlov, Plamen, *The Story – Distant and Close*, Veliko Tarnovo, 2010.
The Chronicle of Theophanes Confessor, Byzantine and Near Eastern History, AD284–813, tr. by P. Magdalino, Oxford, Clarendon, 1997.

CHAPTER 5

Collins, Roger, *The Arab Conquest of Spain, 710–97*, Blackwell, London, 1989.
Conquerors and Chroniclers of Early Medieval Spain, trans. by K. Baxter Wolf, Liverpool University Press, Liverpool, 2011.
Glick, Thomas F., *Islamic and Christian Spain in the Early Middle Ages*, Brill, Leiden, 2005.
Halsall, G., *Warfare and Society in the Barbarian West, 450–900*, Routledge, London, 2003.
Ibn Abd-el-Hakem, *History of the Conquest of Spain*, trans. by John Harris Jones, W. Fr. Kaestner, Gottingen, 1858.
Lewis, David L., *God's Crucible: Islam and the Making of Europe, 570 to 1215*, W. W. Norton, London, 2008.
Olagüe, Ignacio, *La revolución islámica en occidente*, Guadarrama, Barcelona, 1974.
Taha, Abdulwahid Dhanun, *The Muslim Conquest and Settlement of North Africa and Spain*, London, 1989.
Thompson, E. A., *The Goths in Spain*, Clarendon, Oxford, 1969.

CHAPTER 6

Brooks, E. W., 'The Campaign of 716–717, from Arabic Sources', *Journal of Hellenic Studies* 19 (1899), pp.19–31.
Canard, Marius, 'Les expéditions des Arabes contre Constantinople dans l'histoire et dans la légende', *Journal Asiatique* 208 (1926), pp.61–121.
Guilland, Rodolphe, 'L'Expédition de Maslama contre Constantinople (717–718)' in *Études byzantines*, ed. R. Guilland, Presses Universitaires de France, Paris, 1959, pp.109–33.
Kaegi, Walter E., 'Confronting Islam: Emperors versus Caliphs (641–c. 850)' in *The Cambridge History of the Byzantine Empire, c. 500–1492*, ed. J. Shepard, Cambridge University Press, Cambridge, 2008, pp.365–94.
Kennedy, Hugh, 'Byzantine-Arab Diplomacy in the Near East from the Islamic Conquests to the Mid Eleventh Century' in *Arab-Byzantine Relations in Early Islamic Times*, ed. M. Bonner, Ashgate, Aldershot, 2004, pp.81–94.
Kennedy, Hugh, *The Armies of the Caliphs: Military and Society in the Early Islamic State Warfare and History*, Routledge, London, 2001.
Nicolle, David, *The Armies of Islam, 7th–11th Centuries*, Osprey, London, 1982.
The Chronicle of Michael the Great, Patriarch of the Syrians, trans. by Robert Bedrosian, Long Branch, NJ, 2013.
The Chronicle of Theophanes Confessor, Byzantine and Near Eastern History, AD284–813, trans. P. Magdalino, Clarendon, Oxford, 1997.
The History of al-Tabari, Volume XXIV, The Empire in Transition, translated and annotated by David Stephan Powers, State University of New York Press, Albany, 1989.
Treadgold, Warren, *A History of the Byzantine State and Society*, Stanford University Press, Stanford, 1997.
Tsangadas, B. C. P., *The Fortification and Defense of Constantinople*, Columbia University Press, New York, 1980.

CHAPTER 7

Collins, R., *The Arab Conquest of Spain, 710–797*, Oxford, 1989.
Conquerors and Chroniclers of Early Medieval Spain, trans. by Kenneth Baxter Wolf, Liverpool University Press, Liverpool, 1990.
Kennedy, Hugh, *The Armies of the Caliphs: Military and Society in the Early Islamic State Warfare and History*, Routledge, London, 2001.
Mercier, Maurice and Seguin, André, *Charles Martel et la bataille de Poitiers*, P. Geuthner, Paris, 1944.
Nicolle, David, *Poitiers AD732, Charles Martel Turns the Islamic Tide*, Osprey, Oxford, 2008.
Watson, William E., 'The Battle of Tours-Poitiers Revisited', *Providence: Studies in Western Civilization* 2 (1993), pp.51–68.

CHAPTER 8

Beeler, John, *Warfare in Feudal Europe 730–1200*, Cornell University Press, Ithaca, 1971.
Bowlus, Charles R., *Franks, Moravians and Magyars, The Struggle for the Middle Danube, 788–907*, University of Pennsylvania Press, Philadelphia, 1995.
Carey, Brian Todd, *Warfare in the Medieval World*, Pen & Sword, Barnsley, 2006.
Contamine, Philippe, *War in the Middle Ages*, Blackwell, Oxford, 2005.
Delbruck, Hans, *History of the Art of War*, vol. III, trans. Walter J. Renfroe, Greenwood, London, 1982.
Moravcsik, Gyula, *Byzantine Christianity and the Magyars in the Period of Their Migration*, The American Association for the Advancement of Slavic Studies, 2008.
Oman, Sir Charles, *A History of the Art of War in the Middle Ages*, v. I, Greenhill, London, 1993.
Reuter, Timothy, *Germany in the Early Middle Ages, c. 800–1056*, Routledge, London, 1991.
Vasiliev, A. A., *History of the Byzantine Empire*, Madison, 1928.

CHAPTER 9

Amatus of Montecassino, *The History of the Normans*, trans. P. Dunbar and revised with notes by G. Loud, Boydell & Brewer, Woodbridge, 2004.
Brown, Gordon S., *The Norman Conquest of Southern Italy and Sicily*, McFarland & Company, Jefferson NC, 2003.
Chalandon, Ferdinand, *Histoire de la domination normande en Italie et en Sicilie*, Picard, Paris, 1907.
Loud, Graham, *The Age of Robert Guiscard: Southern Italy and the Norman Conquest*, Longman, New York, 2000.
Loud, Graham, 'How "Norman" was the Norman Conquest of Southern Italy?' *Nottingham Medieval Studies* 25 (1981), pp.13–34.
Malaterra, Geoffrey, *The Deeds of Count Roger of Calabria and Sicily and of his Brother Duke Robert Guiscard*, ed. and trans. K. B. Wolf , The University of Michigan Press, Ann Arbor, 2005.
Theotokis, Georgios, *The Norman Campaigns in the Balkans, 1081–1108*, Boydell & Brewer, Woodbridge, 2014.
William of Apulia (Guillaume de Pouille), *La Geste de Robert Guiscard*, ed. and trans. M. Mathieu, Palermo, 1961.

CHAPTER 10

Beeler, John, *Warfare in England, 1066–1189*, Cornell University Press, New York, 1996.
Brown, R. A., 'The Battle of Hastings', *Anglo-Norman Studies* 3 (1980), pp.1–21.
Hern, Ashley, *Mythical Battle: Hastings 1066*, Robert Hale, Wiltshire, 2017.
Lawson, Michelle K., *The Battle of Hastings, 1066*, Tempus, Stroud, 2002.
Morillo, Stephen, *Warfare under the Anglo-Norman Kings, 1066–1135*, Boydell & Brewer, Woodbridge, 1994.
Rud, Mogens, *The Bayeux Tapestry: And the Battle of Hastings 1066*, Christian Ejlers Forlar, 2004.

CHAPTER 11

Carey, Brian Todd, *Warfare in the Medieval World*, Pen & Sword, Barnsley, 2006.
García Fitz, Francisco, 'Was Las Navas a decisive battle?' *Journal of Medieval Iberian Studies* 4 (2012), pp.5–9.
Gomez, Miguel Dolan, 'The Battle of Las Navas de Tolosa: The Culture and Practice of Crusading in Medieval Iberia', PhD dissertation, University of Tennessee, 2011.
Nicolle, David, *Crusader Warfare Volume II, Muslims, Mongols and the Struggle against the Crusades*, Hambledon Continuum, London, 2007.
Nicolle, David, *El Cid and the Reconquista, 1050–1492*, Osprey, London, 1988.
Nicolle, David, *The Armies of Islam, 7th–11th Centuries*, Osprey, London, 1982.
Nicolle, David, *The Moors: the Islamic West, 7th–15th Centuries AD*, Osprey, Oxford, 2001.
O'Callaghan, Joseph F., *Reconquest and Crusade in Medieval Spain*, University of Pennsylvania Press, Philadelphia PA, 2004.
Three sources on the Battle of Las Navas de Tolosa in 1212, available online in: https://deremilitari.org/2014/11/three-sources-on-the-battle-of-las-novas-de-tolosa-in-1212/

CHAPTER 12

Barthélemy, Dominique, *La bataille de Bouvines. Histoire et légendes*, Éditions Perrin, Paris, 2018.
Bartlett, Robert, *England under the Norman and Angevin Kings: 1075–1225*, Oxford University Press, Oxford, 2000.
Bradbury, Jim, *Philip Augustus, King of France 1180–1223*, Routledge, London, 1998.
Carpenter, David, *Struggle for Mastery: The Penguin History of Britain 1066–1284*, London, Penguin, 2003.
Church, Stephen D., *King John: New Interpretations*, Boydell & Brewer, Woodbridge, 2007.
Cox, Eugene L., *The Eagles of Savoy: The House of Savoy in Thirteenth Century Europe*, Princeton University Press, Princeton NJ, 1974.
Duby, Georges, *The Legend of Bouvines, War, Religion and Culture in the Middle Ages*, trans. by Catherine Tihanyi, Cambridge University Press, Cambridge, 1990.
Gilligham, John, *The Angevin Empire*, London, Arnold, 2001.
Verbruggen, J. F., *The Art of Warfare in Western Europe During the Middle Ages, from the Eighth Century to 1340*, trans. S. Willard, R. W. Southern, Boydell & Brewer, Woodbridge, 1997.

CHAPTER 13

Dukes, Paul, *A History of Russia, Medieval, Modern, Contemporary, c.882–1996*, Palgrave, Basingstoke, 1998.
Nicolle, David, *Lake Peipus 1242, Battle of the Ice*, Osprey, London, 1996.
Nicolle, David, *Medieval Russian Armies 1250–1500*, Osprey, Oxford, 2002.
Nicolle, David, *Teutonic Knight 1190–1561*, Osprey, Oxford, 2007.
Nowakowski, Andrzej, *Arms and Armours in the Medieval Teutonic Order's State in Prussia*, Oficyna Naukowa, Lodz, 1994.
Selart, Anti, *Livonia, Rus' and the Baltic Crusades in the Thirteenth Century*, Brill, Leiden, 2007.
The Chronicle of Novgorod, 1016–1471, trans. by R. Mitchel and N. Forbes, London, 1914.
The Livonian Rhymed Chronicle, trans. by Jerry Smith and William Urban, Indiana University Press, Bloomington, 1977.
Urban, William, *The Teutonic Knights: A Military History*, Greenhill, London, 2003.

CHAPTER 14

Babuin, A., 'Τα Επιθετικά Όπλα των Βυζαντινών Κατά την Ύστερη Περίοδο (1204–1453),' (The offensive weapons of the Byzantines in the Later Period (1204–1453)), unpublished PhD thesis, University of Ioannina, 2009.
Bartusis, Mark C., *The Late Byzantine Army, Arms and Society, 1204–1453*, University of Pennsylvania Press, Philadelphia, 1992.
Geanakoplos, Deno John, 'Greco-Latin Relations on the Eve of the Byzantine Restoration: The Battle of Pelagonia – 1259', *Dumbarton Oaks Papers* 7 (1953) pp.99–141.
George Akropolites: The History, trans. by Ruth Macrides, Oxford University Press, Oxford, 2007.
Kanellopoulos, Nikolaos, 'Η οργάνωση και η τακτική του βυζαντινού στρατού στην ύστερη περίοδο (1204–1461)' (The organization and tactics of the Byzantine army in the Later period (1204–1461)), unpublished PhD thesis, University of Thessaly, 2010.
Kyriakidis, Savvas, *Warfare in Late Byzantium, 1204–1453*, Brill, Leiden, 2011.
Livre de la conqueste de la Princée de l'Amorée. Chronique de Morée (1204–1305), ed. J. Longnon, Paris, 1911.
Mihajlovski, Robert, 'The Battle of Pelagonia, 1259: a New Look at the March Routes and Topography', *Byzantinoslavica* 64 (2006), pp.275–284.
Nicephori Gregorae, *Historiae Byzantinae*, CSHB, ed. Immanuel Bekker, Bonn, 1829–1855.
Nicol, Donald M., 'The date of the battle of Pelagonia', *Byzantinische Zeitschrift* 49 (1956), pp.68–71.
To chronikon tou Moreos: a history in political verse, relating to the establishment of feudalism in Greece by the Franks in the thirteenth century, ed. John Schmitt, Methuen, London, 1904.
Wilksman, Juho, 'The Campaign and Battle of Pelagonia 1259', *Byzantinos Domos* 17–18 (2009–2010), pp.131–174.

CHAPTER 15

Annales Placentini Gibellini a. 1154–1284, in MGH SS 18 (1863), pp.457–581.
France, John, *Western Warfare in the Age of the Crusades, 1000–1300*, UCL Press, London, 1999, pp.181–84.
Gravett, Christopher, *German Medieval Armies, 1000–1300*, Osprey, London, 1997.
Herde, P., 'Die Schlact bei Tagliacozzo. Eine historisch-topographische Studie' *Zeitschrift fur Bayerische Landesgeschichte* 28 (1962), pp.741–44.
Herde, P., 'Taktiken muslimischer Heere vom ersten Kreuzzug bis Ayn Djalut (1260) und ihre Einwirkung auf de Schlact bei Tagliacozzo' in *Das Heilige Land im Mittelalter: Begegnungsvraum zwischen Orient und Okzident*, ed. by W. Fischer and J. Schneider, Verlag Degener, Neustadt, 1982, pp.83–94.
Nicolle, David, *French Medieval Armies, 1000–1300*, Osprey, London, 1991.
Nicolle, David, *Italian Medieval Armies, 1000–1300*, Osprey, Oxford, 2002.
Oman, Charles, *The Art of War in the Middle Ages*, (2 vols), Greenhill, London, 1998, I, pp.490–97.

CHAPTER 16

Carey, Brian Todd, *Warfare in the Medieval World*, Pen & Sword, Barnsley, 2011.
Delbrück, Hans, *Medieval Warfare*, University of Nebraska Press, Lincoln, 1990, vol. III.
DeVries, Kelly, *Infantry Warfare in the Early Fourteenth Century, Discipline, Tactics and Technology*, Boydell & Brewer, Woodbridge, 1996.
Gravett, Christopher, *German Medieval Armies 1300–1500*, Osprey, London, 1985.
Hugener, Rainer, 'Erinnerungsort im Wandel. Das Sempacher Schlachtgedenken im Mittelalter und in der Frühen Neuzeit', *Der Geschichtsfreund. Zeitschrift des Historischen Vereins Zentralschweiz* 165 (2012), 135–171.
Miller, Douglas, *The Swiss at War 1300–1500*, Osprey, London, 1979.
Peter Suchenwirts' Werke aus dem 14. Jahrhunderte: Ein Beytrag zur Zeit-und Siltengeschichte, ed. by Alois Primisser, Wien, 1827.
Verbruggen, J. F., *The Art of Warfare in Western Europe During the Middle Ages from the Eighth Century to 1340*, Boydell & Brewer, Woodbridge, 1997.

CHAPTER 17

Atiya, Aziz S., *The Crusade of Nicopolis*, Methuen, London, 1934.
DeVries, Kelly, 'The Battle of Nicopolis', *The Medieval History Magazine* (Issue 2, October 2003), pp.22–27.
DeVries, Kelly, 'The Lack of a Western European Military Response to the Ottoman Invasions of Eastern Europe from Nicopolis (1396) to Mohacs (1526)', *Journal of Military History* 63 (1999), pp.539–559.
Kaçar, Hilmi and Dumolyn, Jan, 'The Battle of Nicopolis (1396), Burgundian Catastrophe and Ottoman Fait Divers', *Revue belge de philologie et d' histoire* 91 (2013), pp.905–34.
Madden, Thomas F., *Crusades: the Illustrated History*, University of Michigan Press, Ann Arbor, 2005.
Nicolle, David, *Armies of the Ottoman Turks 1300–1774*, Osprey, London, 1983.
Nicolle, David, *Hungary and the Fall of Eastern Europe, 1000–1568*, Osprey, London, 1988.
Nicolle, David, *Nicopolis 1396*, Osprey, Oxford, 1999.
The Battle of Nicopolis (1396), according to Johann Schiltberger: https://web.archive.org/web/20090206151155/http://deremilitari.org/resources/sources/nicopolis.htm
Tuchman, Barbara W., *A Distant Mirror: The Calamitous 14th Century*, Random House Publishing Group, New York, 2011.

CHAPTER 18

Christiansen, Eric, *The Northern Crusades*, Penguin, London, 1997.
Cronica conflictus Wladislai regis Poloniae cum cruciferis anno Christi 1410, ed. Zygmunt Celichowski, Poznan, 1911.
Jučas, Mečislovas, *The Battle of Grünwald, Vilnius*, National Museum Palace of the Grand Dukes of Lithuania, 2009.
Nowakowski, Andrzej, *Arms and Armours in the Medieval Teutonic Order's State in Prussia*, Oficyna Naukowa, Lodz, 1994.
Posilge, Johan von, *Chronik des landes Preussen, 1360–1419*, in Scriptores Rerum Prussicarum, vol. 3, Leipzig, 1866.
Turnbull, Stephen, *Tannenberg 1410: Disaster for the Teutonic Knights*, Osprey, London, 2003.
Urban, William, *Tannenberg and After: Lithuania, Poland and the Teutonic Order in Search of Immortality*, Lithuanian Research and Studies Center, Chicago, 2003.

CHAPTER 19

Cooper, Stephen, *The Real Falstaff, Sir John Fastolf and the Hundred Years' War*, Pen & Sword, Barnsley, 2010.
Curry, A., *The Hundred Years' War, 1337–1453*, Routledge, London, 2003.
Davis, Paul K., *Besieged: 100 Great Sieges from Jericho to Sarajevo*, Oxford University Press, Oxford, 2001.
DeVries, Kelly, *Joan of Arc: a Military Leader*, Sutton Publishing, 1999.
Green, David, *The Hundred Years War: A People's History*, Yale University Press, London, 2014.
Nicolle, David, *Orléans 1429, France Turns the Tide*, Osprey, Oxford, 2001.
Pernoud, Régine and Clin, Marie-Véronique, *Joan of Arc: Her Story*, St Martin's Press, New York, 1998.
The chronicles of Enguerrand de Monstrelet, trans. by Thomas Johnes, H. G. Bohn, London, 1853.

CHAPTER 20

Antoche, E. A., 'Les expéditions de Nicopolis (1396) et de Varna (1444): une comparaison,' *Mediævalia Transilvanica* 4 (2000), pp.28–74.
Cartledge, Bryan, *The Will to Survive: A History of Hungary*, Columbia University Press, New York, 2011.
Engel, P., *The Realm of St Stephen: A History of Medieval Hungary, 895–1526*, I. B. Tauris, London, 2001.
Imber, Colin, *The Crusade of Varna, 1443–45*, Ashgate, Aldershot, 2006.
İnalcık, H., 'The Crusade of Varna', in K. M. Setton (gen. ed.), *A History of the Crusades*, 8 vols (Madison, WI, 1855–89), VI: The Impact of the Crusades on Europe, ed. H. W. Hazard and N. P. Zacour, pp. 276–310.
Murphy, Rhoads, 'Ottoman military organisation in south-eastern Europe, c. 1420–1720' in *European Warfare, 1350–1750*, ed. Frank Tallett and D. J. B. Trim, Cambridge University Press, Cambridge, 2010, pp.135–58.
Nicolle, David, *Armies of the Ottoman Turks 1300–1774*, Osprey, London, 1983.
Nicolle, David, *Hungary and the Fall of Eastern Europe, 1000–1568*, Osprey, London, 1988.
Sedlar, Jean W., *East Central Europe in the Middle Ages, 1000–1500*, University of Washington Press, Seattle, 1994.
Setton, Kenneth Meyer, *The Papacy and the Levant, 1204–1571: The fifteenth century*, American Philosophical Society, Philadelphia, 1978.
Shaw, Stanford J., *History of the Ottoman Empire and Modern Turkey, vol. 1: Empire of the Gazis: the rise and decline of the Ottoman Empire, 1280–1808*, Cambridge University Press, Cambridge, 1976.
Turnbull, S., *The Ottoman Empire 1326–1699*, Routledge, London, 2005.

SELECTED BIBLIOGRAPHY

A Companion to the Roman Army, ed. Paul Erdkamp, Wiley-Blackwell, Oxford, 2007.

Atiya, Aziz S., *The Crusade of Nicopolis*, Methuen, London, 1934.

Babuin, A., 'Τα Επιθετικά Όπλα των Βυζαντινών Κατά την Ύστερη Περίοδο (1204–1453)' ('The offensive weapons of the Byzantines in the Later Period (1204–1453)'), unpublished PhD thesis, University of Ioannina, 2009.

Bachrach, Bernard S., 'Vouillé and the Decisive Battle Phenomenon in Late Antique Gaul' in *The Battle of Vouillé, 507CE: Where France Began*, ed. Ralph W. Mathisen and Danuta Shanzer, De Gruyter, Gottingen, 2012, pp.11–41.

––––––––, *Early Carolingian Warfare: Prelude to Empire*, University of Pennsylvania Press, Philadelphia, 2011.

Barthélemy, Dominique, *La bataille de Bouvines. Histoire et légendes*, Éditions Perrin, Paris, 2018.

Bartlett, Robert, *England Under the Norman and Angevin Kings: 1075–1225*, Oxford University Press, Oxford, 2000.

Beeler, John, *Warfare in England, 1066–1189*, Cornell University Press, New York, 1996.

Bowlus, Charles R., *Franks, Moravians and Magyars, The Struggle for the Middle Danube, 788–907*, University of Pennsylvania Press, Philadelphia, 1995.

Bradbury, Jim, *Philip Augustus, King of France 1180–1223*, Routledge, London, 1998.

Brooks, E. W., 'The Campaign of 716–717, from Arabic Sources', *Journal of Hellenic Studies* 19 (1899), pp.19–31.

Brown, Gordon S., *The Norman Conquest of Southern Italy and Sicily*, McFarland & Company, Jefferson NC, 2003.

Browning, Robert, *Byzantium and Bulgaria, A Comparative Study Across the Early Medieval Frontier*, Temple Smith, London, 1975.

Cameron, A., *The Last Pagans of Rome*, Oxford University Press, Oxford, 2011.

Canard, Marius, 'Les expéditions des Arabes contre Constantinople dans l'histoire et dans la légende', *Journal Asiatique* 208 (1926), pp.61–121.

Carey, Brian Todd, *Warfare in the Medieval World*, Pen & Sword, Barnsley, 2006.

Cartledge, Bryan, *The Will to Survive: A History of Hungary*, Columbia University Press, New York, 2011.

Chalandon, Ferdinand, *Histoire de la domination normande en Italie et en Sicilie*, Picard, Paris, 1907.

Christiansen, Eric, *The Northern Crusades*, Penguin, London, 1997.

Church, Stephen D., *King John: New Interpretations*, Boydell & Brewer, Woodbridge, 2007.

Collins, Roger, *The Arab Conquest of Spain, 710–97*, Blackwell, London, 1989.

Cooper, Stephen, *The Real Falstaff, Sir John Fastalf and the Hundred Years' War*, Pen & Sword, Barnsley, 2010.

Coulston, J. C. N., 'Late Roman Military Equipment Culture', in A. Sarantis and N. Christie (eds) *War and Warfare in Late Antiquity*, Brill, Leiden, 2013, pp.463–92.

Curry, A., *The Hundred Years' War, 1337–1453*, Routledge, London, 2003.

Davis, Paul K., *Besieged: 100 Great Sieges from Jericho to Sarajevo*, Oxford University Press, Oxford, 2001.

Delbrück, Hans, *Medieval Warfare*, University of Nebraska Press, Lincoln, 1990, vol. III.

DeVries, Kelly, 'The Battle of Nicopolis', *The Medieval History Magazine* (Issue 2, October 2003), pp.22–27.

––––––––, 'The Lack of a Western European Military Response to the Ottoman Invasions of Eastern Europe from Nicopolis (1396) to Mohacs (1526)', *Journal of Military History* 63 (1999), pp.539–559.

––––––––, *Infantry Warfare in the Early Fourteenth Century, Discipline, Tactics, and Technology*, Boydell & Brewer, Woodbridge, 1996.

––––––––, *Joan of Arc: a Military Leader*, Sutton Publishing, 1999.

Duby, Georges, *The Legend of Bouvines, War, Religion and Culture in the Middle Ages*, trans. by Catherine Tihanyi, Cambridge University Press, Cambridge, 1990.

Dukes, Paul, *A History of Russia, Medieval, Modern, Contemporary, c. 882–1996*, Palgrave, Basingstoke, 1998.

France, John, *Western Warfare in the Age of the Crusades, 1000–1300*, UCL Press, London, 1999, pp.181–84.

García Fitz, Francisco, 'Was Las Navas a decisive battle?', *Journal of Medieval Iberian Studies* 4 (2012), pp.5–9.

Geanakoplos, Deno John, 'Greco-Latin Relations on the Eve of the Byzantine Restoration: The Battle of Pelagonia – 1259', *Dumbarton Oaks Papers* 7 (1953), pp.99–141.

Gilligham, John, *The Angevin Empire*, London, Arnold, 2001.

Glick, Thomas F., *Islamic and Christian Spain in the Early Middle Ages*, Brill, Leiden, 2005.

Gravett, Christopher, *German Medieval Armies, 1000–1300*, Osprey, London, 1997.

Green, David, *The Hundred Years War: A People's History*, Yale University Press, London, 2014.

Guilland, Rodolphe, 'L'Expédition de Maslama contre Constantinople (717–718)' in *Études byzantines*, ed. R. Guilland, Presses Universitaires de France, Paris, 1959, pp.109–33.

Halsall, G., *Barbarian Migrations and the Roman West, 376–568*, Cambridge University Press, Cambridge, 2007.

Hern, Ashley, *Mythical Battle: Hastings 1066*, Robert Hale, Wiltshire, 2017.

Hughes, Ian, *Aetius: Attila's Nemesis*, Pen & Sword, Barnsley, 2012.

Hupchick, Dennis P., *The Bulgarian-Byzantine Wars for Early Medieval Balkan Hegemony*, Palgrave, Basingstoke, 2017.

Imber, Colin, *The Crusade of Varna, 1443–45*, Ashgate, Aldershot, 2006.

İnalcık, H., 'The Crusade of Varna', in K. M. Setton (gen. ed.) *A History of the Crusades*, 8 vols (Madison, WI, 1855–89), VI: 'The Impact of the Crusades on Europe', ed. H. W. Hazard and N. P. Zacour, pp.276–310.

Jučas, Mečislovas, *The Battle of Grünwald*, Vilnius, National Museum Palace of the Grand Dukes of Lithuania, 2009.

Kaçar, Hilmi and Dumolyn, Jan, 'The Battle of Nicopolis (1396), Burgundian Catastrophe and Ottoman Fait Divers', *Revue belge de philologie et d' histoire* 91 (2013), pp.905–34.

Kaegi, Walter E., 'Confronting Islam: Emperors versus Caliphs (641–c. 850)', in *The Cambridge History of the Byzantine Empire, c. 500–1492*, ed. J. Shepard, Cambridge University Press, Cambridge, 2008, pp.365–94.

Kanellopoulos, Nikolaos, 'Η οργάνωση και η τακτική του βυζαντινού στρατού στην ύστερη περίοδο (1204-1461)' ('The organization and tactics of the Byzantine army in the Later period (1204–1461)'), unpublished PhD thesis, University of Thessaly, 2010.

Kennedy, Hugh, *The Armies of the Caliphs: Military and Society in the Early Islamic State Warfare and History*, Routledge, London, 2001.

Kim, Hyun Jin, *The Huns, Rome, and the Birth of Europe*, Cambridge University Press, Cambridge, 2013.

Lawson, Michelle K., *The Battle of Hastings, 1066*, Tempus, Stroud, 2002.

Lewis, David L., *God's Crucible: Islam and the Making of Europe, 570 to 1215*, W. W. Norton, London, 2008.

Lindner, Rudi, 'Nomadism, Horses and Huns', *Past & Present* 92 (1981), pp.2–19.

Loud, Graham, *The Age of Robert Guiscard: Southern Italy and the Norman Conquest*, Longman, New York, 2000.

MacDowall, S., *Catalaunian Fields AD451, Rome's Last Great Battle*, Osprey, Oxford, 2015.

Maenchen-Helfen, Otto J., *The World of the Huns, Studies in the History and Culture*, University of California Press, London, 1973.

Maurice's Strategikon: Handbook of Byzantine Military Strategy, trans. G.T. Dennis (2nd edn.), University of Pennsylvania Press, Philadelphia, 1984.

Mihajlovski, Robert, 'The Battle of Pelagonia, 1259: a New Look at the March Routes and Topography', *Byzantinoslavica* 64 (2006), pp.275–284.

Miller, Douglas, *The Swiss at War 1300–1500*, Osprey, London, 1979.

Mitchell, S., *A History of the Later Roman Empire, AD284–641*, (2nd edn.), Oxford University Press, Oxford, 2015.

Moravcsik, Gyula, *Byzantine Christianity and the Magyars in the Period of Their Migration*, The American Association for the Advancement of Slavic Studies, 2008.

Murphy, Rhoads, 'Ottoman military organisation in south-eastern Europe, c. 1420–1720', in *European Warfare, 1350–1750*, ed. Frank Tallett and D. J. B. Trim, Cambridge University Press, Cambridge, 2010, pp.135–58.

Nicolle, David, *Armies of the Ottoman Turks 1300–1774*, Osprey, London, 1983.

–––––––––, *Crusader Warfare Volume II, Muslims, Mongols and the Struggle against the Crusades*, Hambledon Continuum, London, 2007.

–––––––––, *El Cid and the Reconquista, 1050–1492*, Osprey, London, 1988.

–––––––––, *French Medieval Armies, 1000–1300*, Osprey, London, 1991.

–––––––––, *Hungary and the Fall of Eastern Europe, 1000–1568*, Osprey, London, 1988.

–––––––––, *Italian Medieval Armies, 1000–1300*, Osprey, Oxford, 2002.

––––––––, *Lake Peipus 1242, Battle of the Ice*, Osprey, London, 1996.

––––––––, *Medieval Russian Armies 1250–1500*, Osprey, Oxford, 2002.

––––––––, *Nicopolis 1396*, Osprey, Oxford, 1999.

––––––––, *Orléans 1429, France Turns the Tide*, Osprey, Oxford, 2001.

––––––––, *Poitiers AD732, Charles Martel Turns the Islamic Tide*, Osprey, Oxford, 2008.

––––––––, *Teutonic Knight 1190–1561*, Osprey, Oxford, 2007.

––––––––, *The Moors: The Islamic West, 7th–15th Centuries AD*, Osprey, Oxford, 2001.

Nowakowski, Andrzej, *Arms and Armours in the Medieval Teutonic Order's State in Prussia*, Oficyna Naukowa, Lodz, 1994.

O'Callaghan, Joseph F., *Reconquest and crusade in medieval Spain*, University of Pennsylvania Press, Philadelphia PA, 2004.

Oman, Sir Charles, *A History of the Art of War in the Middle Ages*, v. I, Greenhill, London, 1993.

Selart, Anti, *Livonia, Rus' and the Baltic Crusades in the Thirteenth Century*, Brill, Leiden, 2007.

Shaw, Stanford J., *History of the Ottoman Empire and Modern Turkey*, vol. 1: Empire of the Gazis: The Rise and Decline of the Ottoman Empire, 1280–1808, Cambridge University Press, Cambridge, 1976.

Southern, P. and Dixon, K. R., *The Late Roman Army*, Routledge, London, 1996.

The Cambridge Ancient History (vol. XIII, The Late Empire, AD337–425), ed. A. Cameron and P. Garnsey, Cambridge University Press, Cambridge, 1998.

The Chronicle of Theophanes Confessor, Byzantine and Near Eastern History, AD284-813, trans. P. Magdalino, Oxford, Clarendon, 1997.

Theotokis, Georgios, *The Norman Campaigns in the Balkans, 1081–1108*, Boydell & Brewer, Woodbridge, 2014.

Thompson, E. A., *A History of Attila and the Huns*, Oxford University Press, Oxford, 1948.

Timothy Reuter, *Germany in the Early Middle Ages, c. 800–1056*, Routledge, London, 1991.

Treadgold, Warren, *A History of the Byzantine State and Society*, Stanford University Press, Stanford, 1997.

Tsangadas, B. C. P., *The Fortification and Defense of Constantinople*, Columbia University Press, New York, 1980.

Tuchman, Barbara W., *A Distant Mirror: The Calamitous 14th Century*, Random House Publishing Group, New York, 2011.

Turnbull, S., *The Ottoman Empire 1326–1699*, Routledge, London, 2005.

––––––––, *Tannenberg 1410: Disaster for the Teutonic Knights*, Osprey, London, 2003.

Urban, William, *Tannenberg and After: Lithuania, Poland and the Teutonic Order in Search of Immortality*, Lithuanian Research and Studies Center, Chicago, 2003.

Vegetius, *Epitome of Military Science*, trans. by N. P. Milner, Liverpool University Press, Liverpool, 1993.

Watson, William E., 'The Battle of Tours-Poitiers Revisited', *Providence: Studies in Western Civilization* 2 (1993), pp.51–68.

Wilksman, Juho, 'The Campaign and Battle of Pelagonia 1259', *Byzantinos Domos* 17–18 (2009–2010), pp.131–74.

Wood, I. N., *The Merovingian Kingdoms, 450–751*, Taylor & Francis, London/New York, 1994.

NOTES

INTRODUCTION

1. Clausewitz, Carl von, *On War*, ed. and trans. by M. Howard and P. Paret, Princeton University Press, New Jersey, 1989, p.75.
2. James, William, *The Moral Equivalent of War*, New York, 1910.
3. Munoz-Rojas, D., Frèsard, J.-J., 'The roots of behaviour in war: Understanding and preventing IHL violations,' *International Review of the Red Cross* 86 (2004), pp.189–206, especially p.196.
4. Morillo, S., *What is Military History?*, Polity, Cambridge, 2013, p.4.
5. Morillo, S., Black, J., Lococo, P., *War in World History, Society, Technology and War from Ancient Times to the Present* (2 vols.), New York, 2009, vol. I, p.[x]. *See also* the collection of essays: *Transcultural Wars: from the Middle Ages to the 21st Century*, ed. by Hans-Henning Kortüm, Berlin, 2006, especially part II.
6. Gibbon, Edward, *The Decline and Fall of the Roman Empire*, vol. 3, 1185AD–1453AD, Modern Library, New York, 2000, p.223.
7. Vegetius, *Epitome of Military Science*, trans. by N. P. Milner, Liverpool University Press, Liverpool, 1994, III. 26, p.116.
8. Maurice's *Strategikon: Handbook of Byzantine Military Strategy*, trans. G. T. Dennis, University of Pennsylvania Press, Philadelphia, 1984, VII, p.65.
9. *Leo VI, The Taktika of Leo VI, Corpus Fontium Historiae Byzantinae*, vol. 49, trans. G. T. Dennis, Dumbarton Oaks, Washington DC, 2010, XX. 51, p.554.
10. Harari, Yuval Noah, 'The Concept of "Decisive Battles" in World History', *Journal of World History* 18 (2007), pp.251–266.
11. Clausewitz, Carl von, *On War*, ed. and trans. M. Howard and P. Paret, Princeton University Press, Princeton, 1989, pp.119–20.
12. Keegan, J., *The Face of Battle: A Study of Agincourt, Waterloo and the Somme*, Pimlico, London, 2004, p.18.

CHAPTER 1

1. *Ammianus Marcellinus*, trans. by J. C. Rolfe, Heinemann, London, 1939, vol. III, 31. 13. 19, p.483.
2. Mitchell, S., *A History of the Later Roman Empire, AD284–641*, (2nd edn.) Oxford University Press, Oxford, 2015, p.93.
3. *The Ecclesiastical History of Sozomen*, trans. by Edward Walford, Henry G. Bohn, London, 1846, 7. 22, p.362.
4. The tactical emphasis upon cavalry, according to scholarly consensus, was one of the most notable differences between the armies before and after the fourth century AD: Whitby, M., 'Army and Society in the Late Roman World: A Context for Decline?' in P. Erdkamp (ed.) *A Companion to the Roman Army*, Wiley-Blackwell, Oxford, 2007, pp.515–31; Lendon, J. E., *Soldiers and Ghosts: A History of Battle in Classical Antiquity*, Yale University Press, New Haven, 2007, pp.263–68; Coulston, J. C. N., 'Late Roman Military Equipment Culture' in Alexander Sarantis and Neil Christie (eds) *War and Warfare in Late Antiquity*, Brill, Leiden 2013, vol. II, p.478.
5. For numbers on both halves of the Roman Empire in the fourth century: Jones, A. H. M., *The Later Roman Empire, 282–602, A Social, Economic and Administrative Survey*, Taylor & Francis, Oxford, 1964 (3 vols), vol. III, pp.181–211; Treadgold, W., *Byzantium and Its Army, 284–1081*, Stanford Unversity Press, Stanford C A, 1995, pp.43–59.
6. DeVries, K., *Medieval Military Technology*, Toronto University Press, Ontario, 1992, chapter 1.
7. Vegetius, *Epitome of Military Science*, trans. by N. P. Milner, Liverpool University Press, Liverpool, 1993, I. 20, p.22.
8. Vegetius, *Epitome of Military Science*, II. 15, p.47.
9. Sozomen, p.362.
10. Cameron, *The Last Pagans of Rome*, pp.93–111.
11. Cameron, *The Last Pagans of Rome*, pp.112–24.

CHAPTER 2

1. *Ammianus Marcellinus*, trans. by J. C. Rofle, Heinemann, London, 1939, vol. III, 31. 2, pp.381–95; Matthews, J. F., *The Roman Empire of Ammianus Marcellinus*, Michigan Classical Press, London, 1989, pp.332–42. For the demonization of the Huns in Late Antique Roman sources: Maenchen-Helfen, Otto J., *The World of the Huns, Studies in the History and Culture*, University of California Press, London, 1973, pp.1–17.
2. *The Gothic History of Jordanes*, trans. by C. C. Mierow, Heinemann, London, 1915, p.103.
3. *The Gothic History of Jordanes*, p.107.
4. Bishop Gregory of Tours, *History of the Franks*, trans. by E. Brehaut, Columbia University Press, New York, 1916, p.26.
5. *Sidonius Apollinaris, Poems and Letters*, trans. by W. B. Anderson, Heinemann, London, 1936, poem VII, p.147.
6. Hughes, Ian, *Aetius: Attila's Nemesis*, Pen & Sword, Barnsley, 2012, p.159.
7. MacDowall, Simon, *Late Roman Infantryman*, London, 1994, pp.4–5; ibid, *Catalaunian Fields AD451, Rome's Last Great Battle*, pp.30–31.
8. Heather, Peter, *The Goths*, Wiley-Blackwell, Oxford, 1996, p.176.
9. Maurice's *Strategikon: handbook of Byzantine military strategy*, trans. G. T. Dennis (University of Pennsylvania Press, Philadelphia, 1984) (latest edition 2010), pp.119–20.
10. Maenchen-Helfen, *The World of the Huns*, pp.201–58.
11. Lindner, Rudi, 'Nomadism, Horses, and Huns', *Past & Present* 92 (1981), 15.
12. B. S. Bachrach is a proponent of the view that early medieval commanders could raise armies of more than 50,000 effectives: 'The Hun Army at the Battle of Chalons (451): An Essay in Military Demography' in K. Brunner and B. Merta (eds) *Ethnogenese und Überlieferung: Angewandte Methoden der Frümittelalterforschung*, Vienna and Munich, 1994, pp. 59–67. G. Halsall is of the opposite view, that the 'barbarian' armies of the fourth and fifth centuries could not have been very big: *Barbarian Migrations and the Roman West, 376–568*, pp.144–5. E. A. Thompson remarks 'I doubt that Attila could have fed an army of even 30,000 men': *A History of Attila and the Huns*, p.142, n.1. *See also* S. MacDowall, *Catalaunian Fields AD451, Rome's Last Great Battle*, pp.29–30.
13. MacDowall, *Catalaunian Fields*, p.64.
14. Hughes, *Aetius: Attila's Nemesis*, p.161; J. B. Bury, *History of the Later Roman Empire from the Death of Theodosius I to the Death of Justinian*, New York: 1958, p.294; Abels, R., *Armies, War, and Society in the West, ca.300–ca.600: Late Roman and Barbarian Military Organizations and the 'Fall of the Roman Empire'*, p.66 (teaching documents available in https://usna.academia.edu/RichardAbels).
15. Halsall, *Barbarian Migrations*, p.254.

CHAPTER 3

1. Bachrach, Bernard S., 'Vouillé and the Decisive Battle Phenomenon in Late Antique Gaul' in *The Battle of Vouillé, 507 CE: Where France Began*, ed. Ralph W. Mathisen and Danuta Shanzer, De Gruyter, Gottingen, 2012, p.22.
2. Gregory Bishop of Tours, *History of the Franks*, trans. by Ernest Brehaut, Columbia University Press, New York, 1916, II. 38, p.47.
3. Gregory of Tours, II. 36, p.44.
4. Gregory of Tours, II. 35, p.44.
5. Gregory of Tours, II. 37, p.45.
6. Gregory of Tours, II. 37, p.47. It was standard practice to begin battle by exchanging volleys of arrows when archers were available: Bachrach, Bernard S., *Early Carolingian Warfare: Prelude to Empire*, University of Pennsylvania Press, Philadelphia, 2011, pp.196–97.

CHAPTER 4

1. Hupchick, Dennis P., *The Bulgarian-Byzantine Wars for Early Medieval Balkan Hegemony*, Palgrave, Basingstoke, 2017, pp.7–14; Browning, Robert, *Byzantium and Bulgaria, A Comparative Study Across the Early Medieval Frontier*, Temple Smith, London, 1975, pp.45–53.
2. *The Chronicle of Theophanes Confessor, Byzantine and Near Eastern History, AD284–813*, trans. by P. Magdalino, Clarendon, Oxford, 1997, p.222 (for the year AD501/2), p.243 (for the year AD513/4), p.316 (for the year 538/9) and p.318 (for the year 539/40).
3. Nicephorus, Patriarch of Constantinople, *Short History*, trans. by Cyril Mango, Dumbarton Oaks, Washington DC, 1990, 22, p.71; Theophanes Confessor, Chronicle, p.498.
4. Explained in sufficient detail in Kaegi, Walter E., 'Confronting Islam: emperors versus caliphs (641–c. 850)' in *The Cambridge History of the Byzantine Empire c. 500–1492*, ed. by Jonathan Shepard, Cambridge University Press, Cambridge, 2008, pp.365–94.
5. For more details, see Stickler, Timo, 'The Foederati' in *A companion to the Roman army*, ed. by Paul Erdkamp, Blackwell, Oxford, 2007, pp.495–514.
6. Theophanes Confessor, *Chronicle*, p.498.
7. Treadgold, Warren, *Byzantium and Its Army, 284–1081*, Stanford University Press, Stanford CA, 1995, pp.43–85.

8. Procopius of Caesarea, *History of the Wars*, trans. by H. B. Dewing, Heinemann, London, 1924, VII, xiv. 21–31, pp.269–73; *Maurice's Strategikon: Handbook of Byzantine Military Strategy*, trans. G. T. Dennis (2nd edn.) University of Pennsylvania Press, Philadelphia, 1984, XI. 4, pp.120–26.

CHAPTER 5

1. Glick, Thomas F., *Islamic and Christian Spain in the Early Middle Ages*, Brill, Leiden, 2005, pp.29–30.
2. Olagüe, Ignacio, *La revolución islámica en occidente*, Guadarrama, Barcelona, 1974, pp.73–112, 224–82.
3. Lewis, David L., *God's Crucible: Islam and the Making of Europe, 570 to 1215*, W. W. Norton, London, 2008, pp.123–24.
4. 'Mozarabic Chronicle of 754' in *Conquerors and Chroniclers of Early Medieval Spain*, trans. by K. Baxter Wolf, Liverpool University Press, Liverpool, 2011, 52, p.106; Ibn Abd-el-Hakem, *History of the Conquest of Spain*, trans. by John Harris Jones, W. Fr. Kaestner, Gottingen, 1858, pp.18–22; Glick, *Islamic and Christian Spain*, p.33; Roger Collins, *The Arab Conquest of Spain, 710–97*, Blackwell, London, 1989, pp.134–43; E. A. Thompson, *The Goths in Spain*, Clarendon, Oxford, 1969, p.250.
5. Glick, *Islamic and Christian Spain*, p.32; Abdulwahid Dhanun Taha, *The Muslim Conquest and Settlement of North Africa and Spain*, London, 1989, p.86.
6. Halsall, G., *Warfare and Society in the Barbarian West, 450–900*, Routledge, London, 2003, pp.62–63; Pérez Sánchez, D., *El Ejército en la Sociedad Visigoda*, Salamanca, 1989, pp.129–74.
7. 'Presentation and Composition on Warfare of the Emperor Nicephoros', II. 101–10, in McGeer, E., *Sowing the Dragon's Teeth: Byzantine Warfare in the Tenth Century*, Dumbarton Oaks Research Library and Collection, Washington DC, 1995, p.28.
8. Collins has compared them with the Chansons de Geste – medieval French epic poems that narrate legendary incidents (sometimes based on real events): Collins, Roger, *The Arab Conquest of Spain, 710–97*, Blackwell, London, 1989, p.34.

CHAPTER 6

1. Kennedy, Hugh, 'Byzantine-Arab Diplomacy in the Near East from the Islamic Conquests to the Mid Eleventh Century' in *Arab-Byzantine Relations in Early Islamic Times*, ed. by M. Bonner, Ashgate, Aldershot, 2004, pp.81–94; Kaegi, Walter E., 'Confronting Islam: Emperors versus Caliphs (641–c. 850)' in *The Cambridge History of the Byzantine Empire, c. 500–1492*, ed. by J. Shepard, Cambridge University Press, Cambridge, 2008, pp.365–94.
2. *The Chronicle of Theophanes Confessor, Byzantine and Near Eastern History, AD284–813*, trans. by P. Magdalino, Clarendon, Oxford, 1997, p.538 (AM6208; AD715/16); Canard, Marius, 'Les expéditions des Arabes contre Constantinople dans l'histoire et dans la légende', *Journal Asiatique* 208 (1926), 81.
3. Rodolphe Guilland suggested that Leo went so far as to offer to become a vassal of the Caliphate, but I find his opinion too far-fetched: Guilland, Rodolphe, 'L'Expedition de Maslama contre Constantinople (717–718)' in *Études Byzantines*, ed. R. Guilland, Presses Universitaires de France, Paris, 1959, pp.118–19.
4. *The Chronicle of Theophanes Confessor*, pp.538–9 and p.545; *The History of al-Tabari*, Volume XXIV, *The Empire in Transition*, trans. and annotated by David Stephan Powers, State University of New York Press, Albany, 1989, pp.40–1; Canard, 'Les expéditions des Arabes', p.86.
5. *The Chronicle of Michael the Great, Patriarch of the Syrians*, trans. by Robert Bedrosian, Long Branch, NJ, 2013, p.148; *The Chronicle of Theophanes Confessor*, p.545; Treadgold, Warren, *A History of the Byzantine State and Society*, Stanford University Press, Stanford, 1997, p.938 (n.1).
6. Nicolle, David, *The Armies of Islam, 7th–11th Centuries*, Osprey, London, 1982, p.12.
7. Kennedy, Hugh, *The Armies of the Caliphs: Military and Society in the Early Islamic State Warfare and History*, Routledge, London, 2001, pp.168–69.
8. *The Chronicle of Theophanes Confessor*, p.545; Guilland, 'L'Expédition de Maslama', pp.119–20.
9. Brooks, E. W., 'The Campaign of 716–717', from Arabic Sources *Journal of Hellenic Studies* 19 (1899), pp.24–28.
10. *The Chronicle of Theophanes Confessor*, p.546.
11. Brooks, 'The Campaign of 716–717', p.28.
12. *The Chronicle of Theophanes Confessor*, p.546.
13. For more on the Bulgar-Byzantine political relations between 705 and 717, including the aftermath of the Bulgar victory at Anchialus in 711, which led to the signing of the Treaty of 716 between Tervel and Theodosius III, and was renewed by Leo III on the eve of the siege of the City in 717: Hupchick, Dennis P., *The Bulgarian-Byzantine Wars for Early Medieval Balkan Hegemony*, Palgrave, Basingstoke, 2017, pp.52–53.

CHAPTER 7

1. For a detailed examination of the political and military significance of these razzias: Theotokis, Georgios, 'Border Fury! The Muslim campaigning tactics in Asia Minor through the writings of the Byzantine military treatise Περί παραδρομῆς του κυρού Νικηφόρου του βασιλέως' in *Studies on Mediterranean Culture and History:*

From the Middle Ages through the Early Modern Period, ed. Steven Oberhelman, Athens Institute for Education
& Research (ATINER) Publications, Athens, 2014, pp.13–24.
2. 'The Chronicle of 754' in *Conquerors and Chroniclers of Early Medieval Spain*, trans. by Kenneth Baxter Wolf,
Liverpool University Press, Liverpool, 1990, 80, pp.116–17.
3. Nicolle, *Poitiers AD732*, p.49.
4. Davis, Paul K., *100 Decisive Battles: From Ancient Times to the Present*, Oxford University Press, Oxford, 2001,
p.105; Schoenfeld, Edward J., 'Battle of Poitiers' in *The Reader's Companion to Military History*, ed. by Robert
Cowley, Geoffrey Parker, Houghton Mifflin, New York, 2001, p.366; Nicolle, *Poitiers AD732*, pp.24–34.
5. Kennedy, Hugh, *The Armies of the Caliphs: Military and Society in the Early Islamic State Warfare and History*,
Routledge, London, 2001, pp.168–69.
6. Nicolle, *Poitiers AD732*, p.64.
7. 'The Chronicle of 754', 80, p.117.
8. Nicolle, *Poitiers AD732*, pp.67–9.

CHAPTER 8

1. Kontler, László, *Millennium in Central Europe: A History of Hungary*, Atlantisz Publishing House, 1999; Langó,
Péter, 'Archaeological research on the conquering Hungarians: a review,' in: *Research on the Prehistory of the
Hungarians: Review: Papers Presented at the Meetings of the Institute of Archaeology of the HAS, 2003–2004*, ed.
Balázs Gusztáv Mende, Archaeological Institute of the HAS, 2005, pp. 175–340; in the same volume: Tóth,
Sándor László, 'The past and present of the research on the prehistory of the Hungarians: Historiography,' pp.
45–86.
2. Carey, Brian Todd, *Warfare in the Medieval World*, Pen & Sword Military, Barnsley, 2006, pp. 33; Reuter,
Timothy, *Germany in the Early Middle Ages, c. 800–1056*, Routledge, London, 1991, pp. 142–44.
3. Delbruck, Hans, *History of the Art of War*, vol. III, tr. Walter J. Renfroe, Greenwood, London, 1982, p. 118.
4. Carey, *Warfare in the Medieval World*, p. 34.
5. Morillo, S., Black, J., and Lococo, P., *War in World History: Society, Technology and War from Ancient Times to
the Present*, 2 vols, McGraw-Hill Education, New York, 2009, pp. 100–118.
6. Carey, *Warfare in the Medieval World*, p. 35.

CHAPTER 9

1. Theotokis, Georgios, *The Norman Campaigns in the Balkans, 1081–1108*, Boydell & Brewer, Woodbridge, 2014,
pp.108–113 and 129–30.
2. William of Apulia (Guillaume de Pouille), *La Geste de Robert Guiscard*, ed. and trans. M. Mathieu, Palermo,
1961, II.151–63, p.140.
3. William of Apulia, II.122–38 (p.138).
4. William of Apulia, II.183–91 (p.142); Amatus of Montecassino, *The History of the Normans*, trans. P. Dunbar
and revised with notes by G. Loud, Boydell & Brewer, Woodbridge, 2004, III.40.
5. William of Apulia, II.211–56 (pp.142–6); Amatus of Montecassino, III.40.

CHAPTER 10

1. For both the battles at Fulford Gate and Stamford Bridge: DeVries, Kelly, *The Norwegian Invasion of England in
1066*, Boydell & Brewer, Woodbridge, 1999.
2. *The Gesta Guillelmi of William of Poitiers*, trans. R. H. C. Davis and M. Chibnall, Clarendon, Oxford, 1998,
p.103 (from now on: WP); *Guy of Amiens, Carmen de Hastingae Proelio*, ed. and trans. F. Barlow, Clarendon,
New York, 1999, p.9.
3. William of Jumièges, *The Gesta Normannorum Ducum of William of Jumièges, Orderic Vitalis, and Robert of Torigni*,
ed. E. Van Houts, 2 vols, Clarendon, Oxford, 1992–95, p.167 (from now on: GND).
4. Bachrach, B. S., 'On the Origins of William the Conqueror's Horse Transports', *Technology and Culture* 26
(1985), pp.505–31.
5. *The Anglo-Saxon Chronicle*, trans. M. J. Swanton, Routledge, London, 1998, (E), p.141 (from now on: ANC); *The
Chronicle of Florence of Worcester*, trans. T. Forester, Bohn, 1854, p.170; Beeler, John, *Warfare in England,
1066–1189*, Cornell University Press, New York, 1996, pp.16–7; Lawson, Michelle K., *The Battle of Hastings, 1066*,
Tempus, Stroud, 2002, pp.131–2.
6. *ANC*, (D), p.143; *Carmen*, p.21; Florence of Worcester, p.170.
7. WP, p.131.
8. WP, pp.132–3.
9. Livingston, Michael, 'The legend that just won't die – the arrow in King Harold's eye' in *Medieval Warfare
Special 2017: 1066 – The Battle of Hastings*, ed. Peter Konieczy, Karwansaray, Zutphen.

CHAPTER 11

1. *Letter from Alfonso VIII of Castile to Pope Innocent III*, available online in https://deremilitari.org/2014/11/

three-sources-on-the-battle-of-las-novas-de-tolosa-in-1212/

2.   *The Latin Chronicle of the Kings of Castile*, trans. by Joseph F. O'Callaghan, Arizona Center for Medieval and Renaissance Studies, Tempe, AZ, 2002, 22, p.46.

3.   Nicolle, David, *El Cid and the Reconquista, 1050–1492*, Osprey, London, 1988, pp.9–12; Carey, Brian Todd, *Warfare in the Medieval World*, Pen & Sword, Barnsley, 2006, p.66.

4.   Nicolle, *El Cid and the Reconquista, 1050–1492*, pp.9–23; idem, *The Armies of Islam, 7th–11th Centuries*, Osprey, London, 1982, p.25.

5.   Nicolle, *El Cid and the Reconquista*, p.19.

6.   Nicolle, *El Cid and the Reconquista, 1050–1492*, pp.21–24; idem, *The Moors: the Islamic West, 7th–15th Centuries AD*, Osprey, Oxford, 2001, pp.33–34.

7.   Carey, *Warfare in the Medieval World*, p.67.

8.   Abdesselem, A. Ben, 'al-Ṭurṭūshī', in *Éncyclopaedia of Islam*, Second Edition, ed. by P. Bearman, Th. Bianquis, C. E. Bosworth, E. van Donzel, W. P. Heinrichs. Consulted online on 11 April 2018 <http://dx.doi.org/10.1163/1573-3912_islam_SIM_7650/

9.   Nicolle, David, *Crusader Warfare Volume II, Muslims, Mongols and the Struggle against the Crusades*, Hambledon Continuum, London, 2007, pp.124–25.

10.   Theotokis, Georgios, *Byzantine Military Tactics in Syria and Mesopotamia in the 10th Century, A Comparative Study*, Edinburgh University Press, Edinburgh, 2018, Chapter 8.

11.   *The Latin Chronicle of the Kings of Castile*, available online in https://deremilitari.org/2014/11/three-sources-on-the-battle-of-las-novas-de-tolosa-in-1212/

12.   Verbruggen, J. F., *The Art of Warfare in Western Europe During the Middle Ages From the Eight Century to 1340*, Boydell & Brewer, Woodbridge, 1997, pp.44–46.

13.   *The Latin Chronicle of the Kings of Castile*, available online in https://deremilitari.org/2014/11/three-sources-on-the-battle-of-las-novas-de-tolosa-in-1212/

CHAPTER 12

1.   Gilligham, John, *The Angevin Empire*, London, Arnold, 2001, pp.1–5.

2.   Cox, Eugene L., *The Eagles of Savoy: The House of Savoy in Thirteenth-Century Europe*, Princeton University Press, Princeton NJ, 1974, p.56.

3.   Carpenter, David, *Struggle for Mastery: The Penguin History of Britain 1066–1284*, London, Penguin, 2003, p.284.

4.   Holt, C., *The Northerners*, Oxford University Press, Oxford, 1992, pp.87–95; Painter, S., *The Reign of King John*, Arno, Baltimore, 1949, pp.278–84.

5.   William the Breton, 'Chronicon', in *Oeuvres de Rigord et Guillaume le Breton*, ed. R. F. Delaborde (2 vols), Paris, vol. I, 1882, p.267 (reprinted in Duby, Georges, *The Legend of Bouvines, War, Religion and Culture in the Middle Ages*, trans. by Catherine Tihanyi, Cambridge University Press, Cambridge, 1990, pp.37–54; also reprinted in the *De Re Militari*: http://www.deremilitari.org/RESOURCES/SOURCES/bouvines5.htm).

6.   Verbruggen, J. F., *The Art of Warfare in Western Europe During the Middle Ages, from the Eighth Century to 1340*, trans. S. Willard, R. W. Southern, Boydell & Brewer, Woodbridge, 1997, pp.240–47.

7.   DeVries, K., *Medieval Military Technology*, University of Toronto Press, Ontario, 1992, p.24.

8.   DeVries, *Medieval Military Technology*, p.70.

9.   William the Breton, 'Chronicon', in *The Legend of Bouvines*, pp.40–1.

10.   William the Breton, 'Chronicon', in *The Legend of Bouvines*, p.46.

11.   Theotokis, Georgios, *Byzantine Military Tactics in Syria and Mesopotamia in the Tenth Century, a comparative analysis*, Edinburgh University Press, Edinburgh, 2018, chapters 7 and 8.

12.   William the Breton, 'Chronicon', in *The Legend of Bouvines*, pp.46–7.

13.   Verbruggen, *The Art of Warfare*, p.246.

CHAPTER 13

1.   Tyerman, Christopher, *The Crusades: A Very Short Introduction*, Oxford University Press, Oxford, 2005, p.47.

2.   Otto I's coronation at Aachen by the Archbishop of Mainz: 'Accept this sword with which you are to eject all the enemies of Christ, barbarians and bad Christians. For all power over the whole Empire of the Franks has been given to you by divine authority, so as to assure the peace of all Christians': Widukind of Corvey, *Deeds of the Saxons*, Book II, Chapter 1.

3.   The bishop of Stettin, who persuaded the Crusaders to end their attack on his city: 'If they had come to strengthen the Christian faith . . . they should do so by preaching, not by arms.' Quoted by Christiansen, E., *The Northern Crusades*, Penguin, Harmondsworth, 1997, p.58.

4.   Nicolle, David, *Lake Peipus 1242, Battle of the Ice*, Osprey, London, 1996, p.41.

5.   Nowakowski, Andrzej, *Arms and Armours in the Medieval Teutonic Order's State in Prussia*, Oficyna Naukowa, Lodz, 1994, pp.86–7.

6.   Nicolle, *Lake Peipus 1242*, p.70.

7.   *The Chronicle of Novgorod*, p.87.

NOTES

237

8. Nicolle, *Lake Peipus 1242*, p.69.
9. *The Chronicle of Novgorod*, p.87.
10. Smirnov, I. I., *A Short History of the USSR*, 2 vols, Moscow, 1965, vol. I, p.59.
11. Selart, Anti, *Livonia, Rus' and the Baltic Crusades in the Thirteenth Century*, Brill, Leiden, 2007, pp.168–70. *See also* Ostrowski, Donald, 'Alexander Nevskii's "Battle on the Ice": The Creation of a Legend', *Russian History/Histoire Russe* 33 (2006), 289–312.

CHAPTER 14

1. *Livre de la conqueste de la Princée de l'Amorée. Chronique de Morée (1204–1305)*, ed. J. Longnon, Paris, 1911, lines 97–116.
2. Vásáry, I., *Cumans and Tatars. Oriental Military in the Pre-Ottoman Balkans, 1185–1365*, Cambridge University Press, Cambridge, 2005, pp.63–66.
3. Miklosich, F., Miller, J., *Acta et Diplomata Res Graecas Italasque Illustrantia*, vol. III, Vienna, 1865, pp.239 ff.
4. The best analysis of each party's motives in entering this coalition is Geanakoplos, Deno John, 'Greco-Latin Relations on the Eve of the Byzantine Restoration: The Battle of Pelagonia – 1259', *Dumbarton Oaks Papers* 7 (1953), 99–141 (especially 105–18).
5. Mentioned in the Greek version of the *Chronicle of Morea: To chronikon tou Moreos: a history in political verse, relating to the establishment of feudalism in Greece by the Franks in the thirteenth century*, ed. John Schmitt, Methuen, London, 1904, line 3,653, p.243.
6. Wilksman, Juho, 'The Campaign and Battle of Pelagonia 1259', *Byzantinos Domos* 17–18 (2009–2010), 136–37. Kyriakidis has emphasized that winter campaigns were the exception to the rule for the Nicaean emperors, especially John III and Theodore II: Kyriakidis, Savvas, *Warfare in Late Byzantium, 1204–1453*, Brill, Leiden, 2011, p.138. *See also* Nicol, Donald M., 'The date of the battle of Pelagonia', *Byzantinische Zeitschrift* 49 (1956), 68–71; Geanakoplos, 'Greco-Latin Relations', pp.103–4 and 118–19.
7. Devol, or Deabolis, was a medieval fortress and bishopric in western Macedonia, located south of Lake Ohrid. Its precise location is unknown today, but it is thought to have been located by the river of the same name (River Devol), and on the Via Egnatia.
8. *George Akropolites: The History*, trans. by Ruth Macrides, Oxford University Press, Oxford, 2007, paragraph 80, pp.356–57.
9. Wilksman, 'Pelagonia 1259', 144–45. *See also* Kanellopoulos, Nicholas, Lekea, Joanne K., 'The Struggle between the Nicean Empire and the Bulgarian State (1254–1256): Towards a Revival of Byzantine Military Tactics under Theodore II Laskaris', *Journal of Medieval Military History* 5 (2007), pp.56–69.
10. Kanellopoulos, Nikolaos, Ἡ ὀργάνωση καὶ ἡ τακτικὴ τοῦ βυζαντινοῦ στρατοῦ στὴν ὕστερη περίοδο (1204–1461)' ('The organization and tactics of the Byzantine army in the Later period (1204–1461)'), unpublished PhD thesis, University of Thessaly, 2010, pp.264–73; Babuin, A., 'Τὰ Ἐπιθετικὰ Ὅπλα τῶν Βυζαντινῶν Κατὰ τὴν Ὕστερη Περίοδο (1204–1453)' ('The offensive weapons of the Byzantines in the Later Period (1204–1453)'), unpublished PhD thesis, University of Ioannina, 2009; Bartusis, Mark C., *The Late Byzantine Army, Arms and Society, 1204–1453*, University of Pennsylvania Press, Philadelphia, 1992, pp.322–41.
11. D'Amato, Raffaele, 'The Last Marines of Byzantium, Gasmouloi, Tzakones and Prosalentai, a Short History and a Proposed Reconstruction of their Uniforms and Equipment', *Journal of Mediterranean Studies* 19 (2010), 219–248.
12. Dennis, G. T., *Three Byzantine Military Treatises*, Corpus Fontium Historiae Byzantinae, vol. 25, Dumbarton Oaks, Washington, DC, 1985. *See also* Theotokis, Georgios, 'Border Fury! The Muslim campaigning tactics in Asia Minor through the writings of the Byzantine military treatise Περὶ παραδρομῆς τοῦ κυροῦ Νικηφόρου τοῦ βασιλέως', in *Studies on Mediterranean Culture and History: From the Middle Ages through the Early Modern Period*, ed. Steven Oberhelman, Athens Institute for Education & Research (ATINER) Publications, Athens, 2014, pp.13–24.
13. Kanellopoulos, 'Ἡ ὀργάνωση καὶ ἡ τακτικὴ τοῦ βυζαντινοῦ στρατοῦ', pp.82–83.
14. *Akropolites: The History*, paragraph 81, p.360.
15. This stratagem was used by the Byzantine Emperor Alexius I Comnenus (reigned 1081–1118) against Bohemond of Taranto, son of the Norman Duke of southern Italy Robert Guiscard, during the initial stages of his campaign against Dyrrachium between 1107 and 1108. The stratagem is described in Anna Comnena's *Alexiad*, but it was also recommended by Emperor Leo VI in his military treatise called *Taktika* (written around AD900): *Nicephori Gregorae Historiae Byzantinae*, CSHB, ed. Immanuel Bekker, Bonn, 1829–1855, I, pp.74–75; Anna Comnena, *The Alexiad*, trans. E. A. S. Dawes, In Parentheses Publications, Cambridge ON, 2000, XIII. 4, pp.235–36; Leo VI, *The Taktika of Leo VI*, Corpus Fontium Historiae Byzantinae, vol. 49, trans. G. T. Dennis, Dumbarton Oaks, Washington DC, 2010, XX. 29, p.546.
16. Anna Comnena described the same tactic that was applied by her father, Alexius Comnenus, against Bohemond of Taranto during the latter's campaign in central Greece between 1082 and 1083: Comnena, *The Alexiad*, V. 6, pp.91–93.
17. Leo VI, *Taktika*, XX.51, p.554.

CHAPTER 15

1. Oman, Charles, *The Art of War in the Middle Ages*, (2 vols), Greenhill, London, 1998, I, p.490.
2. Nicolle, David, *Italian Medieval Armies, 1000–1300*, Osprey, Oxford, 2002, p.19.
3. *Annales Placentini Gibellini a. 1154–1284* in MGH SS 18 (1863), pp.457–581 (p.528); Gravett, Christopher, *German Medieval Armies, 1000–1300*, Osprey, London, 1997, p.39.
4. Gravett, *German Medieval Armies*, p.46.
5. Nowakowski, Andrzej, *Arms and Armours in the Medieval Teutonic Order's State in Prussia*, Oficyna Naukowa, Lodz, 1994, p.80.
6. Nicolle, David, *French Medieval Armies, 1000–1300*, Osprey, London, 1991, p.44; Nicolle, *Italian Medieval Armies*, pp.34–35.
7. Vegetius: *Epitome of Military Science*, trans. by N. P. Milner, Liverpool University Press, Liverpool, 2001, III. 7, p.79.

CHAPTER 16

1. Delbrück, Hans, *Medieval Warfare*, University of Nebraska Press, Lincoln, 1990, vol. III, p.573.
2. Carey, *Warfare in the Medieval World*, p.125.
3. Verbruggen, *The Art of Warfare*, pp.159–63.
4. The example of the Battle of Pydna (22 June BC168) clearly illustrates the dangers of operating even a highly professional heavy infantry such as the Macedonian phalanx without adequate support from other arms, such as archers and cavalry. The gaps that were created between the units of the Macedonian phalangites after the first line lost its cohesion during the attack because of the uneven terrain, prompted Lucius Aemilius Paullus to order his legions to strike at exactly that weak spot, attacking the phalangites on their exposed flanks: Goldsworthy, A., *Roman Warfare*, Cassell, London, 2000, p.55; Montagu, J. D., *Greek & Roman Warfare: Battles, Tactics and Trickery*, Greenhill, London, 2006, pp.220–8.
5. Rogers, Clifford J., 'The Military Revolutions of the Hundred Years War,' *Journal of Military History* 57 (1993), pp.241–78, especially 244–52.
6. Morillo, Stephen, 'The "Age of Cavalry" revisited', in D. J. Kagay and L. J. Villalon (eds) *The Circle of War in the Middle Ages: Essays on Medieval Military and Naval History*, Boydell & Brewer, Woodbridge, 1999, pp.45–58.

CHAPTER 17

1. Riley-Smith, Jonathan, *What Were the Crusades?*, Palgrave McMillan, Basingstoke, 2002, p.23.
2. Nicolle, David, *Nicopolis 1396*, Osprey, Oxford, 1999, pp.35–36.
3. Madden, Thomas F., *Crusades: The Illustrated History*, University of Michigan Press, Ann Arbor, 2005, p.184.
4. Nicolle, *Nicopolis 1396*, p.42.
5. Madden, *Crusades: The Illustrated History*, p.185.
6. The Battle of Nicopolis (1396), according to Johann Schiltberger: https://web.archive.org/web/20090206151155/ http://deremilitari.org/resources/sources/nicopolis.htm
7. http://www.theottomans.org/turkce/osmanli_ordu/savaslar2.asp
8. Nicolle, *Nicopolis 1396*, p.37; DeVries, Kelly, 'The Battle of Nicopolis', *The Medieval History Magazine* (Issue 2, October 2003), pp.22–23.
9. Some excellent designs and examples can be found here: http://www.geocities.com:80/normlaw/page4.html
10. Babuin, A., 'Τα Επιθετικά Όπλα των Βυζαντινών Κατά την Ύστερη Περίοδο (1204–1453)', ('The offensive weapons of the Byzantines in the Later Period (1204–1453)'), unpublished PhD thesis, University of Ioannina, 2009, pp.101–2.
11. https://www.metmuseum.org/art/collection/search/35793
12. Nicolle, *Nicopolis 1396*, p.48.
13. Nicolle, David, *Armies of the Ottoman Turks 1300–1774*, Osprey, London, 1983, pp.2–7.
14. Nicolle, *Nicopolis 1396*, p.53.
15. Tuchman, Barbara W., *A Distant Mirror: The Calamitous 14th Century*, Random House Publishing Group, New York, 2011, p.561.
16. Tuchman, *A Distant Mirror*, p.561.

CHAPTER 18

1. Christiansen, Eric, *The Northern Crusades*, Penguin, London, 1997, pp.87–88.
2. Turnbull, *Tannenberg 1410*, p.35.
3. Turnbull, *Tannenberg 1410*, p.25.
4. Nowakowski, *Arms and Armours*, pp.68–70.
5. Nowakowski, *Arms and Armours*, pp.72–74.
6. Nowakowski, *Arms and Armours*, p.80.
7. Nowakowski, *Arms and Armours*, pp.93–94.
8. Urban, *Tannenberg and After*, p.149.

9. Jučas, *The Battle of Grünwald*, p.78; Urban, *Tannenberg and After*, pp.152–53; Turnbull, *Tannenberg 1410*, p.48.
10. Turnbull, *Tannenberg 1410*, p.56.
11. Turnbull, *Tannenberg 1410*, p.68.
12. Jučas, *The Battle of Grünwald*, p.56.
13. Christiansen, *The Northern Crusades*, p.228.

CHAPTER 19

1. Curry, A., *The Hundred Years' War, 1337–1453*, Routledge, London, 2003, p.27.
2. Hewitt, H. J., *The Organization of War under Edward III, 1338–62*, Manchester University Press, Manchester, 1966, p.99; Allmand, Christopher, *The Hundred Years War*, Cambridge University Press, Cambridge, 1988, pp.54–5. Rogers has strongly argued that the chevauchée is a battle-seeking rather than a battle-avoiding strategy: Rogers, Clifford J., 'Edward III and the Dialectics of Strategy, 1327–1360', in *The Wars of Edward III: Sources and Interpretations*, ed. Clifford J. Rogers, Boydell & Brewer, Woodbridge, 1999, pp.265–84; idem, *War Cruel and Sharp: English Strategy under Edward III, 1327–1360*, Boydell & Brewer, Woodbridge, 2000, pp.238–72.
3. Nicolle, David, *Orléans 1429, France Turns the Tide*, Osprey, Oxford, 2001, p.24.
4. Nicolle, *Orléans 1429*, pp.26–7.
5. *The chronicles of Enguerrand de Monstrelet*, trans. by Thomas Johnes, H. G. Bohn, London, 1853, 52, p.544.
6. Nicolle, *Orléans 1429*, p. 38.
7. Curry, *The Hundred Years' War*, p. 76
8. Green, David, *The Hundred Years War: a people's history*, Yale University Press, London, 2014, Chapter 10 ['National Identities: St George and *La Mère France* (1449)']

CHAPTER 20

1. Shaw, Stanford J., *History of the Ottoman Empire and Modern Turkey, vol. 1: Empire of the Gazis: The Rise and Decline of the Ottoman Empire, 1280–1808*, Cambridge University Press, Cambridge, 1976, pp.35–6.
2. Cartledge, Bryan, *The Will to Survive: A History of Hungary*, Columbia University Press, New York, 2011, p.55.
3. Engel, P., *The Realm of St Stephen: A History of Medieval Hungary, 895–1526*, I. B. Tauris, London, 2001, p.285.
4. Turnbull, S., *The Ottoman Empire 1326–1699*, Routledge, London, 2005, p.30.
5. Imber, Colin, *The Crusade of Varna, 1443–45*, Ashgate, Aldershot, 2006, p.29.
6. Turnbull, *The Ottoman Empire*, p.32.
7. Setton, Kenneth Meyer, *The Papacy and the Levant, 1204–1571: The Fifteenth Century*, American Philosophical Society, Philadelphia, 1978, pp.89–90; Sedlar, Jean W., *East Central Europe in the Middle Ages, 1000–1500*, University of Washington Press, Seattle, 1994, p.247.
8. İnalcık, H., 'The Crusade of Varna', in K. M. Setton (gen. ed.), *A History of the Crusades*, 8 vols (Madison, WI, 1855–89), VI: *The Impact of the Crusades on Europe*, ed. H. W. Hazard and N. P. Zacour, pp.308–9.
9. Murphy, Rhoads, 'Ottoman military organisation in south-eastern Europe, c. 1420–1720', in *European Warfare, 1350–1750*, ed. Frank Tallett and D. J. B. Trim, Cambridge University Press, Cambridge, 2010, p.143.
10. Nicolle cites many examples from the Budapest History Museum: Nicolle, David, *Hungary and the Fall of Eastern Europe, 1000–1568*, Osprey, London, 1988, p.46.
11. Nicolle, David, *Armies of the Ottoman Turks 1300–1774*, Osprey, London, 1983, p.8.
12. http://www.turkishculture.org/military/weapons/sword-knives/yatagan-the-turkish-332.htm
13. Compare the accounts of: Anonymous, *The Holy Wars of Sultan Murad Son of Sultan Mehmed Khan*; Jehan de Wavrin, *Extract from the Anciennes Chroniques d' Angleterre*. Both are collected in Imber, *The Crusade of Varna, 1443–45*, pp.95–6 (for Anonymous) and pp.130–31 (for Jehan de Wavrin).
14. Bonfini's Rerum Ungaricarum Decades covers the history of Hungary from its beginnings to the end of 1495: http://www.bvh.univ-tours.fr/Consult/index.asp?numfiche=1232&numtable=B330636101_GF861_REScoffre&url=/resauteur.asp?numauteur=2863-ordre=titre
15. Jehan de Wavrin, in *The Crusade of Varna*, 1443–45, p.131.

INDEX